Read This First

The information in this book is as up to date and accurate as we can make it. But it's important to realize that the law changes frequently, as do fees, forms and other important legal details. If you handle your own legal matters, it's up to you to be sure that all information you use—including the information in this book—is accurate. Here are some suggestions to help you do this:

First, check the edition number on the book's spine to make sure you've got the most recent edition of this book. To learn whether a later edition is available, go to Nolo's online Law Store at www.nolo.com or call Nolo's Customer Service Department at 800-728-3555.

Next, because the law can change overnight, users of even a current edition need to be sure it's fully up to date. At www.nolo.com, we post notices of major legal and practical changes that affect a book's current edition only. To check for updates, go to the Law Store portion of Nolo's website and find the page devoted to the book (use the "A to Z Product List" and click on the book's title). If you see an "Updates" link on the left side of the page, click on it. If you don't see a link, there are no posted changes—but check back regularly.

Finally, while Nolo believes that accurate and current legal information in its books can help you solve many of your legal problems on a cost-effective basis, this book is not intended to be a substitute for personalized advice from a knowledgeable lawyer. If you want the help of a trained professional, consult an attorney licensed to practice in your state.

1st edition

The Lawsuit
Survival Guide

A Client's Companion to Litigation

By Attorney Joseph L. Matthews

First Edition

Second Printing   MARCH 2003

Editor   LISA GUERIN

Illustrations   MARI STEIN

Cover Design   TONI IHARA

Book Design   TERRI HEARSH

Proofreading   ROBERT WELLS AND KATHERINE L. KAISER

Index   PATRICIA DEMINNA

Printing   ARVATO SERVICES, INC.

Matthews, Joseph L.
   The lawsuit survival guide : a client's companion to litigation/by Joseph L. Matthews.
     p. cm.
   Includes index.
   ISBN 0-87337-754-0
   1. Complaints (Civil procedure)--United States--Popular works. 2. Action and
defenses--United States--Popular works. 3. Attorney and client--United States--Popular
works. I. Title.

KF8863.M28 2001
347.73'53--dc21   2001030367

Acknowledgments

Many people at Nolo have had a hand in the project which has become this book. Barbara Kate Repa encouraged the project in its infancy. Shae Irving and Janet Portman did preliminary work on an early manuscript chapter, trying to hammer out an approach that could be most helpful to lawsuit "civilians." And I am very grateful to Mary Randolph, who recognized the project's value and rescued it when it seemed to be floundering.

The book owes its final organizational clarity and consistency to the superb editorial work of Lisa Guerin. It may have been a book when it got to her, but she honed it and polished it to a much finer shape.

Thanks, too, go to the wonderful trial lawyers from whom I have learned so much over the years, not just about the technical aspects of civil litigation but about how to treat human beings—especially their clients—along the way. These fine lawyers include the late Stuart Buckley, Meriel Lindley and especially Dick Duane.

My final and greatest thanks are reserved for someone who combines a comprehensive understanding of the law, a keen and unblinking editorial eye and an unwavering dedication to making the law accessible to all. Steve Elias took a formless mass of words and patiently, tirelessly and always good-humoredly showed me how it could be a book.

Table of Contents

8 Settling a Lawsuit

9 Trial

10 Appeals and Other Post-Trial Proceedings

Index

Introduction

L ike it or not, you're stuck in a lawsuit —whether you brought it yourself or had it dropped on your doorstep. Unfortunately, you may be stuck for a long time, through a lot of ups and downs and a lot of your bank account. If you already have an attorney, you may have little idea what your lawyer actually does and why. All you know for sure at this point is that the lawsuit moves like molasses, could cost a bundle and doesn't seem to offer you a meaningful way to participate in the process.

But it doesn't have to be this way. This book explains each step in the litigation process, guides you through the jumble of legal language and courtroom procedures and offers advice about assisting and working with your lawyer. Lawsuits are complicated, time-consuming and stressful affairs. But with the help of this book and a good lawyer, you can navigate the legal system successfully and get the best possible result with the least possible anxiety.

Section I: The Trouble With Lawsuits

A lawsuit can be an extraordinarily expensive, time-consuming and energy-draining experience, sometimes with life-changing consequences. Nonetheless, many people go through a lawsuit without ever knowing exactly what is happening, let alone taking an active part in important decisions along the way.

A. Why Lawsuits Are So Maddening

There are several reasons for this bleak state of affairs.

First, the adversary process—the lawsuit battle for a winner and loser—has developed into a complex chess game. Obscure legal moves, countermoves, gambits and tactics require highly trained, expensive lawyers. All too often, clients are left confused and unable to follow—much less take an active role in—the proceedings.

Lawsuits also last much longer than most clients expect. Although television dramas might lead us to believe that trials usually start about a week after lawyer and client first meet, it is not unusual for a couple of years—or more—to pass between the start of a lawsuit and the actual trial. Sometimes one or both of the lawyers are partially responsible for this delay. But in many courts—particularly those in urban areas— overcrowding is to blame. These courts simply have more lawsuits ready for trial than available courtrooms at any given time.

Then there is the fake beard of professionalism—that is, the notion that lawyers always know best and that clients, like children or sheep, are better herded than heard from. Some lawyers may use this as an excuse to avoid explaining what is going on and to discourage you from getting involved. Sadly, some lawyers even use it to keep clients from seeing the lawyers' own confusion, lack of work on the case or time and money spent on needless—yet costly—legal maneuvering.

All of this is made worse by the notorious lawyers' lingo. The legal system hides its work behind a twisted mix of Latin, medieval French and entirely made-up words accessible only to those—the lawyers—who speak the language. Although many legal concepts are surprisingly straightforward, the jargon used to describe them is anything but.

Finally, there is precious little plain-language consumer information available to non-lawyers who are caught up in the lawsuit process. That's where this book comes in. It will guide you, step by step, through the litigation maze, explaining legal jargon and procedures along the way.

B. The Informed Consumer

To be an *effective* consumer of a lawyer's services—to get the best "product" at the best price—you have to be an *informed* consumer. The more you understand about your lawsuit, the more you can assist your lawyer—and the more likely you are to end up with a positive result. You will also survive the long process with greatly reduced stress and worry.

Unfortunately, your lawyer may not always take the time to sufficiently explain the lawsuit process. Instead, as your lawsuit slowly wends its way along, you may be frustrated from time to time by some of these unanswered questions:

- What's taking so long?
- Why does it cost so much?
- What's the point of this maneuver or procedure?
- Is it necessary?
- Is it important?
- What risks are involved?
- Are there any alternatives?
- What can I do to help?
- When will we know the outcome?
- What happens next?

Without knowing the pieces of the lawsuit puzzle, you might not even know how or when to ask these questions. Nor will you know what information or assistance to offer your lawyer. And if you do ask a useful question, you might not be able to make sense of your lawyer's answer.

Section II: How to Use This Book

This book can help bridge the gap between you and the legal system. Using simple, everyday language, it explains all the major steps and procedures of a lawsuit. From the very beginning of the process, it describes where your lawsuit is headed, when it will get there and what important tasks you and your lawyer might face along the way.

This Is Not a Do-It-Yourself Guide

This book does not explain how to represent yourself in court or how to do particular legal tasks from start to finish. Instead, it assumes that you are represented by a lawyer who will do the necessary legal work. Although this book can help you work successfully with your lawyer, it won't train you to be your own lawyer. For information on working without a lawyer, see *Represent Yourself in Court* by Attorneys Paul Bergman and Sara J. Berman-Barrett (Nolo).

A. Lawsuits Covered by This Book

Whether you are a plaintiff (suing) or a defendant (being sued) in almost any kind of civil lawsuit, this book is for you. It takes you from the search for a lawyer and the very first papers in the lawsuit right through trial and beyond. Along the way, it explains standard procedures used in both state and federal courts, including variations that occur from courts in one place to courts in another.

Whether your lawsuit arises out of a car accident, a dispute with a neighbor, landlord, tenant, co-owner, employer or employee, a conflict with a business connection, a domestic or business partner or someone who has provided you with services or a product, or almost any other kind of personal or business dispute, this book can serve as your legal companion.

This Book Does Not Cover Every Type of Civil Proceeding

Despite its extremely broad coverage, there are a few kinds of special civil court proceedings this book does not discuss. These include certain parts of cases in bankruptcy, probate (wills, trusts and estates), tax, immigration, workers compensation, family law (divorce, child custody, child support), small claims court or class actions. Many of the procedures described in this book do occur in these lawsuits. However, most courts also have special rules and procedures for each of these types of lawsuits, and these special rules are not covered here.

This book covers only civil lawsuits; criminal cases are not discussed. For information on criminal court proceedings, see *The Criminal Law Handbook* by Attorneys Paul Bergman and Sara J. Berman-Barrett (Nolo).

B. How This Book Is Organized

Each major stage of the lawsuit process is covered here in a separate chapter. The chapters themselves are organized in a simple-to-use question-and-answer format. The questions are those that any non-lawyer caught up in a lawsuit might ask about his or her case. The answers, which often include real-world examples, explain:

- what the legal terms mean

- what a particular procedure is and how it is carried out
- what the procedure is intended to accomplish
- what work the lawyers must do regarding that procedure
- how long the process takes
- what benefits and risks are involved
- how you can help your lawyer
- how to control legal fees and costs, and
- what's coming next.

For almost any civil lawsuit, this book can serve as your personal guide through the litigation maze. When a lawyer says something is happening in your case—or if, for awhile, nothing seems to be happening —this is where you can find an explanation. And it also suggests important questions to ask your lawyer along the way.

C. How to Use This Book

There are several different ways to use this book. You can look over the whole book from start to finish to get a sense of what the entire lawsuit process entails. As your case approaches any particular stage in the lawsuit, you can read closely the chapter that covers that stage.

If you want to know about and prepare yourself for a specific procedure, you can read about it in detail after finding it in the Table of Contents or Index. The Index will send you to the page on which that term first appears. On that page, the term is

highlighted in italic text, such as *Motion for Summary Judgment*. After that first mention, the term will be thoroughly explained in the following paragraphs or pages, often including common examples.

 Warns You of Runaway Legal Bills. Certain legal maneuvers and processes tend to eat up a lot of a lawyer's time and, if you are paying a lawyer by the hour, a lot of your money. This icon alerts you to the danger of high lawyer fees and lawsuit expenses that can easily pile up. These sidebars also suggest some ways to cut your legal costs.

As discussed at each point where this warning sign appears, there may be good reasons to spend money on a particular legal procedure. But because of the high cost, you should discuss the pros and cons in advance with your lawyer. You and your lawyer may then weigh the potential for success and the significance of what might be won against the likely cost and the possibility of losing. You and your lawyer might also discuss alternatives to consider before, rather than after, your money is spent.

This Icon Explains How You Can Help Your Lawyer. You may be very keen to help your lawyer pursue or defend your lawsuit. After all, you're the one who will be most affected by the outcome. Also, at least initially, you probably know more about the dispute than your lawyer. You may want to get involved in the lawsuit just to keep better tabs on the process. And if you are paying hourly attorney fees, you might save considerable money by doing some work that your lawyer would otherwise have to do.

Some lawyers are very good about including their clients in lawsuit tasks. They know that an organized, thorough client can be of great assistance. But many lawyers get so wrapped up in their own role that they don't let their clients know how the clients can help. As a result, a client who wants to be involved might cause friction with the lawyer and run up unnecessary legal bills. Or a client might plunge into a project hoping to be helpful, only to find out later that it was a waste of time and energy. Or a client might just sit and stew, wanting to be involved but not knowing how.

This book makes a special effort to explain what you can do to help your lawyer at each stage of the legal process. For some procedures and maneuvers, there may be very little, if anything, for you to do. For others, however, you may be able to search for and organize information, make sure your lawyer has the necessary facts and prepare yourself for those parts of the lawsuit in which you must participate personally. This icon appears next to tips that speak directly to you, the client, about the ways you can pitch in to help your lawyer. You will find a list of all of these tips, and the page on which they appear, in the Index at the back of this book.

D. A Glossary of Legal Terms

There are a number of legal terms that you will begin to see almost as soon as you open this book. These terms appear through-out the book, some popping up on almost every page. These terms may be familiar to you and most can be understood from the context in which they appear. However, you might not be completely comfortable with their exact meanings—particularly because other terms are also used which are completely or nearly interchangeable. So, as you begin to use this book, you may want to refer back to the following glossary for a handy reminder:

- **party—litigant—side—client—plaintiff—defendant.** A person, business or other organization or entity which sues or gets sued is called a "party" to the lawsuit. "Litigant" is another term for party, used to indicate that a formal lawsuit has begun (as distinguished from a party to a contract, or a party to a dispute that has not yet become a lawsuit). Every lawsuit has at least two "sides," meaning parties with opposing interests in the outcome. In most lawsuits, the party suing is one side (the "plaintiff") and the party being sued is the other side (the "defendant"). A lawsuit may also include countersuits against third parties, in which case it might have more than two sides. (See Chapter 3, Section III.) "Client" refers to a party in the context of the relationship with his or her lawyer. ("A lawyer and client should discuss the procedure before the lawyer begins work on it.")

- **attorney—lawyer—counsel.** These terms are completely interchangeable. They refer to anyone who is authorized to practice law. Each of these terms is used for a lawyer who actively handles lawsuits and appears in court, as well as for someone who gives legal advice but does not handle lawsuits. "Counsel" is more formal than the other two, often used by judges and lawyers when describing a procedure to be followed or a relationship in the lawsuit (as in "Counsel for the opposing side must be notified within ten days," or "Is the witness represented by counsel?"), but it means the same thing.
- **fee—cost—expense.** The money a client pays his or her lawyer for representing the client is called an attorney "fee." (See Chapter 2, Section III.) There are also "fees" paid to the court for filing legal papers and for certain other official court functions. A "cost" is an expenditure, associated with the handling of a lawsuit, made by a lawyer on behalf of a client. Certain kinds of expenditures are considered proper lawsuit costs, and must be paid by the client. And the losing side in a lawsuit usually has to pay the winning side's lawsuit costs. Those amounts spent by a lawyer that are not official lawsuit costs are considered "expenses" that must be borne by the lawyer's office as overhead. Likewise, amounts spent by a client that do not qualify as official lawsuit costs must be borne by the client and cannot be recovered from the opposing side. (See Chapter 2, Section III.)
- **lawsuit—litigation—case—action.** The term "lawsuit" refers both to the initial court papers filed by a person suing someone else ("The lawsuit was filed on February 1st") and to the entire legal process that follows ("The lawsuit took three years from start to finish"). "Litigation" may refer to a particular lawsuit ("The lawyer who represents the defendant in this litigation…") or to all of the various procedures that make up the lawsuit process ("All litigation will be suspended while the two sides seek to mediate their dispute"). "Case" is a general term that is used to refer to a legal dispute whether or not it becomes a formal lawsuit ("Has the lawyer handled a case like this before?"). "Action" is a more technical word for lawsuit. Court personnel sometimes use this term when they refer to a lawsuit by its official identification number ("Action number 12345 will be heard in Courtroom 4 at 9:00 a.m."). It is also a short hand term for a legal right to sue someone. ("The lawyer believes that the conduct described would support an action for damages.")
- **court—jurisdiction—court system.** The federal government and each state maintains its own separate judicial

(court) system. Each of these systems is further divided into smaller sections by district or county. At times this book will mention that a lawsuit procedure is permitted in a certain "jurisdiction," or that some "courts" have different rules or procedures. These terms refer to the court system where the lawsuit is being conducted that, through its particular rules, controls how the lawsuit proceeds. (See Chapter 3, Section I.)

- **judge—court.** Throughout this book you will read about lawyers asking "the court" to make a ruling, or about "the court" ordering that something happen in the case. When used in this way, "court" simply means a "judge." When the book refers to filing documents with "the court," it means giving or sending the papers to the court clerk's office, where they are officially marked as received, placed in the court's file for your case and eventually read by a judge.

- **motion—request—application.** Lawyers frequently ask a judge to order that another party do or refrain from doing something, or to interpret some procedure about which the parties disagree. This is done through a process referred to as making a "motion," "request" or "application." Sometimes one term is used, sometimes another, but all mean the same thing.

- **order—ruling—decision.** During a lawsuit, lawyers frequently ask a judge to interpret some rule or to order the other side to comply with a procedure. (See "motion—request—application" above.) A judge's response to the request is known as a "ruling" or "decision." The official document, or verbal direction, from the judge that precisely states the ruling is known as an "order" or "court order."

- **relief—award—recovery—damages—compensation.** All these terms refer to what a party seeks to win by filing a lawsuit. "Relief" refers to a benefit ordered by a judge or jury. It can include not only money but almost anything else that might be sought in a lawsuit, such as ownership of property or a business, an order for someone to do or stop doing something or termination or enforcement of a contract or lease. Relief may also refer to a temporary benefit ordered by a judge. "Award" similarly refers to what a judge or jury would grant to a party at the end of a lawsuit, but it usually refers only to a sum of money. "Recovery," "damages" and "compensation" all refer to the money one party pays the other at the end of the lawsuit. Unlike "award," these terms include money that changes hands as the result of a settlement between the parties as well as by a judge's or jury's decision. ■

Chapter 1

Lawyers, Fees and Retainer Agreements

One of the first—and most important—tasks a party faces is
choosing a lawyer. Once a
lawyer has been selected, the client will
have to make a formal agreement with the
lawyer about how the lawsuit will be
conducted and how the lawyer will be
paid.

This chapter addresses the process of
selecting a lawyer. The chapter also explains
a client's right to change lawyers. And it
discusses the key elements that must be
contained in any written representation
agreement between a lawyer and client. In
particular, it focuses on the ways in which
a lawyer might be paid, and the extent to
which the client will be responsible for
other expenses of litigation.

You Might Not Need This Chapter.
You may already have hired a lawyer
to represent you in your lawsuit. And you may
be well satisfied with that lawyer's experience
and willingness to meet your needs in the case.
You and the lawyer may also have settled
upon a fee arrangement with which you are
comfortable. If so, consider skipping this
chapter altogether. But even if you already
have a lawyer, it may be a good idea for you
at least to skim this chapter. Information you
can find here about communicating with your
lawyer and about fee arrangements may
enhance your existing relationship. This
chapter also gives information on changing
lawyers, which might come in handy down
the road.

Section I: Choosing a Lawyer

This section raises some key issues to consider when taking that crucial first step of
choosing a lawyer.

1. What is the best way to find a good lawyer?

There is no right or wrong way to look for
a lawyer. Perhaps the best way to find a
good lawyer is through referrals—recommendations from friends, family members,
business associates or local trade or bar
associations. The goal is to find a lawyer who
is able to provide the right kind of representation for a particular client in a particular lawsuit. This means the client might
need to speak with several lawyers before
finding one who seems right for the job.

Many lawyers charge nothing for an
initial meeting to discuss the possibility of
representing a client. However, some
lawyers require potential clients to pay a
consultation fee—a fee for meeting with
the lawyer to discuss the facts and law
relating to the lawsuit and the possibility of
working together. Generally, this fee should
cover any time the lawyer spends reviewing documents, researching the law and
meeting with the client. A client who is unwilling or unable to pay a consultation fee
should ask the lawyer to waive the fee. Even
lawyers who usually charge a consultation
fee will probably meet with a client for free
if they believe the case is a strong one.

Why Hire a Lawyer

This book is written for parties to a lawsuit who have decided to hire lawyers to represent them. Of course, some people choose to go it alone; they represent themselves in court, sometimes with great success. Those considering this option can find information and guidance in *Represent Yourself in Court: How to Prepare & Try a Winning Case*, by Attorneys Paul Bergman and Sara J. Berman-Barrett (Nolo).

Representing oneself is not a good option for everyone or for every type of lawsuit, however. Many people have neither the time nor the inclination to learn the many technical legal rules that apply to every lawsuit, to do the research, investigation and preparation necessary to adequately represent themselves or to determine the realistic value of their case. This is where a good lawyer comes in. A client can expect the lawyer not only to do the legal work necessary to prepare the case for trial, but also to:

- Try to settle the lawsuit, if a settlement can be negotiated that benefits the client. Because lawyers—especially lawyers in the same geographical area who specialize in the same field—tend to know each other, and know how settle-

ments are negotiated, it is generally easier for a lawyer to reach a settlement than it would be for a self-represented person.

- Give the client a reality check. A lawyer with experience litigating similar cases can provide an objective and informed evaluation of the range of likely outcomes if the case goes to trial. This perspective will help the client decide how aggressively to litigate the case and whether to accept (or offer) a proposed settlement.
- Be familiar with the legal rules that apply to the client's lawsuit. Although a self-represented person can certainly learn these rules, it would take a lot of time. And in some cases, the rules are too complex for a non-lawyer to master without some training and experience.
- Be familiar with local court customs, procedures and personalities. A lawyer will have a sense of which judges are most likely to favor a client's side of the dispute, whether a local jury is liable to award high (or low) damages and what to expect from opposing lawyers.

⚠ When searching for a lawyer to handle a dispute that has reached the lawsuit stage, a client should seek referrals specifically to a *litigator* or *trial lawyer*, and preferably to one who has experience with cases involving the same area of law. (See Questions 5-7, below.)

2. Where can I get referrals to an appropriate lawyer?

Lawyer referrals come from many sources.

Lawyers. Lawyers frequently refer cases to one another. Any lawyer probably knows, or knows some other lawyer who knows, a litigation specialist familiar with the area of law involved in a particular case. However, just because a lawyer does the referring does not mean that the lawyer being referred is right for the job. A client must still personally evaluate any lawyer being considered.

Business Associates and Trade Organizations. If a lawsuit arises out of a business dispute, people in the same or other businesses might have been involved in litigation of their own. If so, they may be able provide references to lawyers they used and liked, or warn about lawyers with whom they had bad experiences. Trade organizations or local groups that represent the interests of business owners, such as the Chamber of Commerce, may also have lawyers to recommend.

Conversations With Lawyers Are Confidential

The private conversations between a lawyer and a client are protected from disclosure by the attorney-client privilege. This privilege declares that no one—including other parties, government agencies or courts—can force a lawyer or client to reveal what has been said or written in private between the two. This protection applies even if you have not yet hired the lawyer to represent you, and even if you decide not to hire that lawyer at all. As long as you are speaking with the lawyer about your legal matters, your conversation, and any written communication between you, is protected from anyone else's prying.

This means that when you interview lawyers to decide whether you want them to represent you, you may freely discuss both the facts of your lawsuit and your attitudes toward it. In fact, it is very important that you discuss the case fully and openly. Only if you give the lawyer a complete picture of the case can the lawyer give you an accurate and useful opinion about how the case might be conducted, what its outcome might be and how much it might cost.

Friends and Acquaintances. As an initial referral device, it can be very useful to canvass friends and acquaintances about their experiences with litigation and to get referrals to lawyers whom they found helpful. However, a personal recommendation is never enough. Litigation is complicated, and can vary considerably depending on the parties and area of law involved. A lawyer who does well for one client, or has the time and energy to devote to one case, won't necessarily do as well on another case. Regardless of how highly someone is recommended, clients should always evaluate how the lawyer might handle their particular cases.

Bar Association Referral Service. Many county and city bar associations offer lawyer referral services for the public. Potential clients can contact these services by calling the city or county bar association and asking for the lawyer referral line, or, increasingly, through the Internet. Once the caller describes the type of case for which representation is needed, the service provides the names of local lawyers who specialize in that area of the law. However, most bar associations do not screen lawyers for competency or experience, so a referral is *not* the same as a recommendation. The client must independently evaluate whether the lawyer would be right for the case.

Government Agencies. Certain state and federal government agencies are responsible for enforcing laws that protect the public. For example, the Equal Employment Opportunity Commission (EEOC) enforces the laws prohibiting discrimination in the workplace and the Securities and Exchange Commission (SEC) acts to prevent investors from being defrauded. In some cases, these agencies will get directly involved in a lawsuit, particularly if the lawsuit addresses important and new legal issues in the field. Even if they don't take the case, a few government agencies will provide referrals to local lawyers who handle similar lawsuits. As with referrals from bar associations, however, these referrals may not be screened.

3. Once I have some referrals, what should I do next?

The first step for anyone shopping for a lawyer is to call the lawyers who have been referred by others. Often, a member of the lawyer's staff will question the client about the case and ask who referred the client. If the lawyer is available and interested in the case, client and lawyer will arrange to meet at the lawyer's office.

How You Can Make a Fir st Meeting Successful

Before your first meeting with a lawyer, gather your thoughts and your paperwork. Think about all the important incidents that led to the lawsuit. It is a good idea to write down these events, either in a time-line form or simply as a description—as if you were telling the story in a letter. If you do make a written summary, bring it with you to the meeting with the lawyer. Also bring the names, addresses and phone numbers of witnesses—anyone who might have information about the dispute. And bring any documents—contracts, letters, business records, plans or photographs, for example—that relate to the case.

During this meeting, the client can ask about the lawyer's litigation experience, find out the lawyer's initial view of the case, discuss fee arrangements and legal strategy and check out the lawyer's communication skills. All of these factors—discussed in Questions 5-12—will help the client decide whether to hire the lawyer. Of course, the lawyer will also use this meeting to decide whether to take the case. The lawyer will be thinking about the case's strengths and weaknesses, how lucrative the case might be, how much work the case would require and whether the client and lawyer are likely to get along during the litigation.

4. I have been sued and my insurance company is going to defend me. Can I choose the lawyer who does the job?

Probably not. Many kinds of insurance policies require the insurance company to defend the policyholder in any lawsuit that arises from activity covered by the policy (for example, a policyholder who is sued because of a car accident may be entitled to legal representation through the auto insurance provider). This means the insurance company must provide and pay for a lawyer to defend the policyholder. Usually, an attorney selected by the insurance company handles the defense. Since the insurance company not only has to pay the lawyer but also must pay damages that result from the lawsuit, it gets to choose the lawyer. The lawyer's job, in effect, is to protect the insurance company's money. Because insurance companies are very good at protecting their money, they usually hire very competent attorneys.

An Insurance Company's Conflict of Interest

In some situations, a lawyer for your insurance company might have a conflict of interest in representing you. (Conflicts of interest are discussed in Questions 13 and 14.) This can happen if the amount you might owe as a result of a lawsuit could be greater than your insurance coverage (known as *excess liability*). In such cases, the insurance company has a potential conflict of interest because the lawyer is interested in saving the company's money, not yours. The company's lawyer has little incentive to do much work trying to save you from having to pay the "excess" amount out of your own pocket. In such potential conflict situations, the law in a few states permits the insurance policyholder rather than the insurance company to choose a lawyer—known as *independent counsel*—though the insurance company still has to pay the lawyer. If you believe that what you might owe on a lawsuit greatly exceeds your insurance coverage, consult with an experienced litigation lawyer of your own choosing to find out if you have the right to independent counsel.

5. Are only certain kinds of lawyers permitted to represent me in court?

No. Any lawyer who is licensed to practice in the jurisdiction where the lawsuit is filed is allowed to represent a party in that lawsuit. However, even the smartest, most understanding lawyer in the world may be of little use in a lawsuit if he or she is not experienced in litigation. Surprisingly, most attorneys are not—they handle business transactions, taxes, real estate, wills and a host of other matters, none of which usually gets them near a courtroom. Many other lawyers do some minor or specialized court work but do not handle litigation from start to finish. None of these lawyers is a good bet to represent a party in a lawsuit involving complicated factual or legal issues, or one with a lot of money at stake. Instead, someone suing or being sued is probably best served by a lawyer who regularly handles lawsuits through the entire litigation process, and who has experience actually going to trial.

6. How can I find out if a lawyer has the right litigation experience?

The easiest way is to ask the lawyer directly. Some questions to ask in determining a lawyer's litigation experience include:

- how long the lawyer has been in practice
- how much of that time the lawyer has spent litigating and practicing the type of law in question
- what percent of the lawyer's—not the law firm's—practice involves litigation
- how many trials and arbitrations the lawyer has personally conducted

during the previous five years (the number need not be large—five or six trials and a like number of arbitrations may be plenty)

- how many of those were jury trials, and
- what the results were of those trials.

Your Regular Lawyer Might Not Be Right for This Lawsuit

On a previous occasion in your business or personal life, you may have used the services of a lawyer—and that lawyer may have provided you with excellent legal assistance. So, when you become involved in a lawsuit, you might consider going back to this same lawyer. However, this lawyer may have little or no litigation experience or know little about the area of law that the lawsuit involves. Unfortunately, it too often happens that instead of immediately referring you to an appropriate litigation attorney, your regular lawyer hangs onto your case to try to settle it quickly. Once it becomes clear that you need a trial lawyer, a lot of time may have passed. In smaller, simple cases, this delay causes no harm. But in more complicated cases, valuable opportunities to develop evidence may be lost, and seemingly innocent steps taken by your "regular" lawyer might prove in the long run to be litigation blunders. If your regular lawyer is not qualified to handle your lawsuit all the way through trial, ask that lawyer to refer you—sooner rather than later—to someone who is.

Lawyers are sometimes a bit sensitive when quizzed on their qualifications. But this is information a party to a lawsuit must have before deciding whether to hire the lawyer. If a lawyer cannot gracefully accept such direct questions, that does not bode well for the lawyer's ability or willingness to communicate with the client through the usually long and sometimes very difficult course of litigation.

7. Do lawyers specialize in particular areas of law?

Yes. Like doctors, most lawyers specialize. Some handle divorces, some give tax advice, some work on corporate mergers, some write wills and contracts, some do criminal defense. Some do a little of this and a little of that. But unless a lawyer has at least some experience in the legal area involved in a particular lawsuit, that lawyer might not be the best to handle the litigation.

The facts in every lawsuit are at least somewhat different. On the other hand, every lawsuit has many procedural similarities. This means that it is neither practical nor necessary to look for a lawyer who has experience handling lawsuits that are "exactly" like the client's case. But the lawyer should at least have some experience in the same area of law as the client's case. For example, if a lawsuit involves the break-up of a partnership that ran a florist business, there is no need for a lawyer who has previously handled cases dealing with florists or flowers—but it is important to have a lawyer with experience litigating business partnership disputes.

8. Does a lawyer's fee tell me anything about how good the lawyer will be?

Not necessarily. A less expensive lawyer might be able to do just as well as, if not better than, a more expensive lawyer. There is no direct relation between the fee a lawyer charges and the quality of the work that lawyer would perform in a particular lawsuit. A lawyer who charges high fees may do so because of a large overhead or a large reputation rather than a large talent for litigation. For example, a lawyer with a plush office in a downtown skyscraper may charge considerably more than a lawyer in a smaller office away from the high-rent district, but that plush office is probably not going to help very much during the course of litigation. Or a lawyer's fees may be high because the office is heavily staffed to handle big, corporate litigation. But if a client doesn't need all that firepower to handle a relatively small lawsuit, why pay for it?

9. What should I ask potential lawyers about fees and costs?

When choosing a lawyer, one of the most important considerations is the amount of the lawyer's fee and how it will be calculated. Although this question is addressed in detail in Section III, below, fee arrangements should be discussed at the outset, before a client makes a final decision about hiring a lawyer. If the lawyer will charge by the hour, there should be an open and honest discussion about how much the client can or is willing to pay for the entire litigation. A lawsuit can be conducted in quite different ways—the more aggressively it is waged, the more lawyer hours the client has to pay.

The client should also ask the lawyer for some idea—though it might be quite speculative this early in the process—of how much the client is likely to receive from, or have to pay to, the other side at the conclusion the lawsuit. Once these figures have been discussed, the lawyer can conduct the litigation in such a way that attorney fees remain in balance with what the client stands to gain or lose. If fees get too high despite the lawyer's restraint, the lawyer will know that it might become necessary to push for settlement of the case rather than to continue headlong with litigation.

SO MUCH FOR THE SMALL TALK! HOW MUCH DO YOU CHARGE?

What Is My Case Worth?

At the beginning of the litigation, don't expect a lawyer to give you a bottom dollar assessment of what you can expect to win or lose in your lawsuit. The value of a lawsuit depends on many things; many of them are outside the lawyer's control, and some of them probably haven't happened yet. For example, documents you get from the other side may provide unexpected support for your arguments; a witness you thought would back you up might change sides; or your opponent might hire lawyers who couldn't argue their way out of a traffic ticket. At the outset, your lawyer can only give you some range of the possible outcomes, perhaps including awards in similar cases. As the case progresses, this assessment will become more refined and help you decide whether to settle the case or take it to trial.

10. Should I talk to potential lawyers about my attitudes toward the lawsuit?

Yes. Lawsuits can be extremely hostile affairs. And hostility may be what a client most feels about the opposing party in the lawsuit. If so, the client might want a lawyer to litigate the case as aggressively as possible (and affordable). On the other hand, even if a client has great hostility toward the other party, that client might not want a lawyer to reflect that hostility in conducting the lawsuit because of the aggression it will provoke from the other side—and the accompanying stress and expense.

Some clients have a disagreement but no great ill will against the other side in the lawsuit, and therefore prefer to keep the proceedings calm and civilized. A client might also want the matter settled as soon as possible, even if that means accepting a settlement that is not as favorable as what might be won if the lawsuit were pursued full bore. If so, the client might want the lawyer to steer the proceedings into what is called "alternative dispute resolution" (mediation or arbitration) rather than litigation. (See Chapters 6 and 7.)

Whatever the client's approach, a lawyer should respect it. From the very first discussions between a lawyer and potential client, the client should make sure the lawyer understands the client's approach to the lawsuit and to the other side, and agrees to conduct the litigation accordingly. Some of the specific issues a client might want to discuss with a lawyer up front are:

- how much money is to be spent on the lawsuit, balanced against how much money might be paid to or collected from the other side
- what the client feels is "right" or "fair" and how this can best be achieved
- how much time and energy the client is willing to spend on the lawsuit
- how much control the client wants or expects to have over litigation decisions

- how important it is to the client to end the whole thing as soon as possible, and
- how important it is to the client to exact as much retribution as possible from the other side.

Communication Is Key

There are some important intangibles in choosing a lawyer. How well does the lawyer listen to you? Does the lawyer answer your questions? Do you feel comfortable speaking honestly with the lawyer? Does the lawyer seem willing to accommodate your wishes about how to approach the case? Can you easily understand what the lawyer says? Do you get the sense that the lawyer wants you to know what is going on and to participate in major litigation decisions when appropriate?

These lines of communication will prove important as the lawsuit drags on. The lawyer's willingness to listen and ability to understand may affect how much help you can give the lawyer and whether you can exercise some control over the lawsuit. The lawyer's willingness and ability to explain what is happening in the litigation will likewise affect your capacity to make informed judgments about the case. And your mutual understanding may make the entire process much less stressful.

Learn From Your Lawyer

Good lawyers who litigate cases have a very particular kind of expertise: they know what litigation is like, what results are possible and what kind of toll it can take on a client. Even if you are sure you want to litigate to the death, or settle at the first possible moment, listen to your lawyer's advice on these matters. Your lawyer can offer you a perspective that is informed by experience and usually has the benefit of a little more emotional distance from the issues in the case. Of course, you may not agree with your lawyer's advice; if you don't, your lawyer should accept your decision. But your lawyer's advice and expertise are part of what you're paying for —you may as well get your money's worth.

11. The lawyer I want to hire works in a law firm. Will other people in the firm also work on my case?

Probably. The individual lawyer responsible for all major decisions regarding the litigation —and who actually handles major legal maneuvers and trial if the case gets that far—is known as the *lead attorney*. But in law offices large and small, a certain amount of work on any lawsuit is done by people other than this primary lawyer. Other lawyers in the office (often called *associates), paralegals* (trained legal assistants similar to nurses in a doctor's office) and legal secretaries all will perform tasks during the course of litigation.

This division of labor is due in part to erratic demands on lawyers' time. Also, much legal work is routine and therefore can be done equally well by legal workers with less training (and lower salaries). It is a division of labor that can help or hurt a client. The client benefits if work gets done more quickly and efficiently by others in the office. This might be the case if the lead attorney would not be able to get to the work right away. If the client is paying by the hour, it can be to the client's financial advantage to have routine work done by people with a lower hourly rate. (See Section III.) On the other hand, the client's case might be harmed if important work is left to members of the office with less training or experience.

For these reasons, a potential client should ask who will work on what parts of the litigation. Of course, a lawyer does not know in advance exactly who will do every piece of work. But the lawyer can at least describe how busy he or she is likely to be over the next six months to a year, and therefore how much attention the lawyer can devote to the case. For example, if the lawyer is to begin a big trial within the next few months, the client must realize that this lawyer will have very little time or energy for any other cases during that time.

Also, lawyer and client should discuss which parts of the litigation the lawyer intends to handle personally, such as the trial, depositions of the opposing parties

and key witnesses and preparation of the client for his or her own deposition.

12. Does the size of a law firm affect the quality of the representation it provides?

There is no simple answer to the question of whether a large law firm or a small one is better for any particular case. Most important is the quality of the lead attorney, and excellent lawyers can be found in any size firm. However, it is important that the lead attorney have time for the case. In a big firm, a lawyer may have less time to give to any one case. Also, large firms tend to be highly bureaucratic, so it can be difficult to get personal attention from the lead lawyer and from other staff working on the case. And lawyers in large firms are under pressure to bill many hours of work—whether a case needs it or not. They also tend to spend the client's money freely on litigation expenses.

On the positive side, large law firms have greater resources. They can marshal many people to work on the case, if necessary. They are also better able to front the money for costs in an expensive lawsuit (one requiring a lot of depositions or expert testimony, for example). And a large firm is more likely to have legal staff—paralegals, legal secretaries and less-experienced lawyers—who can do much of the routine legal work in a case at lower cost to a client paying by the hour.

13. Can a conflict of interest prevent me from hiring a lawyer I want?

A lawyer may not represent a potential client if the lawyer's connection to someone or something else creates a *conflict of interest*. A conflict of interest arises when the lawyer's representation of one client might require the lawyer to make an argument, pursue a legal strategy or use information that could harm the interests of another—or former—client of the same lawyer. For example, a lawyer who has represented a business might not be permitted to represent a former partner in a lawsuit against the business. Even connections that have nothing to do with the current dispute, and have ended long before, may create a conflict. For example, the lawyer who previously handled a divorce for one party in a current contract dispute might want to represent an opposing party in a lawsuit about the contract. However, legal rules of ethics hold that the prior relationship creates a conflict of interest. And if the lawyer previously represented parties on both sides of a current dispute, the rules might prevent the lawyer from representing either one in a new lawsuit.

A conflict of interest also may arise when a lawyer sought by one party has already been hired by another party on the "same side" in a lawsuit. For example, if the potential clients are both Plaintiffs, a conflict could arise because the Defendant might have limited resources—the clients would have to compete with each other for the limited assets. And if the clients are both Defendants, a conflict might exist because each could wind up trying to shift legal responsibility onto the other.

14. Can a lawyer represent me despite a conflict of interest?

In some circumstances, the potential benefit to clients of sharing the same lawyer may outweigh the dangers of a conflict of interest. If clients can split hourly attorney fees, rather than pay separate lawyers, they might save a tremendous amount of money. If the same lawyer worked for more than one contingency fee client, the lawyer might offer a reduced rate to each.

This situation may arise when two or more potential clients are Plaintiffs suing the same Defendant. (See Chapter 3, Questions 2 and 3.) Or it can be two or more Defendants being sued by the same Plaintiffs. (See Chapter 3, Section II.)

Parties might share the same lawyer by *waiving a conflict of interest*. The first step in such a waiver is for the lawyer to thoroughly discuss with the parties the various ways in which the conflict might arise during the case. The second step is for the lawyer to advise the clients to seek an outside legal opinion about whether or not to waive the conflict. This would mean spending time and money to go over the situation with a lawyer from a different law firm. A lawyer is obligated to make this suggestion; however, the clients are not obligated to act on it. Finally, the lawyer should explain the conflict in writing and have the clients sign it, to show that the clients have been fully informed of the potential problems.

Section II: Changing Lawyers

This section discusses the circumstances in which a client might change lawyers, and how such a change is accomplished.

15. If I already have a lawyer, can I hire a new one to handle my lawsuit?

Yes. A client might already be represented by a lawyer when a dispute mushrooms into a lawsuit. But the client does not have to stick with that lawyer. An attorney who is good for advice and negotiations might not be suitable for litigation. Or a client might feel that the current lawyer is partly responsible for the dispute winding up in litigation. Whatever the reason—or for no reason at all—a client has the right to change lawyers. And one of the most common times to change lawyers is when a claim or dispute formally becomes a lawsuit.

16. Can I change lawyers after a lawsuit has begun?

Yes. It often happens that a client wants to switch lawyers in the middle of a lawsuit.

There are many reasons why a client might want a change. The client and lawyer might disagree frequently about how the case is being handled. The lawyer might be ignoring the client's requests to keep fees and costs down. Perhaps the lawyer is not keeping the client informed about the progress of the case or of settlement discussions with the other side. Or the lawyer might not seem to be giving the case much attention. Maybe the lawyer and client simply get on each other's nerves.

Whatever the reason, the client almost always has the right to get a new lawyer. The only exception is the rare situation when a client wants to change lawyers right on the verge of trial or during trial itself. In those cases, a judge would have to approve the change, making certain that it would not cause delays that would unfairly affect the other side.

17. If I decide to change lawyers, who gets the fees?

It depends on the fee arrangement with each lawyer. If a client has been paying the first (now former) lawyer by the hour, switching lawyers shouldn't cause any legal fee complications. The client is responsible to the former lawyer for the hours already worked and for costs advanced, but has no additional obligation to that first lawyer once the client hires someone new.

Things are a bit more complicated if the client hired the first lawyer on a contingency fee basis. (See Questions 24-27.) In a contingency fee arrangement, the lawyer gets paid only if the client wins, and the fee owed is a percentage of the money won by the client. A contingency fee is not paid until the case is over, so the former lawyer will not have received any fees when the client hires a new lawyer. The client's new lawyer is also likely to be paid a contingency fee. So, the question becomes how much in total does the client wind up paying and to whom?

The answer is that the client usually pays the same total fees despite switching lawyers. The total percentage fee goes up only if the new lawyer charges a higher percentage rate than the first lawyer, or calculates the fee in a different way regarding litigation costs. (See Question 27, below.)

How the two lawyers divide the total fee will depend on how much work each lawyer has done once the case is over. Fortunately, the client does not usually have to sort out which lawyer gets what. Instead, the lawyers decide on a reasonable division of fees between themselves. To guarantee a share of the fees, the first lawyer may file a court document asking that "reasonable attorney's fees" and unpaid costs be paid out of compensation the client wins in the lawsuit.

18. What is the procedure for formally switching from one lawyer to another?

When a client switches lawyers, the new lawyer should write the previous lawyer a letter, stating that the new lawyer is taking over the case. The client also has to personally inform the first lawyer of the decision to change. The easiest way to do this is for the client to write a brief letter to the first lawyer stating that, as of the date of the letter, the first lawyer's representation of the client is ended. In the letter, the client should also ask the first lawyer to send all the client's files and related materials to the new lawyer. The new lawyer is usually happy to draft this letter for the client.

The first lawyer may ask the client to sign a paper—either in the form of a letter or a document called a *Release*—which formally authorizes the first lawyer to transfer all the files to the new lawyer. The first lawyer may charge a small fee for reviewing the file to remove notes and other work that is personal to the first lawyer, and for copying costs.

If a lawsuit has already begun and the first lawyer has officially filed papers on the client's behalf in the case, the new lawyer has to file, in court, a document called a *Substitution of Attorneys*. This document officially informs the court, the other parties and their lawyers that the new lawyer is now the client's representative in the case. The new lawyer prepares this Substitution of Attorneys, which the client, the new lawyer and the previous lawyer all sign.

Trouble Getting Free of Your First Lawyer?

Lawyers are usually unhappy about losing clients. When you tell your first lawyer that you are switching, the lawyer may try to talk you out of it. Once you make it clear that you intend to make the change, however, most lawyers will sign Substitution of Attorney forms and send the new lawyer your files without further ado. It does occasionally happen, however, that spurned lawyers fail to cooperate. Either because they are still owed money, because they are not satisfied that their right to a contingency fee is protected or for some other reason—laziness, resentment, a belief that the new lawyer has improperly "stolen" the client—they fail to sign papers or send files. But there are things you and your new lawyer can do to shake some sense into your former lawyer. Your new lawyer can go to court to seek a judge's order that the first lawyer cooperate. And help may be available from a local or state bar association.

19. Can my lawyer drop me as a client?

Yes, in some cases. It sometimes happens that a lawyer wants to quit working for a client in the middle of a lawsuit. A lawyer may legitimately want to quit—referred to as *withdrawing from a case*—for any number of reasons: the client may fail to pay the lawyer's fees or litigation costs, the lawyer's health may make it impossible to do a good job on the case, the lawyer may believe that a conflict of interest has arisen or the client and lawyer may strongly disagree about how the case should be handled. A judge would probably permit a lawyer to withdraw for any of these reasons. A lawyer might also want to withdraw for reasons that make good common sense, although a judge might not find them legally sufficient. For example, the lawyer may feel that the case has become too difficult for the lawyer to handle well, the client may be refusing to communicate or cooperate with the lawyer or there may simply be a serious personality clash.

If a lawyer wants to withdraw from a case, it is usually in the client's best interest to let the lawyer do so. A client doesn't want a lawyer who no longer wants to do the job. The lawyer should give the client time to find a new lawyer, during which time the lawyer will continue to protect the client's interests in the lawsuit. Usually, a lawyer who is withdrawing will ask the other side in the lawsuit to delay proceedings while the transition is made. If the delay is not too long, the other side's lawyers usually cooperate. When a new lawyer is found, the client and the old and new lawyers simply execute a Substitution of Attorneys, as described in Question 18, above.

20. Can my lawyer be forced to continue representing me in the lawsuit?

In limited circumstances. Unlike a client, who can change lawyers at any time, a lawyer does not always have the right to immediately withdraw from a case. For example, it is not legally justified for a lawyer to quit just because the case is proving more difficult than originally anticipated. If there is no legally sufficient reason for the lawyer to quit, the client might not want to let the lawyer go—at least not during a crucial stage of the lawsuit—before finding another lawyer to take over.

If there is no new lawyer in place to file a Substitution of Attorneys, the lawyer who wants to quit must seek a judge's permission by filing a *Motion to Withdraw As Counsel*. The lawyer must notify the client of this motion and explain how the client can object. The client may ask the judge to refuse the lawyer's request until another lawyer is ready to take over.

The other side in the lawsuit may also object to a lawyer's request to withdraw. If important litigation procedures are pending, the other side may not want to delay them while the client looks for a new lawyer and that lawyer gets up to speed on the case. In these circumstances, a judge may order the unhappy original lawyer to stay on the case until certain procedures are completed.

Section III: Attorney Fees and Litigation Costs

A lawyer and client must have a clear agreement, from the start of their working relationship, about exactly how the lawyer's fee will be calculated and when the client will be expected to pay it. Lawyer and client must also reach an agreement about which litigation costs the client will be expected to pay and when those payments will be due. This Section discusses the different ways lawyers structure their fee agreements and the kinds of litigation expenses clients may expect to pay. Whatever the arrangement a lawyer and client reach about fees and costs, it should be clearly spelled out in a written representation agreement signed by both lawyer and client (see Sections IV and V, below).

21. What is the range of fees I may be facing if I pay my lawyer by the hour?

The most common form of lawyer compensation is the hourly rate. Unfortunately, those rates range from $75 to $300 per hour—or more. As with most other services, rates tend to be higher in major urban areas. The hourly rate charged for work by less-experienced lawyers in the same office is usually substantially lower than rates charged by more senior attorneys. If the lawyer's office uses paralegals and charges separately for their time, their hourly rate is probably in the $35–$75 per hour range. Most lawyers keep painfully close track of, and charge for, every minute they spend on a case. Lawyers usually mark their work time in tenth-of-an-hour increments (six-minute chunks). So, if they spend even one minute on a case—a quick phone call, reviewing and signing a letter—they bill for a tenth-of-an-hour.

A Lawyer's Time Is Your Money

If your lawyer charges by the hour, the meter is running whenever you have a conversation. Before you pick up the phone or make an appointment, think about whether you really need to talk to your lawyer. A secretary might be able to handle scheduling issues, make sure you get copies of important documents and take care of other basic requests, for example.

If you have questions for your attorney, write them down before you call or visit. This way, you can be sure to get all your questions answered at once and avoid getting charged for a second or third conversation. If you have information you need to share with your lawyer—thoughts about potential witnesses, answers to discovery requests or comments on a pleading, for example—consider writing them down in a letter. Finally, don't use your lawyer—especially not a lawyer you are paying by the hour—as a shoulder to cry on or an emotional sounding board. Lawyers aren't trained as therapists or counselors—but will charge you for their time if you ask them to act like one.

22. What is a retainer?

A lawyer who will be paid an hourly fee may ask the client to pay a lump sum at the beginning of the case to guarantee payment for the lawyer's initial work. Once this "down payment," known as a *retainer*, is received, the lawyer deposits it in a *bank trust account*. Fees are withdrawn from the retainer as the lawyer does work on the case and bills the client for the time. Litigation costs may also be charged against the retainer. (See Questions 30-34, below.)

Some lawyers also require the client to maintain the retainer at a minimum level throughout the litigation. For example, a lawyer might ask that the client deposit an initial $5,000 retainer, and that the client not allow it to fall below $2,000. As soon as the lawyer bills the client for more than $3,000—and takes that amount out of the trust account—the client would be required to deposit enough additional money to push the account back up to $2,000.

23. What can I do initially to control hourly fees?

Because paying by the hour can become so expensive so quickly, a client might want to discuss money-saving measures with the lawyer at the very beginning of the case. Such measures might include:

- **Discounted rate.** Some lawyers will agree to reduce the hourly rate they charge if they work more than a certain number of hours on a case in any one month. For example, a lawyer might charge $150 per hour for the first 20 hours the lawyer works on the case in a month, but then only $100 for every additional hour in that month.

- **Cap on total fee.** By the time most disputes get to the lawsuit stage, both sides have a pretty good idea of how much money is at stake. Based on how much a party stands to gain or lose, a client and lawyer might be able to gauge how much (in lawyer fees) it is worth spending to win, or to protect against losing. For example, if a client is suing to recover $50,000 in damages, the client might want the lawyer to agree to try to settle the lawsuit once legal fees reach $20,000 or so. Otherwise, legal fees might eat up most of the money that could be won. Of course, the client might also win a lower amount, even less than the lawyer's bill. This kind of balancing —legal fees versus the total amount at stake in the lawsuit—should be discussed at the start of the case. If possible, lawyer and client should agree on a maximum fee amount. When legal fees near that figure, the lawyer can push to settle the case— even if the settlement is not as good as the client might have hoped.

- **Prior approval of legal maneuvers.** A client might be able to control some hourly legal fees by making sure the lawyer discusses major legal procedures *before* beginning work on them. A conscientious, client-friendly lawyer will do this anyway—but it doesn't hurt for the client to raise the issue at the outset. (The kinds of legal maneuvers that are likely to eat up a lot of lawyer hours are pointed out to the reader throughout this book.)

- **Careful billing review.** A client paying hourly fees must keep abreast of the lawyer's work. Most lawyers' offices send a client an itemized bill every month. The bill includes, by date, a brief description of the work a lawyer or paralegal has done that month on the case and how long (in tenths of hours) the work took. The client should make sure there have been no major, time-consuming legal maneuvers that the client has not previously heard about from the lawyer. Also, if certain aspects of the case are running up a lot of attorney fees, the client might want to raise the possibility of cutting down in that area of the litigation— for example, taking fewer depositions of minor witnesses. (See Chapter 4.) Finally, if the total lawyer fees will soon become unaffordable or will exceed what the client stands to win in the case, client and lawyer must discuss the possibility of settling the case quickly, rather than continuing with expensive litigation.

24. When would a lawyer work for a percentage of my recovery rather than for an hourly fee?

In certain kinds of cases, lawyers charge what is called a *contingency fee*. Instead of billing by the hour, the lawyer waits until the case is over, then takes, as a fee, a certain percentage of the amount the client has won. If the client wins nothing, the lawyer gets no fee. In this way, the lawyer shares the client's risk of losing or of winning less than expected. A contingency fee also rewards the lawyer for helping to win a higher amount—the more the lawyer wins for the client, the more the lawyer gets. This method of payment was developed to permit lawyers to aggressively represent those people who want to sue for damages but don't have the money to pay a lawyer as the case goes along.

Most commonly, a contingency fee agreement is made for the plaintiff—the person suing—in a personal injury or medical

malpractice case. But it may also be used for individuals who are suing a business or organization for potentially high compensation—in cases involving employment discrimination, harassment or wrongful termination, patent or trademark infringement, personal or business fraud or unfair competition.

25. Will I have to pay a retainer in a contingency fee case?

Perhaps. Some lawyers ask clients to pay a retainer even in contingency fee cases. These retainers act as a guarantee that the lawyer will receive some payment for working on the case. If the client loses or wins only a small award, the lawyer keeps the retainer as payment for services. If the client wins, the lawyer applies the retainer against the attorney fees to be collected.

26. How much do lawyers charge as a contingency fee?

The standard contingency fee in personal injury cases is 33% of the amount of compensation the plaintiff obtains in a settlement. Usually, the fee rises to 40% once the case is set for trial or (in courts where the trial date is set early in the lawsuit) 60 to 90 days before the trial date. Fees rise whether or not the trial actually takes place. The reason for this increase is that a lawyer's work increases tremendously once the case nears trial. Contingency fee rates in other cases are similar, though they can range from 25%–50% depending on the amount of work a lawyer must do, the amount of litigation costs a lawyer must pay, the potential for a large fee and the risk of getting no fee at all.

Although one-third is the standard contingency fee, some lawyers will consider either a lower rate or a mixture of rates, depending on the case. A client might successfully negotiate with a lawyer for a lower rate, perhaps 20%–25% of any settlement before the case is set for trial, if most or all of the following factors are present:

- it seems virtually certain that the client will recover damages—the only question is how much the award will be
- the client is likely to receive a large award, and
- the attorney will not have to do a lot of complicated or time-consuming legal work.

In cases involving a large potential recovery, a sliding scale fee schedule is also a possibility. In these sliding scale arrangements, the lawyer's rate goes down as the compensation goes up. For example, a lawyer might agree to a sliding fee scale of 33% for recovery of up to $100,000 and 25% for all amounts over $100,000. Or a lawyer might agree to a more graduated scale, with 33% up to $100,000, 25% for $100,000 to $250,000 and 15% for all amounts above $250,000. The better the client's case—the more certain it looks that the client will get significant compensation

without need for a trial—the more willing a lawyer will be to negotiate this type of arrangement.

A Lawyer Might Hedge Bets Through a Combination Fee

Your case might have the potential for large compensation—but only with lots of legal work and a significant risk of losing. Because of the risk, a lawyer might balk at taking the case on a pure contingency fee basis. At the same time, because of the enormous work involved, you might not be able to afford to pay the lawyer on an hourly basis.

In such a case, a lawyer might be willing to combine the two types of fee structures, hourly and contingency. In such a *combination fee* or *blended fee* agreement, you pay the lawyer on an hourly basis, but at a reduced rate and only up to a certain limit. Beyond that limit, the lawyer takes no further direct payment from you but instead takes a percentage of the amount you win in the lawsuit. This percentage is considerably lower than in a normal contingency fee case because the lawyer has already been paid an hourly rate. For example, if the lawyer's regular hourly rate is $200 and the normal contingency fee amount is 33% of the client's compensation, the lawyer might agree instead to charge $100 per hour up to a maximum of $10,000, plus 15% or 20% of the final compensation, if any.

27. How is a contingency fee calculated?

There are two different ways in which a lawyer's contingency fee may be calculated. The fee may be calculated as a percentage of the total amount of the plaintiff's settlement or trial award *before* litigation costs are deducted. (See Questions 31-34.) Or, the fee may be calculated based on the amount of compensation *after* costs have been deducted.

The method used—before or after costs are paid—can make a significant difference in the amount a client finally gets to keep when the case is over. A client keeps more if costs are subtracted first. Consider, for example, a contingency fee case in which the client wins $100,000, litigation costs are $20,000 and the lawyer gets a 33% fee. If that fee is collected *before* costs are subtracted, the lawyer gets 33% of $100,000, which is $33,000. From the remaining $67,000, the client must pay the $20,000 in litigation costs, leaving the client with $47,000. On the other hand, if the costs are subtracted *before* the lawyer takes legal fees, the calculation would work as follows. Subtracting the $20,000 in costs from the $100,000 compensation leaves $80,000. The lawyer would get 33% of that $80,000, which is $26,400. The client would keep $100,000 minus the $26,400 legal fee and the $20,000 costs, for a total of $53,600. The client keeps $6,000 more in the second calculation.

Given these figures, it is easy to understand why lawyers almost always calculate contingency fees *before* costs are subtracted. However, in cases where the potential recovery is high but the costs are likely to be very extensive, a client might be able to negotiate this matter with a lawyer. In order to sign up a lucrative case, the lawyer might agree to calculate the contingency fee *after* costs have been paid, or on some compromise figure (for example, the total compensation less 50% of costs). A lawyer is more likely to agree to such an arrangement if the client pays the costs as the case goes along, rather than the lawyer "advancing" the costs. (See Question 33.)

 Your State May Regulate Contingency Fees. Many states have laws restricting the contingency fee percentage a lawyer may charge in certain types of cases. A few states limit contingency fees in all personal injury cases. Other states restrict the amount a lawyer may charge in medical malpractice cases, sometimes in a sliding scale reducing the fee as the recovery amount increases. And a few states restrict the contingency fee rate a lawyer may charge for representing a minor—usually to 25%. If you and a lawyer are discussing a contingency fee, ask whether there is a state law regarding the rate a lawyer may charge in your type of case.

28. Can my lawyer collect fees from the other side?

Perhaps. In most cases, each side in a lawsuit pays its own attorney fees. But in a few kinds of cases, the loser pays the winning side's attorney fees for the entire litigation. If there is a good chance that the client will prevail in such a case, a lawyer might agree to take the case on what is called an *attorney fee award* basis. In this arrangement, the lawyer charges an hourly rate but does not collect it from the client. Instead, the lawyer waits for the court to order that the fees be paid by the other side, once the case is successfully concluded. If the client does not win the case, the client pays no lawyer fees. Sometimes a lawyer will modify this all-or-nothing approach by collecting a small hourly fee from the client along the way, and perhaps also by having the client pay ongoing litigation costs. (See Question 33.)

There are generally three types of cases in which the other side may be required to pay legal fees:

- breach of contract lawsuits, if the contract specifically requires the loser in any legal dispute to pay the winning side's attorney fees
- cases involving violations of state or federal law in which the law itself requires the loser to pay the other side's legal fees (usually a lawsuit against a government entity, or against a business or organization for violation of privacy, safety or anti-discrimination laws), and
- certain types of cases in which state law requires the loser to pay the winner's attorney fees (often family law matters, challenges to a will or trust and certain real estate disputes).

29. Do lawyers ever handle a lawsuit for a lump sum fee?

Although lawyers sometimes charge a flat fee—a one-time only charge, paid in advance, to cover all the lawyer's work—they rarely do so when litigation is involved. The few kinds of litigation for which a lawyer might charge a flat fee are criminal cases, some family law matters (divorce, spousal support, child custody), conservatorship, guardianship and incompetency proceedings, and bankruptcies. In these cases, a lawyer knows at the outset which legal procedures will be necessary and approximately how much time and money they will require. In most other kinds of litigation, however, a lawyer simply would not know how much of a flat fee to set—it is impossible to accurately estimate at the beginning of a lawsuit how much work will be required.

30. What are litigation costs and why should I worry about them?

Many clients are terribly surprised to learn, at the conclusion of their lawsuit, how much their lawyer has spent conducting the litigation. It is a surprise because some lawyers fail to keep clients abreast of the costs being accumulated—and because too many clients fail to pay attention to what their lawyers are spending. The surprise is a terrible one because these costs can run into the thousands of dollars—and because the client may have to pay them all. To avoid surprises, at the very beginning of the lawsuit the lawyer should spell out in the written representation agreement which litigation expenses will be charged to the client and which ones, if any, will be borne by the lawyer's office. The agreement should also specify how and when the client is to pay these costs.

31. What is usually considered a litigation "cost" rather than merely a lawyer's normal business expense?

While the client is usually responsible for paying *litigation costs* incurred during the course of the lawsuit, the client should *not* have to pay for the normal operating expenses of the lawyer's office. At the beginning of the case, a lawyer and client must get straight, and put in the written representation agreement, the costs for which the client will be responsible. Typically, a client pays for any cost that is generated by someone or something beyond the lawyer's office and staff. Of these costs normally paid by the client, the most common are:

- private investigators and process servers
- expert consultants and witnesses, whether or not they actually testify at trial

- court fees, charged to file legal papers and to pay the expenses of jurors
- deposition costs, including the stenographer's hourly fee, the cost of preparing and copying transcripts and any appearance fees or travel costs owed to witnesses
- fees charged by businesses, doctors, accountants and government agencies, among others, for preparing reports or making copies of records and files
- the lawyer's travel costs (such as those incurred taking depositions of distant witnesses)
- extra communications costs, such as long-distance phone calls, messenger and delivery services
- copying costs, and
- special effects, which might include graphs and charts, photo enlargements and other visual and aural exhibits prepared for use in court.

One way a client can keep costs in check is to ask the lawyer to inform the client, in advance, of all depositions and any investigator or expert witness to be used. That way, client and lawyer can discuss the estimated cost versus the expected legal benefit before the money is spent. Also, the client should regularly check monthly bills from the lawyer to see whether there are large costs the client does not understand or did not authorize.

The Modern Cost of Online Legal Research

In recent years, lawyers have begun to use online research services. Although these online research services—like Lexis or Westlaw—can be real time-savers, they also have expensive subscription and usage rates. Because an online service cuts research time for the lawyer, it can save the client money in an hourly fee arrangement. If the lawyer will be paid a contingency fee, however, the client should not be charged extra for the lawyer's online research. After all, the client wouldn't have to pay for time the lawyer spent reading law books in the library, so why should the client have to pay for research done on the computer? Unfortunately, some law offices routinely pass the significant costs of online research on to their clients. Make sure this issue is covered in your fee agreement.

32. Are there expenses I should not have to pay?

Yes. Some lawyers have the nasty habit of padding their bills by charging clients for the law office's normal business expenses, considered "overhead" by most businesses. Common office expenditures for which a client should *not* have to pay include:

- clerical charges, such as secretarial time, word processing or anything characterized as "administrative" costs

- fax charges, and
- charges to use a lawyer's conference room or other internal office space.

33. When will I have to pay litigation costs?

Usually, a lawyer's office calculates litigation costs monthly and includes them in the client's regular bill. At the beginning of a case, a lawyer might ask that a client put down a deposit—either as a separate *costs retainer* or as part of a broader fee retainer —to guarantee payment of costs. In other cases, a lawyer will agree to an *advance of costs*. That means that the lawyer pays the costs and waits to be reimbursed by the client at the end of the case. These arrangements can be made in the following ways:

- **Hourly cases.** When a lawyer charges by the hour, the client usually has to pay the costs of litigation as they are incurred. At the beginning of the case, the lawyer may require the client to put down a costs retainer—a deposit the lawyer puts into a special bank trust account—against which the lawyer draws funds to pay litigation costs. The lawyer's regular bill to the client includes an itemization of these costs. If the client has not given a retainer for costs, the client is expected to pay these costs monthly, along with billed attorney fees.

- **Contingency fee and attorney fee award cases.** There are two ways in which costs can be paid in contingency and attorney fee award cases. The client might pay costs as the case goes along, either directly (as part of a monthly bill) or out of a costs retainer deposit. Or the lawyer might pay costs along the way and be reimbursed out of the client's compensation at the end of the case. Lawyers are willing to do this in some cases because they can often afford to front these costs—and wait months or years for repayment— more easily than their clients.

34. In a contingency fee or attorney fee award case, do I have to pay litigation costs even if I lose the lawsuit?

Perhaps. If the client wins nothing (or wins less than the total costs) and the client has been paying costs all along, that money is gone for good. But if the lawyer has been advancing costs, who ultimately pays will depend entirely on the terms of the representation agreement. If the agreement says that the client is to pay costs, then the client owes the lawyer the total amount of reasonable costs the lawyer's office spent on the case, despite the poor outcome.

In some cases, however, the lawyer agrees to pay some or all of the litigation costs without reimbursement if the client doesn't win enough money to cover those

costs. A lawyer might make this kind of agreement if the lawyer believes there is a good chance of winning a large recovery— this chance makes it worth the risk of having to pay costs if the case doesn't pan out.

Section IV: The Representation Agreement

When a lawyer and client agree on the terms under which the lawyer will represent the client on a particular case, those terms are put in writing and signed by the client and lawyer. This document—called a *fee agreement, retainer agreement* or *representation agreement*—can be a simple letter outlining basic terms or a more formal-looking contract.

The form of the agreement doesn't matter. What matters is that the agreement is clear about certain key issues. This Section discusses the matters that must be included in an agreement. Section V of this Chapter contains sample representation agreements for reference.

35. What important financial issues must be included in a representation agreement?

First and foremost, a representation agreement must explain the lawyer's fee and how it will be paid. That is, it must state how much the lawyer will charge, what fee structure will be used (hourly fee, contingency fee or some combination) and when the lawyer will collect it (monthly from the client, at the end of the case from the client or from the opposing side). If the fee will rise when the case nears trial, the triggering date for that increase should be clearly stated in the agreement. The agreement should also describe anticipated litigation costs, whether the client or the lawyer is to advance them and who must ultimately pay them. And the agreement should cover any agreed-upon retainer deposit—how much the deposit will be, whether it covers fees alone, costs alone or both, and whether the client has to maintain it at a minimum level throughout the case.

36. What other provisions are typical in a retainer agreement?

Because every law office creates its own representation agreements, these contracts vary substantially in language, formality and length. However, some standard terms appear in most of these agreements, including:

- **extent of the representation**—The agreement should make clear that the lawyer will represent the client in all litigation proceedings, including trial. Some agreements exclude certain post-trial proceedings, including appeals or collection of an award if the client wins a judgment. (See Chapter 10.) Sometimes a client has several legal tussles going on simultaneously, so the agreement should define the

specific case the lawyer will handle— that is, the nature of, and parties to, this particular dispute should be specified. If a lawsuit has already been filed, the agreement should identify the case by title and court number.
- **lawyers who will do the work**—The agreement should specify who will be the "lead counsel" on the case and what legal procedures that lead counsel will handle personally. (See Question 11.) If other attorneys in the firm who may handle some part of the case charge different hourly rates, those rates should be specified.
- **no guarantees**—Most representation agreements state that the lawyer does not guarantee any particular outcome in the lawsuit. This prevents a client from complaining—once the case is over—that the lawyer had "promised" to win a particular amount for the client, or to protect the client from a specific level of defeat.
- **ending the representation**—Many lawyers include some standard language explaining when either the lawyer or the client may end their working relationship. Some agreements state that, by signing the agreement, the client agrees that the lawyer can end the representation at any time. Others allow the lawyer to drop the client only under specified circumstances.
- **working together**—Some representation agreements specify how lawyer and client will work together. For example,

an agreement might require the client to be honest with the attorney. Or the agreement might spell out which decisions the lawyer can make alone and which require the client's approval.

37. Must I agree to use the lawyer's standard representation agreement?

Although lawyers develop representation agreements over time to cover most potentially important issues, the standard agreement doesn't always address everything. For example, there might be an unusual fee or cost arrangement not described in any of the lawyer's standard agreements. If so, a lawyer can modify the standard agreement to address the different situation. Adding an addendum to the agreement, on a separate, attached sheet of paper, is a common way to do this. (See Sample Representation Agreement #2, in Section V.) However, a client should not balk at using a lawyer's standard agreement simply because the lawyer drafted it. The lawyer's office has considered many potential problems between lawyer and client in creating this document, so the agreement will cover many issues the client might not have considered. A well-drafted agreement protects both lawyer and client and sets the stage for a positive working relationship. This doesn't mean a client should simply sign whatever the lawyer puts on the table, however. The client should make sure the agreement is fair and accurate before signing.

Make Sure the Agreement Is Accurate

The written representation agreement is an important contract that defines your business relationship with your lawyer. In case of any later disputes between you over fees, costs or the quality of the lawyer's representation, this contract will be the most important evidence of your agreement. While there is no point in arguing with your lawyer over every comma, you must make sure that the contract reflects your understanding of the agreement you have reached with the lawyer. For example, if you have agreed on a particular fee or cost arrangement or have agreed that the lawyer will discuss major expenditures with you ahead of time, make sure that the agreement accurately reflects those discussions. If the written agreement is substantially different than your understanding, ask the lawyer to change it. If the lawyer refuses to conform the agreement to your understanding, or offer you a very good reason why not, this does not bode well for your professional relationship.

38. Can my lawyer and I change our representation agreement once the case is under way?

A representation agreement is just a contract—its terms may be changed at any time, as long as both parties agree in writing. However, a client should never rely on a lawyer's oral promise that their agreement has been changed. Any new terms must be clearly spelled out, in writing. The new contract should refer to the parts of the original written agreement that are being changed and be dated and signed by both lawyer and client.

Either lawyer or client may want to make a change. A client may find that the lawsuit eats up money more quickly than expected or involves much greater sums in potential damages, and so may want to renegotiate the lawyer's fee or arrangements about litigation costs. However, a lawyer is under no obligation to accept such renegotiation. If the lawyer refuses, the client's only option may be to fire the lawyer and hire someone else for the remainder of the case.

As the lawsuit moves along, the lawyer may find the case more complicated than it had seemed based on the client's original information. The lawyer might therefore want to renegotiate fees or cost advances. The lawyer may want to share some of the load with other lawyers in the office or even with a lawyer from a different office. However, the lawyer can't just change the agreement unilaterally; the client must agree to the new arrangement. A good lawyer will thoroughly explain the need for any changes in the agreement, making sure the client understands the lawyer's position —even if the client is not happy about it. If the client does not want to agree to the new terms, client and lawyer should discuss whether the client would be better off with a new lawyer entirely. (See Section II.)

Section V: Sample Representation Agreements

On the following pages are three sample representation agreements. Two are for hourly rate fee arrangements. One is for a contingency fee. Each is somewhat different in form and language—one is a letter, one calls itself an "Agreement" and one is labeled "Contract"—but each serves the same purpose.

None of these samples is meant to be exactly the right form of agreement for any particular lawyer, client or lawsuit, and none of them is a perfect or "standard" document. Lawyers develop their own agreements over time. These agreements may include certain terms required by state ethical rules for the legal profession as well as language the lawyer has devised to address practical matters that commonly arise.

A client need not ask a lawyer to use any specific language from any of these samples. However, if any terms in the lawyer's representation agreement are incomplete or unclear, or do not address issues discussed in these sample agreements, the client should ask the lawyer to explain. If the explanation seems to include something that is not in the lawyer's agreement itself, the client should ask the lawyer to add it to the written document.

Sample Representation Agreement #1

LAW OFFICES OF

TINKER, EVERS & CHANCE

1234 BROADWAY, SUITE 100

OAKMONT, CALIFORNIA 00000

September 12, 20XX

Sheila Q. Public
111 High Street
Oakmont, CA 00000

Re: *Public v. Johnson Contracting Company*

Dear Ms. Public:

We are pleased that you have decided to have us represent you in your legal dispute with the Johnson Contracting Company regarding the construction of your home. This letter is intended to confirm the terms and conditions of our agreement concerning your representation.

We agree that we will assume your representation in this matter to and including any trial of the lawsuit filed in the case, and that we will exert our best efforts to provide you with legal counsel and advice, consistent with the canons of ethics of the legal profession. Obviously, however, we cannot guarantee that those efforts will result in a total or unqualified level of success in this matter.

We agree that Mary C. Tinker, Attorney at Law, will assume responsibility within the office for your representation, including serving as lead trial counsel should the matter go to trial. Ms. Tinker retains the authority to designate other attorneys and paralegals in the office to perform tasks on your case, in her sole discretion.

For these services, you agree to pay us at our current hourly rates: for the calendar year 20XX they are $200 per hour for Mary C. Tinker, Robert Evers and Dean Chance; $150 per hour for all associate attorneys and $75 per hour for paralegals. At the beginning of each calendar year this representation agreement may be updated to reflect any changes in the current hourly rates of the members of our office.

Sample Representation Agreement #1 (continued)

In addition to fees as described above, we will charge you for our actual out-of-pocket costs for the following expenses related to your representation: depositions; service of legal documents; attorney travel; filing and other court fees; photocopies; and non-local telephone charges. In addition, it may be necessary to retain the services of an investigator or expert to consult and perform related services, and to testify on your behalf. If we deem it advisable to have you retain an investigator or expert, we will recommend one to you and will obtain your consent prior to engaging his or her services on your behalf.

You have agreed to give us a retainer in the amount of $5,000, against which we will bill on a monthly basis for services rendered and expenses incurred. If and when such retainer is exhausted, you agree to pay any additional fees and costs within 30 days of receipt of billing from us. Interest at 10% per annum will be added to all unpaid balances of fees and costs 60 days after providing you with a bill for them. If we do not exhaust the entire retainer amount by the conclusion of our representation, we will return the remainder to you within 30 days.

We reserve the right at all times to withdraw from your representation in the event that a conflict arises, or we have a substantial disagreement. Should that occur, we will provide you with notice so that you may have the opportunity to employ other counsel.

Please read this letter carefully. If you are in agreement with its terms, retain this original for your files, sign the enclosed copy and return it to this office. If you have any comments or questions concerning the terms and conditions in this letter, please contact me at your convenience.

Very truly yours,

Mary C. Tinker
for TINKER, EVERS & CHANCE

Read, Approved and Agreed:

Date: _____   _____
                                     Sheila Q. Public

Sample Representation Agreement #2

Hourly Rate Fee Agreement

This Agreement is made this _____ day of _____, 20XX, between Sheila Q. Public ("Client") and Tinker, Evers & Chance ("Attorney").

1. Hourly Rates. Client hereby retains Attorney for the purposes of legal representation and agrees to pay for all services rendered at Attorney's current schedule of fees, dated January 1, 20XX, and attached as Exhibit "A" to this Agreement. Attorney shall be entitled to revise the schedule of fees upon thirty (30) days written notice to Client. Attorney charges for services in increments of 1/10th of an hour.

2. Costs. Client agrees to pay for all reasonable costs advanced by Attorney for client's account. These include, but are not limited to, the costs of: depositions; service of legal documents; attorney travel; filing and other court fees; photocopies; non-local telephone charges; investigators; consultants; and expert witnesses. Before engaging an investigator, consultant or expert on behalf of Client, Attorney will inform Client and will obtain Client's permission.

3. Services. Attorney will charge for all activities undertaken to provide legal services to Client under this Agreement, including but not limited to preparation for and participation in: conferences; court appearances; depositions; legal research, negotiations, personal and telephone conversations, and preparation and review of correspondence, trial preparation materials and legal documents. Client understands that Client is retaining the law firm of Tinker, Evers & Chance and not one particular attorney, and that attorney services to be provided Client will not be performed by any particular attorney. However, it is intended that services will be performed principally by Mary C. Tinker, and that other attorneys or paralegals performing services will have been designated by Mary C. Tinker. The legal services to be performed by attorney for Client are as follows: representation in a legal dispute between Client and Johnson Contracting Company regarding construction of Client's home, including prosecuting on behalf of Client the lawsuit known as *Public v. Johnson Contracting Co*, in the Superior Court of Oakmont County, California, Case No. XXXXXX.

-1-

Sample Representation Agreement #2 (continued)

4. <u>Duties of Attorney</u>. Attorney agrees to perform legal services in an ethical and professional manner and regularly to provide Client with sufficient information concerning the progress of the case to allow Client to make informed decisions concerning the case. Client understands, however, that litigation is an uncertain process and that Attorney cannot, and does not, either guarantee or predict any particular outcome in the case, and that all charges will apply regardless of the ultimate result in the case.

5. <u>Duties of Client</u>. Client agrees to cooperate with Attorney in obtaining and preparing information and materials, responding to discovery requests and such other activities as are reasonably necessary to assist Attorney in representing Client. Client shall be truthful with Attorney, keep Attorney informed of developments which might affect the case, advise Attorney of Client's current address, telephone and whereabouts and timely make any payment required by this Agreement.

6. <u>Billing</u>. Client will be billed monthly for professional fees and for actual costs incurred. Bills are due and payable upon receipt. An account unpaid for more than thirty (30) days from the date of the invoice is considered overdue and interest at the rate of ten percent per annum will be charged on such overdue amounts.

7. <u>Deposit</u>. Client will pay to Attorney a deposit of $5,000 which will be credited towards Client's outstanding professional fees and costs. Client shall at all times maintain this deposit in the minimum amount of $1,000. Any portion of this deposit not so applied will be returned to Client at the conclusion of Attorney's representation of Client.

8. <u>Lien on Recovery</u>. In the event of any recovery or judgment obtained on behalf of Client at a time when any fees or costs owed by Client to Attorney remain unpaid, Attorney shall have a lien on such recovery or judgment in the amount of all such fees or costs.

9. <u>Attorney's Fees/Collection Costs</u>. In the event of a dispute between Client and Attorney arising out of this Agreement which results in litigation or other dispute-resolution procedure including mediation or arbitration, the prevailing party shall be entitled to an award of attorney's fees and costs incurred in connection therewith.

Sample Representation Agreement #2 (continued)

10. <u>Termination</u>. Client has a unilateral right to discharge Attorney and terminate this Agreement without cause by giving Attorney written notice. This Agreement also constitutes Client's consent for Attorney to withdraw as Client's counsel in any pending litigation, administrative proceedings or other matter, and to substitute Client in said proceeding as Client's own attorney for any reason authorized by the Rules of Professional Conduct of the State Bar of California, including, but not limited to, failure to fully honor the fee provisions of this Agreement and refusal to follow Attorney's professional advice on a material matter. Should Attorney wish to withdraw, Attorney shall give reasonable notice to Client. Client agrees that, promptly after such notice and upon Attorney's request, Client will execute such documents as may reasonably be necessary to effectuate the termination of Attorney's representation, including Substitution of Attorneys to be filed with the court.

Client has read, understands and agrees to the terms of the representation Agreement set forth above. Client acknowledges receipt of a copy of this Agreement.

Date: _____   _____
                             Client

Date: _____   _____
                             Attorney

Attachment to Sample Representation Agreement #2

Exhibit A to Fee Agreement

Hourly fee rates for TINKER, EVERS & CHANCE effective January 1, 20XX.

Rate for: Mary C. Tinker, Robert Evers and Dean Chance—$200/hr.

Rate for: associate attorneys—$150/hr.

Rate for: certified paralegal assistants—$75/hr.

Sample Representation Agreement #3

Contract for Professional Services

IT IS HEREBY AGREED between the undersigned <u>Sheila Q. Public</u>, hereinafter "Client," and the law offices of TINKER, EVERS & CHANCE, hereinafter "Attorneys," that said Attorneys shall represent Client in prosecuting a claim for damages, including litigation of the matter to and through trial, arising out of an accident and/or incident which occurred on or about <u>February 10, 20XX</u>.

IT IS HEREBY FURTHER AGREED that the compensation to be paid to Attorneys for said representation regarding the prosecution of said claim shall be one-third (1/3) of the sum paid in settlement of the case or otherwise recovered *before* a date for trial or arbitration thereof has been set. Said compensation amount is to be calculated *before deducting*, from the total sum paid in settlement or recovered, all costs theretofore advanced or incurred by the law firm in the prosecution of the claim.

IT IS HEREBY FURTHER AGREED that the compensation to be paid to Attorneys for said representation regarding the prosecution of said claim shall be forty percent (40%) of the sum paid in settlement of the case or otherwise recovered *after* a date for trial or arbitration thereof has been set. Said compensation amount is to be calculated *before deducting*, from the total sum paid in settlement or recovered, all costs theretofore advanced or incurred by the law firm in the prosecution of the claim.

IT IS HEREBY FURTHER AGREED that Attorneys shall advance all of the costs of processing the claim and related litigation, including: court costs, filing fees, service of process fees, jury fees, deposition costs, investigative fees, reporter fees, expert consultation, appearance and testimony costs, witness fees, travel costs, photocopying costs and the cost of non-local telephone calls.

IT IS HEREBY FURTHER AGREED that if there is a recovery in the matter, either before or after a date set for trial or arbitration, Attorneys are to receive, in addition to attorney fee compensation, reimbursement for the full amount of any such costs advanced or incurred. Client agrees to repay Attorneys for such costs advanced or paid out of the sum paid in settlement or otherwise recovered in the case.

-1-

Sample Representation Agreement #3 (continued)

IT IS HEREBY FURTHER AGREED that if there is no settlement of the claim or other recovery, Attorneys shall receive nothing from Client for legal services and shall not be reimbursed by Client for any costs advanced by Attorneys. Client shall, however, be obligated to pay any other party's costs if awarded by the court.

IT IS HEREBY FURTHER AGREED that Attorneys are entitled to, and this Agreement shall constitute, a lien on any settlement amount, judgment or other recovery by Client arising out of this case, for Attorneys' fee compensation and for costs advanced by Attorneys on behalf of Client in the prosecution of this case.

This Agreement covers only the handling of Client's claim and resultant litigation, if any, arising out of the accident and/or incident described herein. Any other matters handled by Attorneys on behalf of Client are not included in or covered by this Agreement, and Client shall pay Attorneys separate, additional compensation, as negotiated and agreed between Attorneys and Client, for any such additional services.

Date: _____   _____
                                   Client

Date: _____   _____
                                   Attorney

I acknowledge that I have received a duplicate copy of this Agreement signed by both Attorney and Client.

Date: _____   _____
                                   Client

Chapter 2

Working With Your Lawyer

The relationship between lawyer and client often comes under considerable pressure during the long course of litigation. And how well the lawyer and client manage their relationship can significantly affect the client's lawsuit experience. A good working relationship can both increase the odds of a positive result and reduce the client's miseries along the way.

This Chapter describes how to work successfully with a lawyer. It discusses attitudes and approaches a client can take to enhance the lawyer-client relationship. And it explains what a client can expect—and a few things not to expect—from a lawyer.

1. How much information should I give my lawyer?

Everything. Bringing information—documents, names of witnesses, conversations and explanations—to the lawyer's attention is always a good thing. It is the lawyer's job to sift through the information and determine what is useful and what is not. A fact the client thought was insignificant might turn out to provide the basis for a solid defense or a creative legal argument. And the sooner the lawyer knows about a piece of information, the better prepared the lawyer can be to use it or respond to it.

As soon as a client hires a lawyer, the client should show or tell the lawyer everything that might pertain to the dispute. And the client must continue this policy of full disclosure throughout the litigation process. A client should bring to the lawyer's attention any information the client discovers, remembers or otherwise learns of during the course of the lawsuit.

2. Should I tell my lawyer things that might hurt my case?

Yes. A lawyer is under the strictest legal instructions never to reveal anything a client tells the lawyer. The protection provided by this attorney-client privilege extends to information provided by the client to any member of the lawyer's staff, or to anyone hired by the lawyer to work on the case. (See Chapter 4, Section VI.)

Given the very broad protection of the attorney-client privilege, a client should tell

the lawyer all negative and potentially damaging information as well as those facts that might help. If a client tells the lawyer about potential problems, the lawyer can develop legal tactics to counter or explain them—that is part of a lawyer's job. It is the things a client does *not* tell the lawyer that often cause the most trouble—if the lawyer is caught by surprise by a damaging piece of information, it might be too late to control the harm it causes.

Don't Ask Your Lawyer to Lie or Hide Things

It is inevitable that some of the information you turn over to your lawyer will be more harmful than helpful to your case. It is a basic part of your lawyer's job to minimize the legal consequences of this negative information. You and your lawyer can brainstorm together about how best to keep this information from coming to light, if possible.

However, do not expect your lawyer to help you hide or lie about information—documents, the identity of witnesses or harmful facts—that the other side has properly requested. Such conduct by your lawyer would violate professional rules and perhaps even break the law. Your lawyer has a professional and personal life beyond your case and will not be willing to risk the serious penalties that such conduct might bring.

3. How can I best help my lawyer do a good job?

In sidebars throughout this book, a client can find specific guidance about how to help a lawyer with the legal procedure under discussion. But there are some general things a client should always do during the course of a lawsuit to make life easier for the lawyer. When a lawsuit goes more smoothly for the lawyer, it saves time and money for the client and can lead to a better outcome in the case.

Among the things a client should do are:

- Search thoroughly for documents and other information relating to the dispute. A client often has much easier access to lawsuit information than the lawyer has, and may have information the lawyer would not even know to request.
- Carefully prepare summaries, descriptions, time-lines and other materials a lawyer has requested to help understand the dispute. At the beginning of the lawsuit, everything the lawyer knows about the case will come from the client: making sure this information is accurate will save time and money.
- Answer thoroughly any written questions or discovery requests from the other side, if the lawyer asks for the client's help in responding.
- Promptly respond to the lawyer's requests. During litigation, a lawyer often works under tight deadlines. The more time a client gives a lawyer

to digest material the client provides, the better job the lawyer can do of using that material in preparing legal papers. If a client is simply unable to respond quickly, the client should tell the lawyer as soon as possible so the lawyer can seek an extension or rearrange other matters to accommodate the delay.

- Keep the lawyer posted on the client's schedule and availability. There are certain events in a lawsuit in which the client must participate. Most can be postponed or moved up to fit the client's schedule if the lawyer is given enough advance warning.

4. Should I expect my lawyer to explain what is going on in the lawsuit?

Yes, to some extent. During litigation, lawyers tend to get lost in their legal battles with the opposing lawyers. Keeping their clients fully and regularly informed about what's going on is not always a high priority. Clients, on the other hand, often feel left out of the loop entirely. The lawsuit charges (or stumbles) toward a conclusion, fees and costs soar, but the client sits in the dark.

Each chapter of this book highlights ways in which a client can participate in major decisions about litigation procedures. But there should also be a regular flow of information from lawyer to client about the progress of the lawsuit. A lawyer may do

this without any prompting from the client —some lawyers regularly call their clients just to keep the clients up-to-date. But if a lawyer does not maintain such contact, it is up to the client to stay in touch with the lawyer and the lawsuit.

The trick for the client is to do it but not overdo it. A client can establish his or her own regular schedule—bi-weekly or monthly, for example—for calling the lawyer to ask for an up-date on the case. During these calls, the client can also raise any specific questions about particular procedures or maneuvers. After a few of these calls, the lawyer will probably get the idea that the client wants to hear about the lawsuit on a regular basis and may start initiating the conversation.

It is not a good idea, however, for a client to call every few days with a long list of questions, or to demand a blow-by-blow description of everything the lawyers have been doing. If the client is paying by the hour, this can become a very expensive habit. But regardless of how the lawyer is being paid, such close monitoring can seriously strain attorney-client relations. The lawyer is likely to be irritated at having to answer detailed questions about things to which only the lawyer need pay attention. And worse, the lawyer may feel mistrusted, which does not bring out the best work from anyone. Unless the client has good reason to be concerned about what the lawyer is doing, the best approach is generally to stay in touch but let the lawyer do the work he or she is paid to do.

You and Your Lawyer Will Have Your Ups and Downs

Once a lawsuit begins, you and your lawyer are likely to spend a lot of time together. Your relationship on just this one case may last for several years or more. Sometimes, it will seem that you and the lawyer have just won a great lawsuit battle. But there may also be times when it seems you are losing the entire war. And your tolerance of each other will vary with these changing fortunes of the lawsuit.

Your ups and downs will also vary because of things that have little to do with how the lawsuit will end—legal delays that keep the lawsuit from moving or the unpleasant personality of an opposing lawyer or judge, for example. And some things that lead you and your lawyer to bump heads will have nothing at all to do with your case. The stresses of other business or personal life may sometimes leave one of you with little time or patience for the other.

It is almost inevitable that you and your lawyer will go through these difficult periods. But as long as they are not too frequent or long-lasting, they should not cause you to look for another lawyer. Similar problems would await you with someone else. And a change of lawyers can cause great delay and unnecessary expense. So, as long as you have not lost confidence in your lawyer's ability or commitment to your case, hang in there. A lawsuit is a long, rough ride, and each of you will have to take some lumps.

5. How much can I rely on my lawyer's advice?

There is an old expression in the legal profession that a lawyer's advice is his or her stock-in-trade. And while it is never a good idea to follow advice blindly, legal advice is precisely what a client needs from a lawyer. Once the decision has been made to hire a particular lawyer—because of the lawyer's experience, reputation and interest in the case—a client should trust that the lawyer's actions and recommendations will be sound, absent some reason to suspect otherwise.

A client informed about the legal process can be a better consumer of a lawyer's advice. This book explains legal procedures and maneuvers and suggests ideas for the client to consider when discussing them with the lawyer. If the client understands the proceedings and asks the lawyer good questions, the lawyer can provide more comprehensive, and therefore better, advice. There are certain things only the client can decide: Does this settlement meet my needs? Am I willing to go to trial? Is continuing to litigate too stressful and costly for me? But the lawyer will always have a wide edge in litigation experience and understanding various legal courses of action. And so a client should give great consideration to a lawyer's advice. In the end, that advice is a big part of what the client is paying for.

Don't Blame Your Lawyer for the Whole Legal System

As your lawsuit wends its way along, you may very well become frustrated, angry, even disgusted with the legal process. Litigation seems to take forever. Some rules make no sense. You have little say in what happens. And every painfully detailed maneuver costs money.

Because most of your direct contact concerning the lawsuit is with your own lawyer, there is a tendency to blame your lawyer for every misery the lawsuit rains down on you. Your lawyer is certainly a voluntary member of the legal profession and judicial system. But it is unlikely your lawyer had anything to do with making the rules that drive you crazy—and certainly your lawyer had no significant role in establishing the adversary legal system this country uses to settle disputes. Unless your lawyer seems to be taking advantage of the legal process to increase fees or to avoid doing work on your behalf, try to remember not to hold the lawyer personally responsible for the whole lousy thing.

6. While the lawsuit is going on, may I keep trying to settle the dispute on my own?

Often a lawsuit arises between people who have known each other for some time. Because of these personal relationships, a client may be tempted to try talking to people on the other side of the lawsuit while the lawyer is doing legal battle. Although such private conversations may seem to make sense, they are not usually a good idea—and sometimes violate lawsuit rules.

Once a lawsuit has begun and a party to the dispute is represented by an attorney, all communications with that party should take place through the lawyers. Ethical rules prohibit lawyers from talking directly to the opposing party in a lawsuit. The lawyers are expected to speak only to their own clients, to independent witnesses and to each other. The reason for this rule is simple: it prevents lawyers from trying to pry confidential information out of a party represented by a lawyer, including information protected by the attorney-client privilege. If a client receives any contact—a phone call, letter or effort to talk in person—from a party or lawyer on the opposing side (or anyone speaking on their behalf, such as an investigator or paralegal), the client should immediately report the matter to his or her own lawyer.

Although no rule prohibits it, a client should not attempt to directly contact any opposing party to the lawsuit or any witness to the lawsuit. The client must assume that any conversation with the opposing party or a witness for the other side will immediately get back to the opposing lawyer, and be used in whatever way possible against the client. If the client unwittingly reveals information or legal strategy—even something as simple as the identity of a witness or the existence of evidence proving the client's claims—the results can be disastrous.

A client should even refrain from discussing the dispute with friendly witnesses. Although it is not unlawful to speak with a witness, it might appear that the party is trying to influence what that witness will say. Of course, some witnesses would rather talk to the client—a person they know—than to the lawyer. If a client wants to talk to a witness, the client should discuss it with the lawyer first. Together, client and lawyer can decide whether the conversation makes sense, what questions the client should ask and what topics the client would do best to avoid.

There Are Ways to Talk If It Seems a Good Idea

During the course of your lawsuit, you might hear things from friends, acquaintances or business associates that suggest your opponent would like to talk to you about ending the lawsuit. If so, you should not contact your lawsuit opponent directly. But there are some things you can do. First, you can pass the information on to your lawyer and ask the lawyer if it seems an appropriate time to explore a settlement with the other side. (See Chapter 8.)

If the lawyers are unable to reach a settlement without you and the other side sitting down face to face, that, too, can be arranged. The lawsuit can be suspended temporarily so that you and your opponent may sit down together in a process known as "mediation." (See Chapter 6.) With the help of the lawyers and a professional mediator, you and your opponent may be able to hash things out face to face—and put an end to the lawsuit.

Chapter 3

Getting a Lawsuit Started: The Pleadings

How You Can Help Your Lawyer

When someone decides to begin a lawsuit, the lawyer representing that person prepares a document called a *Complaint*. This is the first of the initial set of lawsuit papers known as the *pleadings*. The person for whom a Complaint is prepared is called the *Plaintiff*; the person being sued is referred to as a *Defendant*; together, Plaintiff and Defendant are called *parties* to the lawsuit. In reply to the Complaint, a Defendant must file one of several kinds of documents, known as *responsive pleadings*.

Plaintiff's and Defendant's pleadings have three basic purposes:

- they set out each side's version of the basic facts
- they offer each side's general arguments about the legal bases of their claims or defenses, and
- they get the whole lumbering litigation process moving.

This chapter explains what these initial pleadings are and how they accomplish these purposes.

Section I: The Complaint

A person, business or organization suing someone else is a *Plaintiff* in the lawsuit. To get the litigation started, Plaintiff's lawyer prepares a document called a *Complaint*. The Complaint is delivered to whomever is being sued, called *the Defendant*, and is filed with the court.

Filing Papers with the Court

Much of a lawsuit is conducted on paper. Each side prepares written statements and legal arguments, which are delivered to the opposing side in the lawsuit and sent to the court in which the case is being litigated. Because of time limits and deadlines for most lawsuit procedures, lawyers frequently say a document "needs to be filed." What lawyers mean by "filing" is formal delivery to the court clerk's office, which notes the date on which it was received and places the document in the court file created for your lawsuit. Some courts now also allow electronic or "paperless" filing—filing documents electronically, using the Internet.

1. What are the basic elements of a Complaint?

A Complaint names the people directly involved on both sides of the lawsuit: all the Plaintiffs suing and all the Defendants being sued. The Complaint also tells a Defendant where the case has been filed and describes the dispute, setting out the basic facts on which Plaintiff bases the lawsuit. It also refers to the legal theories Plaintiff—or rather, Plaintiff's lawyer—believes make the Defendant legally responsible for the problems about which Plaintiff is complaining. Finally, the Complaint

Deciding to File a Complaint

Filing a Complaint sets a lawsuit in motion. And once it's moving, a lawsuit quickly eats up time, energy and money. For this reason, most people involved in disputes don't rush into court immediately; instead, they try to resolve their problems informally, by talking to each other directly or through lawyers. At some point, however, it might be necessary to abandon these informal discussions and get a lawsuit started. You should think about filing a Complaint in these circumstances:

- **You've reached an impasse with the other side**—You may be ready to file a lawsuit because your attempts to settle your dispute have gone nowhere. However, it is often a good idea to give your lawyer a chance to negotiate with the other party or party's lawyer, at least for a short time, before filing a lawsuit. Lawyers sometimes can come up with settlement scenarios that you and your opponent have not considered. And sometimes the other side's lawyers can make a settlement more attractive by explaining to their clients what a lawsuit would entail.

- **You want to shock the other side into reacting**—A lawsuit quickly gets someone's attention. Even if you intend to continue negotiations and don't relish the idea of litigation, merely filing a lawsuit can sometimes move the other side to make a reasonable settlement offer (particularly if you have been trying to settle a dispute with someone's stubborn insurance company).

- **You need immediate help from the court**—Sometimes, you simply cannot wait to file a lawsuit. You may need a court to step in immediately to prevent destruction or damage to your property or the ruining of your business. Or, you may need a court to settle an ownership dispute so that you can move ahead with personal or business plans.

- **You've run out of time**—There is a legal time limit, known as the *Statute of Limitations*, within which a Complaint must be filed. The time limit varies depending on the type of dispute (contract, personal injury, etc.) and the rules of the jurisdiction and court where the dispute arose. If a Complaint is not filed within that time, the person who might have filed it forever loses the right to sue. So if the Statute of Limitations regarding your dispute may soon run out, your lawyer has to file a Complaint.

states what the Plaintiff wants to obtain or achieve through the lawsuit, such as monetary compensation, establishment of ownership or other rights or preventing Defendant from engaging in specified future conduct.

2. May there be more than one Plaintiff in the same lawsuit?

Yes. Often, more than one person wants to sue the same Defendant for the same misconduct. Obvious examples are:

- several people hurt in the same car accident
- spouses suing for financial or other losses that affected both
- co-workers suing an employer for the same conduct, or
- business partners suing in a commercial dispute.

In such situations, two or more people or organizations may be able to join as Plaintiffs in the same Complaint. The rule is that two or more people may sue together if their claims "arise out of the same dispute". In general, this means that each of their problems with the Defendant occurred because of the same or similar actions by the Defendant (though not necessarily at the same time).

Several Hats on One Head Means Several Plaintiffs

Someone filing a lawsuit, particularly in a business dispute, may be acting in several capacities at the same time. A Defendant may have harmed both the Plaintiff's individual interests and the interests of Plaintiff's business. Plaintiff's business may be divided into several entities, such as a corporation, partnership and/or one or more publicly identified business units, often called dba's ("doing business as"). If each of these entities or interests has been harmed by a Defendant's conduct, then each may and should be named in the Complaint as a separate Plaintiff—even though underneath all the hats sits only one real head.

3. Are there advantages to joining with other Plaintiffs in the same lawsuit?

Multiple Plaintiffs may enjoy some advantages. They can share information, one lawyer can do the same work for more than one client or, if there is more than one lawyer, they can divide the lawsuit tasks. This might mean fewer lawyer hours and other costs for each client. And having more than one Plaintiff in the same lawsuit sometimes exerts added pressure on the Defendant to settle the case.

Joining with other Plaintiffs in the same lawsuit is not always in a Plaintiff's best interest, however. If one Plaintiff has a more complex case, the simpler case may get stuck waiting for the other part to wend its way through litigation. Or, the Plaintiffs may have different goals. For example, one Plaintiff may be much more interested, willing or financially able to fight a long hard legal battle while the other Plaintiff wants to reach a simple, inexpensive conclusion as soon as possible.

Sometimes, two Plaintiffs want to pursue different legal strategies. One Plaintiff's legal strategy might require more time, energy and legal fees than another Plaintiff wants to spend. Or one Plaintiff may raise allegations against the Defendant that the other Plaintiff does not want to make. For example, one Plaintiff may want to pursue a simple case of breach of contract, seeking only to get his or her money back, whereas another Plaintiff may want to claim fraud, seeking large extra monetary compensation.

Finally, Plaintiffs are not the only ones who have a say in this matter. If a Defendant is sued in two separate lawsuits that are in some way related, the Defendant may ask the court to combine the two lawsuits into one. (See Chapter 5, Section IV.) On the other hand, if several Plaintiffs have joined in one complex lawsuit against a Defendant, the Defendant may ask the court to split the big lawsuit into two or more smaller ones. (See Chapter 5, Section IV.)

One Lawyer or Two?

If you are joining with someone else as Plaintiffs in the same lawsuit, you may each have your own attorney. But in some circumstances—if there is no conflict of interest (see Chapter 1, Section I)—you can instead use the same lawyer. If you are paying by the hour, it may be considerably cheaper for you to use the same lawyer and share costs and legal fees with the other Plaintiff. It may also help move the case more quickly—as a general rule, the fewer lawyers there are, the faster cases get resolved.

Although there can be advantages to having one lawyer represent two or more Plaintiffs, there might also be advantages to having your own, separate lawyer. You may be better able to influence how the litigation is conducted if the lawyer is answerable only to you. And if two law offices work on one case, more work might get done, putting more pressure on the Defendant. If Plaintiffs' lawyers are able to cooperate, the litigation may move more efficiently—which could benefit both Plaintiffs.

4. Where is a Complaint filed?

For many lawsuits, only one court is legally available. But in other instances a Plaintiff's lawyer has some choice about where to file a Complaint. There are three decisions to make in determining where the Complaint gets filed:

- Is it filed in state or federal court?
- Which level of court (upper or lower) is used?
- Which geographical location is appropriate?

State or federal court. There are two entirely different court systems—federal and state. Most cases must be filed in state court. A case may be filed in federal court only if federal law specifically allows that type of lawsuit. The two main categories of cases that can be filed in federal court are those involving enforcement of federal laws or rights (called cases with a *federal question*), and those between residents of different states (called *diversity* cases). Lawsuits that involve both federal and state laws generally may be filed in either state or federal court.

Level of trial court. In some state judicial systems, there are two levels of courts in which a lawsuit can be litigated and tried. In these *trial courts*, there may be a higher level court for more complicated cases (often called *Superior Court*) and a lower level court for smaller, simpler cases (called *Municipal Court, District Court* or *Court of Common Pleas*). There is often a limit on the amount of money a party may recover in the lower level trial court. Some lower level trial courts also limit the type or number of legal procedures permitted, in an effort to make the proceedings more efficient and less costly.

Location of the court. A Plaintiff cannot file a lawsuit just anywhere. The county or district where a lawsuit is filed must have some logical connection to the dispute. The geographic area where a lawsuit is filed is referred to as *venue*. Most state and federal courts have numerous geographical locations. Federal trial courts are divided into different districts, and sometimes into smaller subdivisions within districts. State trial courts are usually divided by county (some larger counties have more than one district) or by city.

Venue is proper—meaning a lawsuit may be filed in that geographical area—in the district where the defendant resides, where a contract was formed or where the activities giving rise to the dispute took place. Sometimes a lawsuit may be filed in one of several different venues. For example, if different Defendants live in different counties or districts, or the dispute arose in one place but a Defendant lives in another, a lawyer may be able to choose among two or more possible venues.

5. How do my lawyer and I decide where to file the lawsuit?

Sometimes, only one venue is proper for a dispute. If a lawsuit may be filed in one of several courts, however, the Plaintiff has to decide where to bring the case. Factors to consider in making this decision include:

- **Time.** Cases move considerably more quickly in some courts than in others, due to local rules or courtroom back-log. If no other consideration out-weighs it, a Plaintiff's desire to resolve the case quickly may suggest one court over another. On the other hand, many courts have what are called "fast track" programs that force lawyers and litigants to meet very short litigation deadlines. If a lawyer believes that it would be better to have more time to prepare and pro-cess the lawsuit, it might be better for the litigant to avoid a "fast track" court.

- **Convenience.** One court might be more convenient than another because of its proximity to Plaintiff's home, the office of Plaintiff's lawyer or the residences of most witnesses.

- **Court procedures.** Some courts—including many lower level state trial courts—have simple procedures that move a case along more quickly and less expensively. A court with more elaborate procedures might make liti-gation more complicated for lawyers and more expensive for clients. How-ever, if a case is complex or other-wise difficult to prove, a lawyer might advise choosing a court where more thorough procedures are available—despite the increased time and ex-pense. Also, many lower level trial courts have limits on the amount of money that can be awarded, which may preclude filing a particular case there.

- **Judges and juries.** Not all judges and juries are created equal. A lawyer may know the judges in one court better than those in another. The judges and juries in one court may be more or less receptive to certain kinds of cases or litigants. For example, judges and juries in well-to-do suburban areas tend to be less sympathetic to people injured in accidents and to individuals suing corporations. And some courts may be notoriously less accommodat-ing to minority and women litigants and lawyers than other courts.

- **Jury verdicts.** In federal court, a jury's verdict must be unanimous. In some state courts, however, a jury in a civil trial can return a verdict with a less than unanimous vote. This increases the odds that a jury trial will result in a verdict—and decreases the chance of a deadlocked jury (and expensive retrial). If a Plaintiff has considerably fewer financial resources than Defen-dant, Plaintiff's lawyer might advise filing the lawsuit in a court that does not require a unanimous verdict.

6. How does my lawyer decide whom to name as Defendants?

The question of what person, business or organization to sue—technically speaking, whom to name in the Complaint as a Defendant—often has an obvious answer. If you've had an accident or dispute with an individual or a business, that person or business will be the one and only Defendant. Sometimes it's not that simple, however. For example, an employer may be legally responsible for an employee's actions, so perhaps both should be sued for the employee's misconduct. Or if a business is owned by more than one person, or by another company, all owners should be named as Defendants. Similarly, both the driver and the owner of a car may be legally responsible for a car accident; if road conditions contributed to the accident, the city or county could be on the hook as well.

There is no limit to how many Defendants may be named in a single lawsuit. It is Plaintiff's lawyer's job to determine who *might* be legally responsible. To help the lawyer, a client should provide the identities of anyone even marginally connected to the dispute. The lawyer can then sort out whom to include as Defendants. Sometimes, however, neither the Plaintiff nor Plaintiff's lawyer are certain, among several possible Defendants, who did what or who is legally responsible. In that situation, all potentially responsible persons should be named in the Complaint. If it turns out, as the case moves along, that certain Defendants clearly have no legal responsibility, Plaintiff's lawyer can easily release them from the lawsuit. Or the Defendants themselves can ask a judge to cut them loose.

Finding a Defendant Who Can Compensate You

Your lawyer wants to name as Defendants in the Complaint every person or organization that might be legally responsible for any damages you have suffered. In part, this is because it is not always clear at the outset of a lawsuit who is most legally responsible. But naming all possible Defendants has another purpose: it increases the likelihood that at least one of them might be financially capable of compensating you.

Sometimes, the Defendant most responsible for your damages has few assets and no insurance coverage. A Defendant who has a lower degree of legal responsibility might nonetheless have plenty of resources to pay its share of your damages. A common example is an employee who injures someone while at work. The employee, who is primarily responsible for the injuries, may have little or no money. The employer, on the other hand, maintains insurance to cover just such a situation, and so must be included as a lawsuit Defendant.

7. What if I don't know all the potential Defendants?

Sometimes, a Plaintiff knows or suspects that certain people or businesses are at least partially responsible for the problems that have led to the lawsuit without knowing exactly who they are. Or a Plaintiff may know for certain that someone is responsible but not know that person's name. However, a Plaintiff may want or need to file a Complaint before discovering the identity of every Defendant. To accommodate Plaintiffs in this situation, the law allows the Complaint to name what lawyers call *Doe Defendants* (after the fictitious name "Doe" they are given in the Complaint). These Doe Defendants serve as placeholders for the actual Defendants whose names Plaintiff does not yet know. Their real names can be substituted in once they are learned. By naming Doe Defendants, a Plaintiff's lawyer insures that Defendants discovered later can be added to the lawsuit. Because it is so difficult to predict whether additional Defendants will spring up in the course of litigation, Plaintiff's attorneys routinely include Doe Defendants in the Complaint.

8. What kinds of facts belong in the Complaint?

One of the main purposes of the Complaint is to disclose the Plaintiff's version of the facts. Whatever the facts are, they must be sufficient to pin legal responsibility on a Defendant. Otherwise, the Defendant may have the Complaint thrown out of court before the lawsuit even gets started. (See

Section II.) On the other hand, the Complaint need not include every nasty, irritating, incompetent or otherwise negative thing every Defendant ever did or said. Nor must the Complaint include every fact that might be proved in the case. It is the lawyer's job to strike a balance—enough facts, but not too many—in the Complaint's allegations.

Just the Facts, Ma'am.

Striking the right balance in stating the facts can help hold down the expense of the lawsuit. Factual allegations are like red flags to litigating lawyers; they are likely to spend time and energy trying to prove or disprove them. If certain facts alleged in the Complaint turn out not to be crucial to a determination of legal responsibility, all the activity generated by the allegations may prove to have been a waste. And if any of those unnecessary facts or added details turn out to be false, you might lose some of your credibility in the eyes of a jury.

The client's role is to provide all information that might have anything to do with the dispute, being clear with the lawyer about what things the client knows for certain and what other things the client believes to be true but does not know for sure. The lawyer's job is to sort all this out and generate a focused Complaint that gets to the heart of the matter.

How You Can Help Your Lawyer Prepare the Complaint

Information is the key to any lawsuit. At the beginning of a case, almost everything your lawyer knows about the dispute comes from you. So the quality of the Complaint your lawyer prepares may depend on how thoroughly and accurately you provide that information.

There are several things you can do to help your lawyer prepare the Complaint:

- If you have not done so already, write down a time-line or narrative description of all the important events that led to the dispute.
- List the names and addresses of anyone who might know something about the dispute, along with a description of who they are and what information they might have.
- Give your lawyer all key documents you have—contracts, letters, business records, emails and photographs—that relate to the case. Include any correspondence you have had with the other side about trying to settle the dispute.
- Let your lawyer know about any similar legal disputes in which either you or your lawsuit opponent has been involved.
- Tell your lawyer about any privacy concerns you have regarding personal or business information. This may help the lawyer craft the Complaint in such a way that the lawsuit does not invite unwanted prying.

As you educate your lawyer, you must include the bad news. Tell your lawyer everything that supports your position and everything that undermines it. Your lawyer must consider the negative facts in planning the lawsuit, which begins with the Complaint. These conversations with your lawyer are confidential; you need not worry that your lawyer will have to reveal these facts to anyone.

9. How does a Complaint spell out the Defendant's legal liability?

One of a lawyer's primary tasks in preparing a Complaint is to fit the facts into legal theories that show exactly why the Defendant should be held responsible for Plaintiff's troubles. Each legal theory is described in a separate section of the Complaint called a *cause of action*. For example, the facts may show that a Defendant refused to live up to the terms of a contract. Plaintiff's lawyer might include in the Complaint one cause of action for breach of contract and another for fraud, based on promises the Defendant made but never intended to keep.

Lawyers tend to include a number of different causes of action in the Complaint. Often, each cause of action describes the same event or conduct but with a different legal slant. Multiple causes of action increase the likelihood that the case can be won on at least one of the underlying legal theories, even if the others fail. For example, one cause of action may depend on facts that turn out to be easier to prove than others. Or all the facts may turn out to support one legal theory but not another. Including different causes of action protects the Plaintiff

—at the beginning of the lawsuit, Plaintiff's lawyer won't know what facts finally will be proven, what seeming facts will disappear into thin air and what previously unknown facts will drop from the sky.

Plaintiffs' lawyers sometimes include particular causes of action (such as fraud) because they raise the possibility of punitive damages against the Defendant, and other causes of action (such as breach of contract) because they might permit the award of attorney fees. (Punitive damages and attorney fees are discussed in Questions 10 & 12.)

10. How does the Complaint explain what I want the court to do?

The final section of a Complaint is called the *Prayer* (and like other prayers, it asks for considerably more than is likely to be received). The Prayer states what *relief* the Plaintiff wants: what the Plaintiff wants the court to order the Defendant to do, such as pay the Plaintiff money, take a specific action or stop doing something. A Plaintiff might ask for a variety of things, depending on the nature of the case. The basic categories of relief are:

- **Compensatory damages.** Compensatory damages compensate the Plaintiff for any losses or injuries caused by the Defendant's conduct. In many courts, the Plaintiff does not specify how much money is sought. Instead, the amount is to be determined later

"according to proof" (what the facts show as the case develops). In some courts, the Plaintiff is expected to state, in the Complaint, the specific dollar amount sought. Since the Plaintiff may have only a vague idea of damages at the beginning of the lawsuit, most lawyers pick a round number large enough to cover all possible damages. Obviously, this amount will never be recovered in full. (This tends to produce hysterical media reports that so and so is "demanding millions." The reason for the large figure—the need to ask for enough to properly compensate the Plaintiff—is seldom explained.) Sometimes compensatory damages are broken down further in the Complaint, into categories known as *special damages* and *general damages*. *Special damages* refer to money owed or spent as a result of the Defendant's conduct; a common example is medical bills resulting from an accident. *General damages* refer to money the Plaintiff contends has been or will be lost but which cannot be calculated exactly. These general damages compensate Plaintiff for injuries that do not easily translate into dollars and cents, such as the pain and suffering endured as a result of physical injuries, the discomfort and emotional injury suffered from discriminatory conduct or the damage done to personal or business reputation because of a libel or slander.

Think Twice Before You Claim Certain Damages

In general, you and your lawyer will want to include in the Complaint a reference to each of the consequences—all the things you have lost or suffered—resulting from the Defendant's actions. You must include any types of "damages" for which you want a judge or jury to award you compensation.

However, it is not always a good idea to include every possible claim of damages. If you contend that you have been harmed in a certain way, the other side will be permitted to question you closely about these damages. You may be forced discuss aspects of your personal or business life that you would rather not disclose.

If you allege that you suffered "emotional distress," for example, the other side may be permitted to examine records of any psychiatric, psychological or other therapeutic treatment you have undergone, even if it covers personal matters not related to the lawsuit. And the doctor or therapist with whom you consult might be subject to face-to-face examination about your treatment. Similarly, if you claim that the Defendant caused your business to suffer damages that are difficult to measure, the other side might be allowed to delve deeply into your business practices and financial records.

- **Punitive damages.** Also called *exemplary damages*, punitive damages are money that a judge or jury makes a Defendant pay the Plaintiff as a kind of punishment, similar to a fine. Punitive damages are awarded when the Defendant has committed particularly outrageous acts, such as when the Defendant has engaged in intentional or highly reckless misconduct, fraud, misappropriation of funds, activity dangerous to the public or invasion of privacy. The amount of punitive damages varies according to how awful the Defendant's behavior was, how serious the consequences were and how much the Defendant is worth (that is, how much it would take to make the damages be a real punishment). Punitive damages are also available if the Defendant violates a specific law that expressly provides for such damages. For example, laws that prohibit discrimination in employment and housing allow for punitive damages awards. Some laws limit punitive damages to an amount three times greater—referred to as *treble damages*—than the compensatory damages awarded in the case. Punitive damages are more likely to be awarded, and more likely to be high, when the Defendant is a large corporation rather than an individual or small business, and more likely if the Defendant engaged in a long pattern of conduct rather than a single nasty act. However, a lawyer may decide to include a request for punitive damages even if there isn't much chance of winning a large amount. The mere *possibility* of punitive damages may make the Defendant more likely to settle the case on terms more favorable to Plaintiff.

- **Equitable relief.** In addition to asking for money, a Complaint may request that the court sort out the parties' respective rights to property or other interests. For example, a court may order the *rescission* of a contract, meaning that the parties' responsibilities under the contract are declared at an end. Conversely, a court may order *specific performance* of a contract, meaning that both parties must follow through on their obligations under the agreement. Or, a court may order the dissolution of a partnership or corporation and a division of its assets and liabilities. Equitable relief may also include a court order that a Defendant take some action, or refrain from doing so. For example, a court may order Defendant to move a fence that encroaches on Plaintiff's property or stop using a business name similar to the one Plaintiff uses. This kind of court order is known as a *permanent injunction.* (Temporary injunctions are also sometimes available long *before* a case is finally resolved; the special steps and rules regarding temporary injunctions are discussed in Chapter 5, Section II.)

What Is My Case Worth?

You don't have to decide what your case is worth—how much you are likely to be awarded if you win at trial, as well as the (lower) amount you might realistically expect the other side to offer in settlement— before filing the Complaint. At that point, it is probably too soon for you and your lawyer to have a very good idea of what the case is worth. In the Complaint, the lawyer simply needs to ask for a figure at least as high as you could possibly imagine winning. Nonetheless, it is important to consult with your lawyer early in the process about what a realistic range of damages might be.

In making this assessment, you need to know whether a request for punitive damages is realistic or is merely a litigation tactic. If you are paying your lawyer by the hour, you also need to know the likelihood that the other side will be required to pay your attorney fees. Realistic assessments of settlement and verdict amounts may go up or down—and perhaps both—as the lawsuit progresses. But by regularly asking for your lawyer's current sense of the "value" of the case, you should be able to gauge how much you are willing to spend on the litigation and how much the other side would have to offer for you to settle the case.

11. Can my Complaint ask the court to settle a dispute even if I haven't yet suffered any harm?

In certain cases. Normally, a person may not file a Complaint until he or she has actually been harmed as a result of someone else's actions. Otherwise, the courts would be flooded with people who merely worry that someone was about to do them wrong. But there are a few situations in which a court will make a decision in advance to avoid a future problem. This kind of lawsuit is called an action for *Declaratory Relief*. The court is asked to "declare" (clarify) the rights and obligations of both parties, so that they can carry on their daily business without a legal uncertainty hanging over their heads.

Declaratory relief is used to settle a number of different kinds of questions, the most common of which are:

- who is obligated to do what under the terms of a written contract
- who is covered by an insurance policy, and to what extent
- what are the rights of property owners, such as determining boundaries of adjacent properties or ownership of property among several claimants (called a lawsuit to *quiet title*), and
- whether and how a specific local, state or federal law applies to a particular business, property or organization.

12. Can my Complaint ask the other side to pay my legal fees?

Sometimes. In most lawsuits, each side must pay its own attorney fees. But in some cases, the losing side in the lawsuit may be forced to pay the winning side's fees. Since attorney fees can be enormous, the possibility of recovering them from the other side is sometimes more important than the amount of damages won. If the Plaintiff can't afford to pay a lawyer, the possibility that attorney fees will be paid by the loser might be the major incentive for a lawyer to take the case.

Regardless of how a Plaintiff and lawyer have arranged for the lawyer to be paid, the lawyer will often include in the Complaint a cause of action that supports an award of attorney fees against the other side. Even if there is little likelihood of winning the lawsuit based on that particular legal theory, the mere possibility that the other side might have to pay Plaintiff's lawyer fees might make them more likely to settle the case on terms more favorable to Plaintiff.

Attorney fees typically are awarded in several kinds of lawsuits:

- **Contract disputes.** Many contracts require the losing party in any dispute over the contract to pay the winner's fees.
- **Lawsuits to enforce protective laws.** Many state and federal laws, notably those designed to protect individuals against discrimination by businesses and institutions, provide that a losing Defendant must pay the attorney fees of the Plaintiff who was wronged. These attorney fee provisions are written into the protective statutes themselves.
- **Lawsuits against the government.** A lawsuit by a private individual or business against a local, state or federal government agency is permitted only if there is a specific law on the books that allows such a lawsuit. Often, such laws also permit a person who successfully sues the government to obtain attorney fees.

- **Lawsuits by the government.** If a government agency files a lawsuit against an individual, business or organization, the government may be entitled to attorney fees if the government wins the case.

13. Can my Complaint ask the other side to pay my litigation costs?

Yes. The losing side in a lawsuit is usually ordered to pay the costs incurred by the winning side, so a Complaint always includes a formal request that they do so. In most states, these costs include fees charged by the courts to file legal documents, jury fees and deposition costs, which can run quite high. However, official litigation costs do not include many expenditures for which a lawyer charges the client. For example, the costs of copying, long-distance phone calls, messenger services and consultations with experts do not have to be paid by the losing side.

14. Do I have to swear under oath that the facts in my Complaint are true?

In some states, a Plaintiff must sign a form accompanying the Complaint in which the Plaintiff states under oath that the facts—though not the legal rigmarole—in the Complaint are true. In other states, this oath, called a *Verification*, is optional. Verification of a Complaint has two effects.

In courts where it is required, it is intended to prevent people from filing Complaints full of wild allegations they have no way of knowing or proving. Swearing that a fact in a Complaint is true is like testifying to that fact in court; the sworn allegation in a Complaint ties the Plaintiff to that fact for the rest of the lawsuit. If the Plaintiff or other witnesses later contradict that sworn fact, the Plaintiff will have to explain the contradiction to the judge or jury. The other effect of a verified Complaint, in some states, is that it requires a verified and detailed Answer from the Defendant. If the Complaint is unverified, the Defendant generally can file a blanket denial. (See Section II.)

15. Once the Complaint is filed in court, what happens next?

The lawsuit may not proceed until the Plaintiff gets a copy of the Complaint into the hands of the Defendant—a procedure known as *service of process*. Until service of process has occurred, the court has no jurisdiction (legal authority) over the defendant. In addition to the Complaint, the Defendant must be "served" with a document called a *Summons*: the court's official notice to the Defendant that the lawsuit has been filed. The Summons contains prescribed language, usually on a pre-printed form, explaining to Defendants what it means to be served with a Complaint, how they may respond, how long they have to do so and what happens if they don't.

Holding Back on Service May Simplify a Lawsuit

As explained above, Plaintiff's lawyer needs to name as Defendants everyone who might conceivably bear some legal responsibility for the harm suffered by Plaintiff. But some of these Defendants may have only minimal responsibility, or few resources from which to pay compensation. Forcing them into the lawsuit might require them and Plaintiff to spend resources needlessly. The solution is to name them as Defendants but wait to serve them with the Summons and Complaint. Unless local "fast track" rules require service of process within a particular time period, the legal time limit for serving a Defendant is usually considerably longer than the time for filing a Complaint. By waiting to serve, the Plaintiff can include marginal Defendants in the Complaint but exclude them from the actual litigation, at least until their involvement is required.

There are several ways in which a Summons and Complaint may be served on a Defendant.

- **Personal service.** A Complaint and Summons may be hand-delivered to the Defendant. If the Defendant is a corporation, the papers are delivered to the corporate officer whom the company has designated for that purpose. This can be done by someone in the Plaintiff's lawyer's office or by a professional process server. A client can make personal service easier for the lawyer to arrange, and therefore cheaper for the client, by providing recent, detailed information about where the Defendant lives and works. In most states the Plaintiff is not allowed to be the person who hand-delivers the Complaint.

- **Substitute service.** Often a would-be Defendant knows a Complaint is coming and is anxious to get on with the process, or is at least willing to accept the inevitable. If so, some courts do not require Plaintiff to serve the De-

fendant personally. Instead, Plaintiff's lawyer may send the Complaint and Summons by registered mail to the Defendant's home or business (or lawyer's office, if the Defendant already has an attorney). Accompanying the mailed Summons and Complaint is a form, called *Acknowledgment and Receipt* or *Acknowledgment of Service*, which the Defendant signs and sends back to Plaintiff's lawyer. This form acknowledges that the Defendant has received the Summons and Complaint, which satisfies the court that Service of Process has been accomplished. Most courts also permit a type of substitute service if the Defendant is dodging the process server or simply cannot be located. In these situations, a copy of the Complaint is handed to any adult found at the Defendant's residence. Another copy is then sent to the Defendant at that address by registered mail.

- **Constructive service.** If neither personal service nor substitute service is feasible, courts have various procedures known as *constructive service*, which allow a Plaintiff to serve the Complaint even if the Defendant's whereabouts is unknown. In some courts, Plaintiff's lawyer may do this by mailing the Complaint to the Defendant's last known residence and place of work, and listing the summons in the "Legal Notices" section of a local newspaper. However, it is risky to depend on constructive service. If the Defendant's "last known address" is not the person's most recent residence or workplace, a court might not consider the constructive service legally suffi-cient. In that case, any legal procedures taken against the Defendant will be ineffective.

16. What are Defendant's options in responding to my Complaint?

Once the Complaint is served, a Defendant has several options. The Defendant might file an Answer (see Section II), which would immediately set the lawsuit in motion. Depending on how thorough Plaintiff's Complaint is and whether or not it is verified, the Answer might be a flat denial of everything in the Complaint, or it might be a point-by-point admission and denial of specific facts. The Answer may also include specific legal theories, known as affirmative defenses, which argue that Defendant should not be held responsible for Plaintiff's troubles. (See Section II.)

Rather than answer the Complaint right away, a Defendant may challenge the Complaint's legal validity and ask a judge to order the Plaintiff to "amend" it (do it over again). If a Plaintiff receives one of these responses to the Complaint—a *Motion to Quash, Demurrer* or *Motion to Strike* (see Section II)—Plaintiff and Plaintiff's lawyer must decide whether it is worth the time, money and delay to oppose it in court. If

the Plaintiff's lawyer believes a judge is likely to agree with the Defendant's lawyer's argument, both lawyers can informally agree that Plaintiff will amend the Complaint if Defendant drops the challenge. In other words, Plaintiff can simply concede the point, saving the time and expense of fight-ing a fruitless legal battle.

If such a compromise is not possible, or if for some other reason Plaintiff's lawyer believes it is important to fight the chal-lenge, Plaintiff's lawyer will reply as to any other motion. (The process for making and opposing a motion is explained in Chapter 5, Section I.) However, even if the Plaintiff loses in court on one of these motions or Demurrers, the judge will almost always permit the Plaintiff to amend the Complaint and file it again—unless it appears to the judge that the Plaintiff flat out doesn't have a case.

Who Pays for Redoing the Complaint. If your Complaint must be amended—particularly if it must be amended more than once—and you are paying your lawyer by the hour, you may want to ask your lawyer why the Complaint was flawed in the first place. Perhaps you have a very difficult case to ar-ticulate and the lawyer is doing as well as possible. Drafting complaints is as much art as science. Even the best lawyers, trying to squeeze in an argument that might put more pressure on the Defendant, prepare Com-plaints that have to be amended. Often the lawyer has taken the calculated risk of putting extra ammunition into the Complaint, knowing that some of it might have to be removed if challenged by the Defendant. If your lawyer had a good reason for the way in which the first Complaint was prepared, you may have to accept the need for an amendment as the result of a tactical decision that did not work out perfectly—one of the unfortunate but normal costs of litigation.

17. Once the lawsuit is underway, can my lawyer amend the Complaint?

Yes. Often, the Plaintiff learns new information that changes the case after a Complaint has been filed. If these new facts point to a new Defendant, additional legal theories or increased damages, the Complaint should be amended to include them. The contents of the Complaint determine what evidence and legal arguments the Plaintiff may present at trial—and that determines what a judge or jury may decide in a verdict. A Plaintiff may voluntarily file an *Amended Complaint* that reflects the new information. It is not uncommon for a Plaintiff to do this two or three times over the course of the litigation. However, once a Defendant has filed an Answer to the Complaint, the Plaintiff must get a judge's permission to file an Amended Complaint. The Defendant may object, but unless discovery has been completed (see Chapter 4) and would have to be repeated because of the Plaintiff's changes, or trial would have to be postponed, a judge usually permits the amendment.

18. How does my lawyer file an amended pleading?

The simplest way to file an amended Complaint or Answer (see Section II) is to get the other side's permission. The lawyer for the party who wants to amend presents a consent form—called a *Stipulation to File Amended Complaint (or Answer)*—to all the other parties in the case. If the other parties sign the Stipulation, the lawyer for the amending party presents it to the court along with a proposed *Order Permitting Filing of Amended Complaint (or Answer)* and the amended pleading itself. A judge will usually sign the order if the parties all agree to the amendment.

Why would the other parties agree without a fight to allow an amendment to the pleadings? If it is early in the lawsuit and the new information does not represent a complete reversal of facts or change in legal theories, a judge would likely allow the amendment. So agreeing to the amendment saves all the parties from wasting time and money fighting it out in court.

If any other party refuses to agree to an amendment, however, a judge will have to decide whether to allow it. The amending party must file a legal document called a *Motion for Order Permitting Amendment to Complaint (or Answer)*, accompanied by a Declaration or Affidavit (sworn statement) by the party or the party's lawyer explaining what the new information is, why it is only now coming to light and what effect it might have on the litigation. Any party opposed to the amendment may file its own documents stating the reasons for its opposition. (For an explanation of the standard procedure for going to court on a motion, see Chapter 5, Section I.)

19. How does a judge decide whether to allow an amended pleading?

In deciding whether to grant permission to file an amended Complaint or Answer, judges apply a rather vague-sounding standard: Would permitting the amendment cause "undue prejudice" to the other side? Translated, this means that the judge considers:

- **Timing.** The longer the lawsuit has been going on, the less likely a judge is to permit an amendment. As the case approaches trial, less time remains to investigate and prepare arguments about new facts or legal issues that an amended pleading might raise.
- **Impact.** A judge is more likely to permit an amendment that makes only a minor change in the Complaint or Answer than one that changes the lawsuit's direction by adding a whole new set of facts or entirely new legal theories. Judges particularly disfavor amendments that would force the parties to do extensive additional investigation or repeat time-consuming discovery in order to explore the new matter. If a witness or evidence that would have to be reexamined is no longer available, a judge almost surely will not allow an amendment. A judge is also less likely to permit an amendment if it would require costly additional legal work by a party who cannot afford it, such as an individual in a lawsuit against a large business or organization.
- **Fault.** A judge is more likely to permit an amendment if the failure to include the new information or legal theory in the original pleading was not the amending party's fault—for example, if the party just uncovered the information during the discovery process. On the other hand, if the party seeking to add new material should have known about it at the time of the original pleading, a judge may look less kindly on the request to amend.

Section II: Defending Against a Complaint: Responsive Pleadings

Shortly after a Complaint has been delivered to a Defendant, the Defendant must reply by filing legal papers called *responsive pleadings*. There are several sorts of responsive pleadings:

- a flat denial of everything in the Complaint
- a partial denial that admits certain facts
- a total or partial denial, topped off with a claim that Plaintiff or some third party—rather than Defendant—

is legally responsible for Plaintiff's troubles

- a contention that the Complaint has technical flaws
- a challenge to the court's authority over this particular lawsuit or this Defendant, or
- a request that a judge decide the lawsuit immediately in Defendant's favor, based on the Complaint alone.

Each type of response is discussed in this Section, including the tactical matters a lawyer and client must consider in choosing among them.

If You Are Served With a Complaint, Get a Lawyer Now

If you are served with a Complaint, you have only a limited time—usually 20-30 days from receipt—in which to file a response. Although the Plaintiff's lawyer might give you extra time to respond—called an *extension of time*—there are no guarantees. There can be serious legal consequences if you fail to file a response within the allotted time, including the possibility that the court will order Plaintiff the winner by default. If you have not hired a lawyer by the end of your time to respond, call the attorney representing the Plaintiff (this lawyer will be identified in the Summons), explain that you do not yet have a lawyer and ask for an extension of time to respond. Then get to a lawyer of your own as soon as possible.

20. What is an Answer?

The simplest response to a Complaint is called an *Answer*. An Answer does not attempt to stop the lawsuit by challenging the legal sufficiency of the Complaint. Instead, an Answer denies the most important factual allegations and legal theories of the Complaint while allowing the litigation to move on to the next stage. How thorough and complex an Answer is depends on tactical considerations, and sometimes on the rules of the court in which the lawsuit has been filed. The Answer typically takes one of the following forms:

General Denial. In some courts, if the Complaint is not verified (see Section I), the Defendant is permitted to file a one-sentence Answer that simply denies everything in the Complaint. A general denial says something like "Defendant denies each and every allegation of the Complaint and each of its Causes of Action, and asks that Plaintiff take nothing by his (her) Complaint." By filing a general denial, the Defendant makes the Plaintiff wait for discovery (see Chapter 4) to learn the details of Defendant's side of the story. If a general denial is permitted, it is the easiest and least time-consuming type of Answer for a lawyer to prepare.

Specific Admissions and Denials. In some courts, a general denial is not allowed. And a general denial is typically not allowed in any court if the Plaintiff verified the Complaint. (See Section I.) Instead, the Defendant's lawyer must answer, paragraph for paragraph, each allegation in the Complaint.

How You Can Help Your Lawyer Prepare an Answer

If you and your lawyer are required to file only a general denial to the Complaint, your lawyer won't need your help to prepare the Answer. However, you must still give your lawyer a full accounting of all the facts pertaining to the dispute and copies of all relevant documents, correspondence and other written materials, so that the lawyer can advise you whether a countersuit is appropriate. (See Section III, below.)

If you and your lawyer must file specific admissions and denials in your Answer, you can help your lawyer by:

- Preparing a time-line or narrative description of all the important events that led to your dispute with the Plaintiff

- Carefully reviewing the Complaint. For every fact alleged in the Complaint, write out for your lawyer your version of that fact, explaining why the two versions differ

- Admitting to your lawyer those allegations by Plaintiff that are true. Your lawyer needs to know about any negative facts as early as possible to begin preparing to counter them

- Giving your lawyer every important document you have— correspondence, business records or photographs—that relates to the case, and

- Telling your lawyer about any other disputes you have with the Plaintiff. Your lawyer may want or need to prepare a countersuit for you against the Plaintiff about these other disputes. (See Section III.)

21. How forthcoming should I be in my Answer?

If a Defendant must file an Answer that specifically admits or denies each allegation in the Complaint, extreme caution is the watchword. A Defendant should admit only those allegations that state the very obvious —for example, that Defendant resides in a particular county or that Defendant owned a certain car on a certain day. Most facts in the Complaint are subject to more than one interpretation. Until a Defendant is certain what the implications of an admission might be, a denial is always the better course of action.

Some allegations in the Complaint will be obviously true while others will be flat-out false, or at least questionable. A Defendant can admit the parts that are obviously true while denying the rest. For example, a paragraph in the Complaint might state that the Defendant owned and operated a business on a certain date and was solely responsible for the safety of persons visiting the business's premises. The Defendant might admit that she owned and operated the business (if ownership is not in dispute) but deny that she was solely responsible for visitors' safety (since the visitor is also partly responsible, as well as the property owner).

If a Defendant does not yet know whether the facts alleged in a particular paragraph of the Complaint are true, an Answer may simply state that Defendant has insufficient knowledge either to admit or deny that allegation.

More Than One Defendant—How Many Lawyers?

You might not be the only Defendant named in a Complaint. If the other Defendants are very close or related to you, you may be able to use the same lawyer and file the same responsive pleadings. This could help both of you present a coordinated defense and save money. However, different Defendants usually need different lawyers. Even if you and another Defendant are *mostly* on the same side, you may wind up facing different levels of liability for Plaintiff's damages. In such a situation, a lawyer might be forced to choose between admitting blame for one client or the other. That would be an impermissible conflict of interest for the lawyer and a bad spot for you. If you learn that the same lawyer might be representing you and another Defendant, ask the lawyer as soon as possible about conflicts of interest. And be prepared for the response that even a close friend or partner needs a separate lawyer. (See Chapter 1, Section I, regarding conflict of interest and choosing a lawyer.)

22. Does an Answer contain legal arguments?

Yes. An Answer is not limited to denials of the factual allegations in the Complaint. An Answer may also assert specific legal reasons (called *affirmative defenses*) why the Defendant is not responsible for the Plaintiff's damages. Examples of affirmative defenses include the *Statute of Limitations* (Plaintiff filed the lawsuit beyond the legal time limit), *Release and Satisfaction* (Plaintiff is not entitled to any money because defendant already paid all that was owed) and *Assumption of Risk* (Plaintiff was responsible for his or her own accidental injuries). In an affirmative defense, a Defendant may include facts that the Plaintiff did not include in the Complaint.

23. What happens if my responsive pleadings aren't filed in time?

It is not uncommon for a Defendant to fail to file an Answer or other responsive pleadings within the time allotted by court rules. Some fail to pay attention to time limits; others are unable to find a lawyer in time. If for any reason a Defendant fails to file a responsive pleading in time, Plaintiff's lawyer may "take" the Defendant's *Default*. To take a Default, Plaintiff's lawyer files papers notifying Defendant that if he or she continues to ignore the lawsuit, Plaintiff will ask a judge to declare the case over—in legal parlance, to enter a *Default Judgment*—and award Plaintiff all relief requested in the Complaint.

If the Defendant has a reasonable excuse for not filing a responsive pleading in time—illness, failure to receive the Complaint or inability to find a lawyer—the judge usually will not enter a Default Judgment.

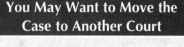

Instead, the judge will allow the Defendant to file a late Answer or other responsive pleading. Because judges are usually willing to give Defendants another chance, a Default Judgment is used more as a prod to get the litigation moving than as a way to win the whole case. However, in certain kinds of proceedings in which time is crucial—such as "unlawful detainer" actions that seek to evict a tenant—judges are not as forgiving of Defaults. In those cases, judges grant extra time only if the excuse is a particularly good one, and then only grant a very short extension for Defendant to respond.

You May Want to Move the Case to Another Court

When you are served with a Complaint, you may find that the court where it has been filed is inconveniently located for you or your lawyer. If so, you may be able to move the lawsuit to a court in a different location, by filing a *Motion for Change of Venue*, discussed in Chapter 5, Section IV.

Sometimes the Plaintiff files a lawsuit in state court, though it could also have been filed in federal court. (See Question 5, Section I.) If your lawyer would be more comfortable litigating the case in federal court or there are technical advantages to litigating in federal court (the requirement of a unanimous verdict, for example), your lawyer might try to move the lawsuit to federal court using a process known as *removal*.

24. What can my lawyer do if the Complaint doesn't make any valid legal claims against me?

To win a lawsuit, a Plaintiff must state in the Complaint and prove in court a set of facts and a legal theory that establish the Plaintiff's rights and the Defendant's responsibility for Plaintiff's damages. This combination of facts and legal theory is referred to as a *legal claim* or a *claim upon which relief may be granted*.

Special Appearance to Challenge the Court's Authority Over the Defendant

By filing any responsive pleading discussed in this Section, a Defendant makes an *appearance* in the case. By appearing, a Defendant concedes that the court is proper for the lawsuit and has *jurisdiction*—legal authority—over the Defendant. But what if you want to argue that the court has no jurisdiction over the lawsuit, or over you? How can you make that argument without appearing and conceding that very jurisdiction? Courts permit what is called a *special appearance* (as distinguished from the normal, *general appearance*), a kind of legal "time-out" during which a Defendant may file papers and appear in court without automatically giving the court jurisdiction. Most commonly, a special appearance is made to object to the court's jurisdiction (because the Defendant resides out of state, for example) or to challenge whether service of process was properly accomplished. (See Section I.)

Sometimes a Complaint—even if everything it alleges is true—simply does not state a valid legal claim. The Complaint might contain some technical legal flaw, be filed in an improper court or fail to present facts that fit any legal theory establishing Defendant's responsibility. For example, a Complaint might allege that Plaintiff was injured in a fall on the way into Defendant's store without stating any facts showing that Defendant was careless or otherwise responsible for the accident. Or, a Complaint might detail all the ways in which a partner's mistakes sank a business, but fail to show why that proves anything other than poor business judgment. In these situations, Defendant's lawyer may ask the judge to throw out the Complaint because of its failure to properly or adequately state a legal claim against the Defendant. This is done in a document called a *Motion to Quash the Complaint*, also called a *General Demurrer*.

Going Through the "Motions"

Any responsive pleading other than an Answer—one that seeks to defeat, delay or alter the Complaint, for example, must be filed in the form of a *motion*. The term motion simply refers to the process of getting a legal question into court so a judge may make a decision on it. The *moving party*—the party who wants the court to take some action—must file legal papers asking a judge to grant (approve) the motion. The other side—called the *opposing party*—may file papers asking the judge to deny the motion. Motions are discussed in detail in Chapter 5, Section I.

25. If the judge rules that the Complaint doesn't state a legal claim against me, what happens next?

Even if there is a solid legal basis for filing a Motion to Quash or a Demurrer, it is not always worth the trouble. Even if the Complaint is thrown out, a judge is likely to give the Plaintiff another chance to get it right by filing a new version, called an *Amended Complaint.* (See Section I.) If the Plaintiff amends the Complaint, the Defendant has to start again by filing an Answer or another responsive pleading. Months might go by before the lawsuit really gets going. And if the Defendant's attorney is paid by the hour, the Defendant might end up spending a lot of money on this process without getting any significant benefit.

In a few circumstances, however, a Motion to Quash or General Demurrer might

actually win the case for the Defendant, or at least put the Plaintiff in such a difficult position that the Defendant will be able to settle the case quickly and advantageously. This can happen when the problem with the initial Complaint is not easily fixed, raising the possibility that an Amended Complaint would not fare any better than the first one.

26. Can my lawyer object only to certain parts of the Complaint?

Yes. Often, a Complaint states one or more valid claims against the Defendant but also contains extra matter that the Defendant would prefer to keep out of the lawsuit. For example, a Complaint might include irrelevant personal matters that the Defendant does not want dissected and discussed. The Plaintiff might include a claim that is clearly unsupported by the facts alleged, which would be good to knock out of the lawsuit early so that the Defendant's lawyer doesn't have to spend time and energy contesting it. Or, a Complaint might request certain relief—for example, punitive damages—that is not legally allowed for Plaintiff's claims. In any of these situations, the Defendant's lawyer may file a *Motion to Strike*, also called a *Special Demurrer.* This procedure does not claim that the entire Complaint is invalid or that it fails to state a cause of action. Instead, it merely asks a judge to delete certain parts of the Complaint.

Motion for More Definitive Statement

If a Complaint has vague or ambiguous language, or skimps in its factual descriptions, some courts allow Defendant's lawyer to file a *Motion for More Definitive Statement*. This motion does not challenge the Complaint's validity but merely asks a judge to order the Plaintiff to make it more precise. Is this a worthwhile use of your lawyer's time? Usually not. Complaints are not *required* to be complete or terribly precise—so even if it is granted, such a motion probably won't accomplish much. Besides, your lawyer has the rest of the litigation to pin down the Plaintiff's facts. On occasion, however, your lawyer might file such a motion to force the Plaintiff to reveal something early on about the direction of Plaintiff's case. Your lawyer may want to find out precisely what Plaintiff knows or is complaining about. The Complaint might even be so vague that your lawyer can't respond properly—or even figure out what dispute underlies the lawsuit. In these situations, filing a motion makes sense. The procedure will probably only cause a minor delay in the case and may provide your lawyer with a bit of useful early information.

27. Can I have the Plaintiff's whole case against me tossed out of court at the outset?

Sometimes a Complaint includes facts that would prevent the Plaintiff from winning a court case against the Defendant. If so, the Defendant's lawyer may file a *Motion to Dismiss*, or *Motion for Judgment on the Pleadings*, which argues that even if everything in the Complaint is true, the Plaintiff still cannot hold the Defendant legally responsible. Unlike a *Motion to Quash* or a *General Demurrer*, if a judge grants a Motion to Dismiss, Plaintiff is generally not given another opportunity to file an improved Complaint.

This kind of motion is most often used to raise some technical legal matter. For example, Defendant might argue that the events described in the Complaint occurred outside the appropriate Statute of Limitations (the legal time limit), or that Plaintiff failed to take some step legally required before a Complaint may be filed. If the Defendant's lawyer thinks there is a legitimate shot at winning this kind of motion, it is probably worth a try—if Defendant wins, the lawsuit would be over. Because this kind of motion often depends on a single technical legal question, it is often fairly simple for a lawyer to prepare. Some courts require Defendant to file an Answer at the same time; this avoids delay if the Defendant's Motion to Dismiss is denied.

Section III: The Defendant Strikes Back: Countersuits

A person who is sued can do more than just defend against the action. Defendant may also file a "countersuit" against anyone the Defendant thinks is responsible for the dispute, or for related problems. Defendant can file a countersuit against the Plaintiff, against Co-Defendants in the Plaintiff's original Complaint or against third parties whom the Plaintiff has not sued. A Defendant may also bring up other legal gripes against the Plaintiff, even if they have nothing to do with the problems described in the Plaintiff's Complaint.

A countersuit is treated, legally, as a completely new Complaint. A Defendant who files a countersuit not only remains a Defendant in the original Complaint, but also becomes a type of Plaintiff called a *Cross-Plaintiff, Cross-Complainant* or a *Counter-Claimant*. And whoever is sued in the countersuit—including the original Plaintiff —becomes a *Cross-Defendant* or *Counter-Defendant*. If a countersuit is filed, it becomes connected to the original Complaint. From that point on, all proceedings, including trial, will include both the original suit and the countersuit, and all facts developed in the litigation may be used to prove or disprove either case, as if it were all one big lawsuit.

The Countersuit Name Game

Depending on the parties sued and the court system, a countersuit might be called a *Cross-Complaint, Cross-Claim, Counter-claim, Third Party Claim* or *Impleader*. In some courts, all countersuits are called Cross-Complaints, whether filed against a Plaintiff, Co-Defendant or third party. In other court systems, a countersuit against the Plaintiff is called a Counterclaim, while a countersuit against a Co-Defendant or a third party is called a Cross-Claim. And in federal court, countersuits against third parties are called Impleaders.

28. When can a Defendant file a countersuit?

A countersuit is usually filed at the same time that the Defendant files an Answer. If the Defendant has already filed an Answer but later decides to file a countersuit, the Defendant will probably need a judge's permission.

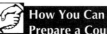 **How You Can Help Your Lawyer Prepare a Countersuit**

A countersuit may serve several purposes. It can put extra pressure on the Plaintiff to settle or drop the original Complaint. It allows you to raise negative facts about the Plaintiff that otherwise would not have come up in the lawsuit. It might give you a convenient opportunity to get a different dispute into court without having to initiate a new lawsuit. And in some circumstances, it provides your only chance to have a court decide a related dispute you have with the Plaintiff. (See Question 30, below.)

In order for your lawyer to know whether a countersuit should or must be filed for you, you have to provide information to the lawyer well beyond responding to what's included in the Complaint. You must discuss with your lawyer all other disputes you have with the Plaintiff, whether or not they are directly related to the dispute described in the Complaint. For each of these disputes, you must present information to your lawyer exactly as if you were a Plaintiff and your lawyer were preparing a Complaint. (See Section I.)

29. What kinds of claims can I raise in a countersuit, and against whom?

In a countersuit, a Defendant may raise any claims against the Plaintiff regardless of whether they are related to the dispute described in the Plaintiff's original Complaint. This encourages people who are already in court to hash out all the different problems they have with each other in one legal action, rather than wasting court time with separate lawsuits. For example, if the Plaintiff's Complaint charges a neighbor with destroying a fence on their property line, the Defendant may countersue to complain that the Plaintiff's tree roots are undermining the Defendant's foundation. However, the fact that a Defendant *may* file a sepa-

rate, unrelated countersuit against the Plaintiff does not mean the Defendant *must* join it to Plaintiff's lawsuit. If the subject is unrelated to the Plaintiff's Complaint, Defendant may choose to file a separate lawsuit.

A Defendant is also permitted—but not required—to file a countersuit against a Co-Defendant or a third party. But a countersuit against anyone other than the Plaintiff may only include claims related to the disputes described in the Plaintiff's original Complaint. For example, a plumber may be named as a Defendant in a dispute with a homeowner over plumbing repairs. The plumber would be permitted to countersue against the general contractor for any matters pertaining to this homeowner's project, but would not be allowed to countersue the contractor for problems with different construction projects. For those, the plumber would have to file a separate lawsuit.

Anyone Who Is Countersued Must Act Like a Defendant

If you are a Plaintiff or a Co-Defendant in a lawsuit and you are served with a countersuit by a Defendant, you become what is called a *Cross-Defendant* in that countersuit. You must file a responsive pleading to that countersuit just as if you had been named as a Defendant in a separate lawsuit. You may use any of the responsive pleadings available to any Defendant in an original lawsuit. (Responsive pleadings are described in Section II.)

30. Are there some issues that I *must* raise in a countersuit?

Yes. If a Defendant has a claim against the Plaintiff that is related to the dispute raised in the Plaintiff's original lawsuit, the Defendant *must* include that claim in a countersuit or forever lose the right to bring it to court. A Defendant may *not* wait to file a separate lawsuit against the Plaintiff concerning the same dispute. Because of this rule about *related claims*, Defendant must tell his or her lawyer about all possible claims against the Plaintiff. A Defendant should be sure to describe anything the Plaintiff might owe the Defendant, and any damages Defendant may have suffered because of the Plaintiff's conduct. The lawyer can then determine whether these matters are legally "related" to the dispute described in the Plaintiff's Complaint, and therefore must be raised in a countersuit.

Countersuits and Contingency Fees Don't Mix

If you are a Plaintiff who has retained your lawyer on a contingency fee basis and you now find yourself named as a Defendant in a countersuit, your contingency fee agreement probably does *not* cover your defense to the countersuit. Your lawyer took your original case assuming that the contingency fee would pay for the work of pursuing your lawsuit; that fee was *not* calculated to include the extra work of defending you against your own potential losses.

If you find yourself in this position, you will have to work out a separate defense arrangement with a lawyer. You can usually negotiate a separate hourly fee arrangement for your lawyer to defend you in the countersuit. If you have insurance coverage, your insurance company may pay your lawyer on an hourly basis to defend you. Or, the insurance company may provide and pay for a separate lawyer to defend your countersuit. (Contingency fees, insurance payment for lawyers and hourly fee arrangements are discussed in Chapter 1.)

Section IV: Litigating on Behalf of a Minor: Guardian ad Litem

Sometimes, a child is directly involved in events that result in a lawsuit. For example, a child may cause, or be injured in, an accident. In such lawsuits, the interests of the child must be represented. But in most states, a minor—usually, a child under age 18—does not have the right to sue or be sued. Courts deal with this gap in the law by appointing someone to stand in for the child for purposes of the lawsuit. The stand-in is called a *Guardian ad litem* ("for the lawsuit").

31. What is a Guardian ad litem?

The position of Guardian ad litem is much more limited and temporary than that of a full legal guardian. A Guardian ad litem is permitted to make decisions for the child regarding the lawsuit only, for as long as the lawsuit continues. Even this authority is limited, because two of the most important decisions about the lawsuit—the child's lawyer's fee and the amount of any settlement—must be approved by a judge.

32. Who can be appointed Guardian ad litem?

Normally, a parent is appointed Guardian ad litem. Either parent, or both, may be appointed. In the case of divorced or separated parents, the parent who has legal custody of the child is usually appointed Guardian ad litem, but if both parents agree, either parent may serve in the role.

A legal guardian, grandparent or other responsible adult may also serve. If someone other than a parent with legal custody applies to serve as Guardian ad litem, or if one parent applies but the other objects, the judge may select the parent, or other adult, the judge believes would best serve the child's interests.

Your Child Might Need a Separate Lawyer

If you and your child have both been injured—for example, in a car accident—by the actions of a third party, your child might need to have someone other than you serve as Guardian ad litem. In some circumstances you might also need separate lawyers. This might become necessary if the Defendant has insufficient resources (such as insurance coverage) to pay both of you what you fairly deserve. A lawyer who represented both of you in this situation would be in an impossible spot: more money for one client means less for the other, yet the lawyer must represent the interests of both. This kind of conflict might require that either you or your child get another lawyer. Because you would have this same conflict of interest, you would not be the proper person to serve as Guardian ad litem.

The problem of a lawyer's conflict of interest is discussed in Chapter 1, Section I.

33. How is a Guardian ad litem appointed?

If a child needs to be represented in a lawsuit, a lawyer for the parent or other adult files a *Petition for Appointment of Guardian ad litem*. This document asks the court to appoint a parent or other adult as the child's representative for the lawsuit. This Petition is filed immediately before, or at the same time as, the other initial papers in the lawsuit—the Complaint, if the child is suing (see Section I), or the Answer or other responsive pleading, if the child is being sued (see Section II).

34. What are the terms of a Guardian ad litem's appointment?

A judge spells out the terms of appointment in a document called an *Order Appointing Guardian ad Litem*. It names the Guardian and sets the specific conditions of the appointment, which may include:

- ongoing court review at certain stages of the proceedings
- court approval of payment terms to the child's lawyer
- court approval of any final settlement of the case
- placing lawsuit money obtained for the child in a special bank account until the child turns 18, and/or

- requiring that any award or settlement be spent only for specific purposes (such as the child's health or education) except with prior approval of the court.

Once a parent or other adult has been appointed, the Guardian is authorized to hire a lawyer to represent the child, sign all lawsuit papers pertaining to the child, direct the child's lawyer regarding conduct of the litigation and make all decisions relating to the child's position in the lawsuit (except those specific decisions that a judge must first approve).

The Court Keeps an Eye on a Child's Attorney Fees

After the appointment of a Guardian ad litem, the lawyer chosen to represent the child may have to ask the court to approve the lawyer's fee. Most states have laws restricting the amount a lawyer can charge to represent a minor. Other states have no actual law but do have customarily lower fees for representing minors. In contingency fee cases, for example, the lawyer's fee to represent a minor is usually 25% of the recovery, rather than the normal 33% for an adult. In hourly fee cases, the courts may have a prevailing rate that is the maximum they will approve for a child.

Chapter 4

Discovery

How You Can Help Your Lawyer

Discovery is a set of legal procedures that a party may use to get lawsuit-related information from another party or from people and businesses that are not parties to the lawsuit. A party may ask not only for "facts" but also for the identity of others who may know something about the case, for documents that pertain to the case and for examination of physical objects and property connected to the dispute. The scope of discovery—the kind of information that a party can force someone to reveal—is extremely broad, though there are some limits. For the most part, discovery takes place outside the courtroom, with lawyers and parties exchanging written information and sitting through face-to-face questioning sessions. However, lawyers sometimes must file motions asking the court to resolve disputes about discovery. Discovery motions are discussed in Chapter 5, Section VII.

Section I: An Overview of Discovery

This section describes generally what lawyers are seeking in the discovery process, the various procedures available and how each is used to elicit different kinds of information. After this section, each discovery device is discussed in detail (Sections II through V), followed by an explanation of the limits placed on discovery (Section VI).

Discovery Rules Vary From Court to Court

Every jurisdiction makes its own rules governing discovery. Federal court has its own set of rules, as does each state. On top of that, individual courts—each federal district and each county or other division of state court—frequently add their own local discovery rules. Despite these separate rules, the major discovery procedures addressed in this chapter operate in essentially the same way from court to court. Because details sometimes vary, however, from time to time you may read that "in certain courts ... " or "in some jurisdictions ... " a rule is slightly different.

1. What kinds of information can a party obtain through discovery?

The basic rule of discovery is that a party may obtain any information that pertains—even slightly—to any issue in the lawsuit, as long as the material sought is not legally "privileged" or otherwise protected. (Privileges and other limits on discovery are explained in Section VI.) In discovery, a lawyer can even request information that might not be admissible at trial, as long as it relates to an issue in dispute. The information sought during discovery need only "tend to lead to admissible evidence." For example, it is common to ask in discovery about what was said in a conversation, even though the information would probably not be admissible in court because repeating what someone said is usually considered "hearsay."

Because of the great latitude regarding what is "discoverable" (what may be obtained in discovery), lawyers regularly ask for:

- anything a witness has seen, heard or done in connection with the dispute or the parties to the dispute
- what anyone has said at a particular time and place, or at any time about a certain subject
- the identity of anyone who might know something about the dispute or the damages suffered by either party
- a detailed description of the way a business or other organization regularly conducts itself
- almost any document generated by or in the possession of an individual or business if it pertains at all to the dispute, and
- a witness's personal and business history (with deeper background probing permitted about a party than about a non-party witness).

Discovery Can Get Very Personal

You are likely to be surprised and distressed by the detailed questions the other side can properly ask during discovery. Your personal background, education, domestic arrangements and entire work history may all be fair subjects for inquiry. If a lawsuit involves a business, most of that business's records may be subject to review and the people who operate the business may be quizzed in great detail about how the business was run.

If your a lawsuit claims a personal injury, your medical records will be scrutinized by the other side and you will be subjected to extraordinarily close questioning about your injuries and their effect on your work and personal life. You may even have to undergo a physical examination by a doctor chosen by the Defendant. And if your lawsuit claims emotional injury, your mind becomes a fair subject of inquiry—records of psychological treatment are opened to the other side and your treating therapist may be subjected to direct questioning about your entire emotional history.

However, there are some limits on the kinds of probing a lawsuit opponent can do. They are discussed in detail in Section VI of this chapter. As a client, you can help protect yourself by becoming familiar with these limits and alerting your lawyer when you believe certain information sought by the other side goes too far. But you must also recognize that the lawsuit will include discovery that you will find uncomfortable or irritating—and there may be little you or your lawyer can do to prevent it.

2. What is an interrogatory?

Interrogatories are written questions asked by one party to another. They must be answered under oath. The responses become part of a party's sworn testimony about the case and might be used as evidence in court, including trial. (Interrogatories are discussed in detail in Section II.)

3. What is a request for production?

In a request for production, one party asks another for physical evidence relating to the lawsuit, usually documents that pertain to the case. These are most often business records, but they might also be personal documents such as appointment books and letters. Requests for production may also ask to inspect, and sometimes test, physical objects and property. (Requests for production are discussed in detail in Section III.)

4. What is a request for admissions?

Using a request for admissions, a party may ask another party to admit, under oath, that a certain fact is true or that a document is genuine. An admission can save both parties from spending time and money trying to prove or refute an obvious, specific fact. (Requests for admissions are discussed in Section IV.)

5. What is a deposition?

A deposition is the face-to-face questioning of a witness—a party to the lawsuit or anyone else—by the lawyers in a case. Any party may initiate a deposition. Lawyers for all parties have a right to attend the deposition and to pose questions to the person being deposed (called "the deponent"). The questioning usually takes place in the office of the lawyer who is taking the deposition, not in a court. The answers of the deponent are given under oath and recorded for later possible use as evidence. (Depositions are discussed in Section V.)

6. Are there other discovery procedures?

In addition to interrogatories, requests for production, requests for admissions and depositions, there are a few other discovery procedures in common use. For instance, documents can be obtained from people or organizations who are not parties to a lawsuit by use of a *subpoena duces tecum* or a *deposition subpoena*. If questions about a litigant's physical condition are part of the lawsuit—such as in a personal injury case—one side may request that the other party undergo a physical examination by a doctor selected by the requesting party. This procedure is called a *request for independent medical examination (IME)*. (Discovery subpoenas and requests for an

IME are discussed in Section III, along with requests for production.)

7. When does discovery start and how long does it last?

Generally, a party may begin discovery as soon as that party formally becomes part of the lawsuit by filing, or being served with, a Complaint. (See Chapter 3). However, some states impose a ten to 30-day waiting period at the beginning of the case before discovery may begin. Some courts also prohibit the Plaintiff from starting discovery during a waiting period at the beginning of a case, unless and until the Defendant does. Once underway, discovery continues until a cut-off date set by law or by a judge overseeing the case. This date usually falls about 30 days before trial or arbitration.

8. Do the parties have to turn over some types of information without using a formal discovery procedure?

Yes. To cut the time and cost of discovery, a few courts (including all federal courts) require the parties to exchange basic information at the very beginning of a lawsuit. This eliminates the need for the other side to request it through one of the formal discovery devices discussed in this chapter. Called *automatic disclosure* or *mandatory disclosure*, this process usually occurs within 90 days after the Defendant has filed

its first responsive legal papers in the case. Depending on the court, the parties may be required to exchange some or all of the following information:

- names, addresses and phone numbers of witnesses—called *occurrence witnesses* or *percipient witnesses*—who are likely to have direct information about disputed facts
- copies, descriptions or locations of crucial documents or physical objects in the possession or control of a party
- an estimate and calculation of the monetary damages either side claims, and
- copies of any insurance policies or agreements that might cover damages awarded in the lawsuit.

9. What's the point of all these discovery maneuvers?

Discovery can be an exhaustive—and exhausting—examination of every conceivable detail related to a case. At times, a client may wonder if all this searching for and arguing over details is worth it. But discovery plays a crucial role in any lawsuit: it allows a party to gather the facts that will prove his or her case. As long as a lawyer's efforts seem to pursue one or more of the following goals—and have not been reduced to petty arguing with the opposing lawyers—a client should support the lawyer's thorough use of discovery's varied tools:

- **Uncovering all the facts.** The most basic discovery task is to uncover the facts of the dispute underlying the lawsuit and to establish crucial, perhaps previously unknown facts that might determine its outcome. For example, a Plaintiff who learns that a warped stair was built 30 years ago and has never been checked for damage will have an easier time showing that the building owner was at fault for Plaintiff's fall. On the other hand, the building owner might have a stronger case after learning that the Plaintiff was carrying packages and not holding onto the railing when the fall occurred.

- **Pinning down information.** Discovery permits each side to establish a fact—for example, that a car's headlights were off—once and for all. This prevents people from changing their stories later on, once they realize that a different answer would be more advantageous or they have been influenced by other people's statements.

- **Finding holes in the other side's story.** One of the main tasks in discovery is to find contradictions in the other side's story. Because there are many forms of discovery, the same information can be sought several times in several different ways. A party who doesn't really know what happened—or who knows but is not telling the truth—might wind up providing contradictory answers to crucial questions. If so, those contradictions can be used against the party when the case goes to arbitration or trial and in attempts to reach a settlement. It is a lawyer's and client's job throughout the discovery process not only to uncover these contradictions, but also to avoid making any conflicting statements that the other side can use.

- **Preserving information.** It takes months or years for a case to go to trial. During that time, evidence may become unavailable. Witnesses may die, disappear, forget or move beyond the reach of the court. Physical evidence may be lost or destroyed. Once evidence is pinned down in discovery, however, it can be used at trial no matter how long the case takes to get there.

- **Examining and testing physical evidence.** Some cases turn on the exact dimensions, composition or condition of a physical object: the strength of a beam; the workings of a car's brakes; the extent of damage to someone's knee; or the soundness of a building's foundation. Discovery provides an orderly process—no need to sneak around in the dark with hidden cameras—by which one side may examine an object that someone else controls.

- **Establishing a witness's background.** Many questions asked in discovery seek information about a party's or other witness's personal history, education and work experience. This sort of probing may sometimes seem to go well beyond what pertains to the lawsuit. But the courts permit some inquiry into personal background in order to place each witness—and therefore the witness's testimony—in context. For example, a party's level of education might help explain how well the party understood technical legal requirements. Or, an employee's lack of training or experience operating heavy equipment might be important in determining whether an employer was legally careless in putting the employee behind the wheel of a forklift.

- **Identifying or eliminating parties.** Sometimes discovery shows that someone other than a party in the lawsuit is legally responsible for what happened. If so, that person or organization can be added to the lawsuit as a party. Sometimes, an original party turns out to be blameless. That party can then be released from the case, which simplifies matters for the parties that remain.

- **Establishing liability or absolute defense.** Sometimes discovery brings out facts that stop a lawsuit dead in its tracks. For example, discovery might show that crucial events occurred beyond the legal time limit—the Statute of Limitations—for filing a lawsuit. Or, discovery might show that a govern-

ment agency is legally immune (cannot be sued) for the type of injury claimed.

- **Opening the door to settlement.** At the beginning of a lawsuit, the parties may be far apart in their perceptions of what occurred and what a fair outcome would be. ("I'll sue 'em for all they're worth!" versus "They'll never see a penny!") Once facts have emerged in discovery, however, these positions may shift considerably. Evidence may alter the parties' original ideas of what happened, and therefore of what a fair resolution would be. Or, a party may realize that its version of events simply cannot be proved. Such doses of reality frequently lead to settlement.

Section II: Interrogatories

This section explains interrogatories: written questions that the lawyer for one party prepares and sends to the other party to answer, under oath.

10. To whom may interrogatories be sent?

Interrogatories may be sent only to an actual party in a lawsuit, either Plaintiff or Defendant. They may not be sent to someone who is not officially a party, regardless of that person's connection to the dispute.

For example, interrogatories may be sent to a business that is suing or being sued. But they may not be sent to individual owners or employees of the business, regardless of how much they know about the dispute, unless they are named as parties to the lawsuit.

11. What kinds of information do interrogatories typically seek?

Interrogatories may ask for a wide range of information, including:

- **A party's background.** Many interrogatories are directed at the personal, business or corporate history of a litigant. Discovery rules permit a party to delve broadly into the background of opposing parties, including residences, educational history, work experience and financial status of individual parties, and the organizational structure and identity of officers of businesses or other organizations.
- **Facts of the case.** Interrogatories may ask for a party's version of the facts—what happened, when, who did and said what—as well as the identity of anyone with information about what happened.
- **Identification of documents.** The other side's documents can provide information about witnesses, admissions of wrongdoing and a wealth of other evidence crucial to a lawsuit's success. But early in the case, a lawyer won't

know what sorts of documents the other party possesses. Interrogatories can be used to obtain this information. The documents may then be obtained through a "request to produce." (See Section III, below.)

- **What the other side contends.** Interrogatories may be used to learn precisely what one side in the lawsuit contends the other side has done. For example, in a car accident case, one of these *contention interrogatories* might ask whether one party contends that the other party failed to signal before making a turn. In a case for breach of contract, an interrogatory might ask whether one party contends the other side failed to perform certain work or performed work improperly. Contention interrogatories may also ask for the basis of a party's beliefs—the specific facts upon which a party relies in making such contentions.

12. Who decides what interrogatories to ask the other side?

"Drafting" interrogatories—deciding what information to seek and how to phrase the questions—usually requires the training and experience of a lawyer. A client may be able to help by giving the lawyer a description not only of the facts of the dispute but also of the background and business practices of the opposing side.

Some Interrogatories Are Standard, Some Are Specially Devised

Interrogatories that ask for the opposing party's personal and business background are virtually the same for every case. Instead of recreating these interrogatories for each lawsuit, a lawyer usually just copies standardized versions—known as "form interrogatories"—out of a legal handbook. The same goes for the basic interrogatories in any particular type of lawsuit; for example, there are some form interrogatories for every contract case, every employment case and every car accident case. Choosing these standard interrogatories takes little time. In fact, a paralegal may do it rather than the lawyer—which will save you legal fees if you are paying your lawyer by the hour.

Although some interrogatories may be standard, many others will have to be specially formulated to fit the particular facts of your case. Your lawyer must devise these questions carefully so that the other party cannot use some clever loophole to avoid disclosing important information. The careful crafting of interrogatories takes skill and a certain amount of time. If you are paying hourly legal fees, you should understand that your lawyer probably had to individually draft many of the interrogatories for your case—even though they may sound simple or obvious. If it seems that you have been billed many hours for relatively few interrogatories, ask your lawyer how many of them had to be specially fashioned for your case and why.

13. Do I personally answer interrogatories received from the other side?

It is the party, not the party's lawyer, who must answer interrogatories under oath. But good lawyers help their clients answer interrogatories. Although the information must come from the client, the lawyer can help the client understand how much or how little information needs to be provided. The lawyer may also suggest ways of saying things that are accurate but avoid broad or unnecessary statements that might harm the client's case or reveal private or otherwise confidential information.

When a lawyer receives interrogatories for the client to answer, the lawyer should first determine which questions need not be answered at all. Then the lawyer usually asks the client to prepare rough draft answers to the remaining questions. The lawyer might discuss the questions with the client before the client prepares the rough draft. But the lawyer will certainly go over the answers with the client before they are put in final form and returned to the other side. Because slight differences in wording might later prove significant, it is important for a client and lawyer to carefully review answers to interrogatories before the client swears that they are accurate and sends them to the other side.

How You Can Help Your Lawyer Answer Interrogatories

Answering interrogatories is a joint effort between you and your lawyer. Before you begin, your lawyer must determine whether you have to answer every interrogatory. And your lawyer must carefully review your answers to make sure you have not said more to the other side than you need to. (See Question 13, above.)

But much of the responsibility for answering interrogatories falls squarely on your shoulders. Here are some steps you can take to do the best possible job:

- **Do your homework.** You are required to answer interrogatories with more than just what you can remember at the moment. You must search your personal or business records for the information requested, though you are not required to check sources beyond your own records. If you are replying on behalf of a business or organization, you must ask other officers and employees what they know about the particular subject. (This kind of thorough searching can also be very useful to you. It can help your lawyer prepare the case and prevent information from surfacing by surprise later on. If you are paying your lawyer by the hour, doing your own thorough searching might also cut down on fees.)

- **Give complete answers.** You must answer questions fully. If the other side believes that your answers are incomplete, they might ask the court to order you to amend your answers. To avoid this expensive hassle, answer questions

as completely as you can the first time around.

- **Be brief.** The flip side of answering fully is to use as few words as possible. Writing long answers, or giving more information than necessary, might harm your case. You may inadvertently give the other side more facts than they requested, revealing information that they would otherwise not have known.

- **Alert your lawyer.** Sometimes, your lawyer does not realize that a particular interrogatory asks you to reveal confidential or extremely personal information. If this happens, you should bring the matter to your lawyer's attention before attempting to answer the question. The lawyer can then determine if the information might be protected by a legal privilege or privacy right. (See Question 14 and Section VI.) Then you and your lawyer together can decide the best way to approach the problem.

- **Try out different answers on your lawyer.** There are often several ways to answer an interrogatory. This may be simply a matter of wording. Or, it might involve different interpretations of what the question asks or what needs to be included in the answer. If you have doubts about a question or your answer, discuss it with your lawyer before putting an answer in final form. This may include writing out rough drafts of different proposed answers and asking your lawyer which one works best for your case while still properly responding to the question.

14. Do I have to answer every interrogatory?

No. Some interrogatories legally need not be answered. This is one reason why a lawyer should review the questions before the client begins working on responses. The lawyer can then tell the client not to bother answering certain improper questions. Instead, the lawyer writes down objections to those questions, including the legal basis for refusing to answer, and sends the objections—along with the answers to proper questions—to the other side.

A lawyer will object to interrogatories that improperly seek information. An interrogatory is objectionable if it asks for:

- private, privileged or otherwise confidential information
- information that has no possible relevance to the lawsuit, or
- information that is equally available to the party that is asking.

Sometimes, an interrogatory seeks appropriate information but is improper in form. Generally a lawyer will object to the form of these interrogatories (as vague or too broad, for example) but ask the client to respond anyway. By objecting to form, the lawyer reserves the right to object if the other side later attempts to use the interrogatory responses as evidence at trial.

Objections to interrogatories are discussed in detail in Section VI of this Chapter. When objectionable interrogatories are asked (and they often are), it is the lawyer's job to interpose an objection rather than having the client provide an answer.

15. How are interrogatories typically used in litigation?

The party's signed interrogatory responses become part of the party's sworn testimony in the case. They may be used as evidence when either party asks a judge to decide important issues—even the entire case—before trial. (See Chapter 5, Sections VIII.) The answers may also be used to support or contradict other statements the party makes, including statements the party later makes at arbitration or trial.

If, during arbitration or trial, a party's testimony differs from that party's interrogatory responses, the interrogatory answers may be used to *"impeach"* (contradict) the party. That is, the interrogatory answer can be read to the judge or jury to show that the witness changed his or her testimony. For example, the Defendant in a car accident case might testify at trial that he or she carefully looked in every direction "before I moved into the intersection" where the accident happened. The lawyer for the opposing party might then read out the Defendant's interrogatory answer, in which the Defendant wrote "I checked in both directions as I entered the intersection." The difference between checking for other cars *"before* I entered" and *"as* I entered" the intersection might be important in deciding who was at fault for the accident. The Defendant would be forced to explain which statement is accurate and why the answers are different.

16. When do lawyers send interrogatories?

Interrogatories are usually among the first discovery devices used in a lawsuit. Sets of questions are often sent to the opposing party in the first few weeks or months of litigation. Interrogatories are sent early because they can provide a lawyer with a long list of people and documents related to the case. The lawyer can then follow up using other discovery devices such as depositions and requests for production. In courts that allow numerous interrogatories (see Question 19), a lawyer commonly sends follow-up interrogatories later in the case. These follow-up questions can be used to pin down details about evidence obtained through other discovery procedures.

17. How long does a party have to respond to interrogatories?

A party usually has 30 to 45 days to respond to a set of interrogatories. Because a lawyer must review answers before they are put into final form and returned to the other side, a client should get them to his or her own lawyer at least a few days before the deadline.

18. What happens if I can't respond to the interrogatories in time?

Usually, a party is able to answer interrogatories within the time provided. But a party may need more time if questions require a search for documents or discussions with others who are not readily available, or if the party's lawyer will be unavailable for awhile and unable to review the party's answers. In those instances, it is common practice for a lawyer to ask the other side for a few more days or weeks—known as an *extension of time*—to return the answers. These requests are usually granted—the other side will likely need a similar courtesy at some point during the long lawsuit process.

Although it is common practice for a party to grant an extension of time to respond to interrogatories, a litigant should not assume that this will happen. If the lawyer or party on one side regularly ignores the normal deadlines and repeatedly asks for extensions of time, the other side may stop being agreeable. Sometimes, a lawyer for the other side is simply inflexible, always demanding that responses be completed within the prescribed time period. In either case, if the answering party fails to get the responses back in time, there can be very negative consequences. A court may impose fines and payment of the other side's attorney fees if they have to go to court to get a response. (See Chapter 5, Section VII). In extreme cases, failing to answer on time may also limit the testimony or objections a party can use at trial.

19. How many interrogatories can be asked?

Some jurisdictions have limits, usually 25 to 50, on the total number of interrogatories each party may send to another. A limit is particularly likely in lower level courts, commonly called "Municipal" or "Common Pleas" courts. (See Chapter 3, Questions 4-5.) However, there are exceptions to these limits. Often one or both sides feel they need extra interrogatories. Most jurisdictions allow the lawyers to make an agreement between themselves—called a stipulation—that each side may send extra interrogatories. In any jurisdiction, a lawyer may request a judge's permission to ask extra interrogatories; judges generally allow at least a few over the limit.

20. What happens if one party doesn't think the other has answered interrogatories properly?

Lawyers from opposing sides frequently disagree over whether one or another interrogatory is proper, whether an objection to an interrogatory is justified or whether an answer is complete. If such a disagreement arises, lawyers are required to first discuss the matter—in legal lingo, to *meet and confer*—either by phone or in person, to see if they can come to a compromise. If the two sides remain at loggerheads, then each has the option of going to court. (The procedures for going to court about discovery are discussed in Chapter 5, Section VII.)

21. What happens if I come across new or different information after my responses have been sent to the other side?

After interrogatories have been answered, a party may learn new information that would alter, add to or contradict the earlier responses. In some jurisdictions, a party has what is called a *continuing duty to respond*: a legal obligation to provide the new information to the other side whenever it is discovered or remembered. In other jurisdictions, however, there is no such duty; the party must only provide information that is accurate as of the time the interrogatories are answered. When a client first prepares proposed answers to interrogatories, the lawyer should explain whether there is a continuing duty to respond. And even if there is no such duty, the client should always report new information to his or her own lawyer. This gives the lawyer a chance to consider how the new information can help or hurt that case and whether to reveal the information to the other side.

Section III: Requests for Production of Documents and Physical Evidence

Often the most tedious—yet in many lawsuits the most important—discovery tool is the *Request for Production of Documents*. A company's records may show how it has conducted its business, made decisions or treated its workers and customers. When it comes to long-term business patterns and performance, documents are often more revealing than the memories and descriptive powers of witnesses. (For example, it was internal emails more than witness testimony that recently convinced a judge to find that Microsoft had violated federal antitrust laws.)

This section explains several separate but related procedures—*Requests for Production of Documents, Requests for Inspection of Property, Subpoenas Duces Tecum, Deposition Subpoenas (Records Only)* and *Requests for Independent Medical Examination*—that allow a party to obtain copies of documents, to inspect and test physical objects and in some cases to examine another party's physical condition. By using these devices, a litigant can inspect virtually any piece of written, electronic or physical evidence related to the lawsuit, subject to the limits on discovery discussed in Section VI.

How You Can Help Your Lawyer Prepare a Request for Production of Documents

A lawyer's work in identifying documents to be requested, preparing the requests, sometimes going to court to obtain documents and painstakingly reviewing each document received, can be a time-consuming process. If you are paying your lawyer by the hour, it can also be an expensive one. But the lawyer who gives short shrift to this task does so at the risk of missing key pieces of evidence. And if you lose patience with your lawyer's slow but careful work, you may well be sabotaging your own case.

There may be ways to help your lawyer in this process, which can save you money and allow your lawyer to find documents that might otherwise be difficult to locate. This is particularly true in business or employment litigation, where you may have experience or inside information about how the other side keeps its records. Here are a few suggestions:

- **Give an overview.** You may be able to help your lawyer understand what types of documents to request by explaining the structure of the other side's business. This might include a description of the responsibilities of different divisions or offices and the roles of different executives and management-level employees.
- **Explain recordkeeping practices.** If you know how the opposing side keeps its records, including what different records are called, what software is used and how information is stored, share this information with your lawyer.

- **Go over the documents produced.**
Once your lawyer receives another party's documents, ask your lawyer whether it would be helpful for you to review them. If you are familiar with the other side's business, you can explain the functions of different types of documents, identify individuals named in the documents and flag important papers for your lawyer's special attention.

22. What kinds of things can I include in a request for production or inspection?

A party to a lawsuit may request that another party provide copies of any business, organization or government records, personal documents, compilations of data, internal memoranda, manuals, correspondence and almost anything else that has been reduced to writing, printing, computer disk or electronic file if those records relate, directly or indirectly, to the dispute or to the amount of damages claimed.

A party may also ask to inspect, examine, measure, test, photograph and take samples of any physical object, including land or a physical structure, under the control of another party. For example, if a contractor is being sued for faulty work on a house, the contractor's lawyer's may request that a construction expert enter the home to inspect the work. Similarly, in a car accident case, either side might request permission to examine and test the other car's brakes or other equipment.

23. Whose documents and property can I inspect?

By sending a request for production, a party may inspect, examine and copy documents or objects owned, possessed or controlled by any other party to the lawsuit. A judge's permission for such a request is not usually required, though in some jurisdictions the requesting party's attorney must draw up a statement—known as a *Declaration* (or *Affidavit) in Support of Request for Production* or *Affidavit of Good Cause*—explaining under oath why inspection or production of the material is necessary to a fair resolution of the lawsuit.

24. Can I obtain documents or inspect property under the control of a non-party?

Yes. A party may copy or inspect documents and property controlled by someone who is *not* a party in the lawsuit if the records or objects might have some bearing on the case. For example, the police report on a traffic accident may be obtained even though the city and its police are not parties to the lawsuit. Or, a business that is not a party to a lawsuit may have records of its transactions with another company that is being sued; a lawyer may want to inspect those records to examine the business practices of the company being sued.

Documents or property belonging to someone who is not a party are obtained by sending that person or organization a *Subpoena Duces Tecum*, a *Subpoena for Production/Inspection* or a *Deposition Subpoena for Records*. Although these legal papers are technically subpoenas—court orders to appear—in most jurisdictions they are sent directly by the lawyer who wants the material, without the need for prior court approval. These subpoenas do not require that the responding party actually appear in person, as long as copies of the requested documents are delivered to the lawyer requesting them.

 Agreeing to Exchange Documents Instead of Going to Court. In a few jurisdictions, a party must go to court for permission to inspect another party's documents or other property. However, both sides can save time and money by agreeing ahead of time to reasonable, run-of-the-mill exchanges of documents. Then, rather than hearing arguments in court, a judge can merely rubber-stamp the lawyers' agreement. Such an agreement for a mutual exchange is called a *Stipulation*.

In some jurisdictions, the only way to force a non-party to produce records or other things is to issue a *Subpoena Duces Tecum re Deposition*. This cumbersome process requires that the non-party with the documents actually appear in person at a scheduled deposition,

complete with court reporter and all the other lawyers in the case. (See Section V.) To save time, money and hassle for all concerned, your lawyer might instead try contacting the person or entity that has the documents or other things and asking to examine or copy them informally.

Unfortunately, this informal process does not guarantee that the person or organization agreeing to the request will provide every document in its possession. Your lawyer might decide that it is too risky to rely on informal arrangements if the documents are important and the other person or organization has any reason to hold back some of its information. In that instance, your lawyer's caution is well-taken; it is likely worth the extra time and money for the more formal procedure.

25. Can I fight a request to produce or inspect?

There are several reasons why a party may legitimately refuse to produce documents, or other property, the opposing side requests. For example, the documents might reveal confidential material, may refer to private personal matters or may simply have nothing to do with the dispute. (The legal justifications for refusing to respond to a discovery request are explained in Section VI.)

When a party does not want to produce something requested by another party, the lawyer for the resisting party informs the other side by written *objection*, which states the legal reason for not providing the material. The lawyer for the requesting party must then decide whether to pursue the matter. Often, opposing lawyers will discuss the matter with each other, seeking a compromise whereby some material might be produced while other material is withheld. If no agreement can be reached and the requesting lawyer believes the requested material should be turned over, that lawyer may go to court to seek a judge's order—called an *Order to Compel Production*—requiring the documents or other objects to be produced. (See Chapter 5, Section VII.)

How You Can Help Your Lawyer Respond to a Request for Production

When your lawyer receives a request for production of your written or electronic documents or inspection of your property, he or she will review it carefully to consider whether you are legally obligated to produce the items requested. Because you probably know your documents or property better than your lawyer does, you should also personally go over each item requested, with the following questions in mind (see Section VI for a complete discussion of the limits on discovery information):

- Does it ask for something private or confidential?
- Does it ask for something you don't have or can't produce?
- Does it ask for something to which the other side also has access?
- Does it ask for something you have already produced?

- Does it ask for documents arranged in categories that do not correspond to the way the records have been kept? In other words, would it require you to reorganize the documents before producing them?
- Does it ask for categories of documents that are too broad? That is, does it ask for a group of documents the great majority of which have nothing to do with the dispute (for example, "records of all emails sent and received over the previous three years")?
- Does it simply ask for too much? That is, would you have to do a tremendous amount of work to produce documents that have information of little or no value in the case?

If you answer yes to any of these questions, discuss the matter with your lawyer to see if the lawyer should object to that request. Once you and your lawyer have decided what documents you should produce, organize them in a way that will help your lawyer keep track of them. The documents may be produced in the same order—files, sets or categories—in which they are regularly kept, or they can be reordered to match the specific requests to which they respond.

26. Who pays for the production of documents or testing?

The cost of copying documents, or of inspecting and testing a physical object, is borne by the party who requests the information. If an expert is required to analyze the document or electronic files or a physical object, the requesting party also pays that cost. However, copying, inspecting and analyzing are not the only expenses associated with requests for production. The collection and organizing of documents may require considerable labor by the responding party or employees. And a lawyer being paid by the hour may run up a sizable bill reviewing the documents before releasing them to the other side. These expenses are *not* reimbursed by the party seeking the documents and instead are borne by the party providing them.

27. Is a party always required to actually produce physical objects?

Some physical objects may be important to a case but difficult to produce for the other side to inspect—a computer system's hard drive, for example, or an inoperable car. Others may be impossible to "produce"—a house, fence, wall or other immovable object. In these situations, the requesting party must be permitted to enter the responding party's property—or other place where the object is located—and conduct an inspection on the spot.

The time and place of the inspection must be agreeable to both sides, along with the duration of, and other limits on, the inspection. The parties may also need to agree on the qualifications of the inspector. For example, a responding party might be completely within its rights to demand that

anyone roaming around in a computer hard drive be a computer expert who is not likely to ruin its data.

The timing of, and limits on, these on-site inspections can sometimes be difficult to work out. Disputes over inspection requests are more likely to wind up in court than disputes over simple document production. (See Chapter 5, Section VII.)

28. How long do I have to gather the documents the other side has requested?

A party usually has 30 days to respond to a request for production. However, this time limit may be, and often is, extended by mutual agreement, for the convenience of lawyers or clients. If a party would have trouble gathering, organizing and reviewing the requested documents within the allotted time, that party's lawyer may ask the other side for an *Extension of Time* within which to produce the items. If the extra time seems reasonable, the request is usually granted, in part because the other side will probably need similar courtesies sometime during the course of the lawsuit. Reasonable extensions are also usually granted because, if refused, the party producing the documents could ask a judge to grant the extra time. If the request for more time was reasonable, the judge could order the party who refused the extension to pay for the other lawyer's time in going to court to get it. (See Chapter 5, Section VII.)

You Must Produce Documents in Reasonable Order

If you get a request for a ton of documents, you may feel like getting some revenge on the other side by dumping copies of all of them loose into a huge box, shaking it vigorously two or three times and then spraying it with a hose, just for good measure.

Satisfying as that may be for the moment, it can cause you grief in the long run. The law requires that you turn over documents in the same order and condition in which they are maintained in the usual course of business. So, if you send the other side the big messy box, they have the right to send it back to you, demand that you present it in proper form and charge you for the time it took them to review it and send it back. You may also have to pay your own lawyer for the time spent brokering this exchange, as well as for the lawyer's time organizing the documents properly.

29. Can the other side inspect my medical records?

In limited circumstances. In most lawsuits, a party's physical condition and medical history are off limits. But in some cases, a party's physical condition is central to his or her claims in the lawsuit. The most common example is a personal injury action, in which the Plaintiff asserts that the other side's conduct caused the Plaintiff physical

harm. The legal question of who was at fault in such a case may depend on whether the injured person's pre-existing physical condition contributed in some way to the accident. Did a bad knee cause a fall? Did poor eyesight prevent the Plaintiff from noticing a danger? And the amount of compensation in these cases depends on the extent of the injuries.

Because the Plaintiff has raised questions about his or her own physical condition by filing an injury lawsuit, courts permit a Defendant to closely examine the Plaintiff's medical history, including access to some of the Plaintiff's medical records. However, the Defendant may not rummage around in the records of every doctor the Plaintiff has ever seen. A Defendant may inspect only those records directly related either to possible causes of the accident or to the resulting injuries. For example, if Plaintiff claims a leg injury, the Defendant may have access to records of an orthopedist who treated the injury but not to records of the Plaintiff's cardiologist, gynecologist or psychologist.

30. Can I be forced to submit to a medical examination?

Possibly. When a Plaintiff places his or her medical condition in question by filing a lawsuit that claims physical injury, a Defendant usually has the right to force Plaintiff to undergo a physical examination—referred to as an *Independent Medical Examination*

(IME)—by a doctor of the Defendant's choosing. An IME might also be appropriate if a party claimed that a physical or mental condition excused that person's failure to fulfill a legal duty, such as the performance of contract obligations or employment terms. Some courts also allow a psychiatric IME of a Plaintiff who claims to have suffered serious emotional distress because of the Defendant's actions. However, an IME is *not* permitted merely to test an opposing party's mental acuity, credibility or capacity to recall.

In many jurisdictions, an IME may only be obtained by court order or written agreement between the parties. In other jurisdictions, no court order is required. Instead, a written request is sent directly from one lawyer to another. If an IME is held, the doctor who conducts the examination must prepare a written report of the examination, of any tests conducted and of the doctor's opinion concerning the medical condition in controversy. Each side gets a copy of that report. The party who requested the IME must pay the entire cost of the examination, tests and preparation of the doctor's report.

31. Can I challenge a request for an Independent Medical Examination?

When a request for an IME is made, the party who is to be examined has several possible responses. If the exam seems appropriate and its terms—the type of

doctor, the time and place and the scope of the proposed exam—are reasonable, the party should probably agree rather than spend time, energy and money fighting it. Even if an exam might be proper in general, however, the terms proposed may be objectionable. For example, the time or place might be inconvenient, the doctor in question might not be an expert in the specific medical field at issue, proposed testing might be too intrusive or uncomfortable or the scope of the proposed examination might be too broad.

A party can also object to the entire exam, either because the party's physical condition is not sufficiently related to the issues in the case or because the examination is not likely to disclose useful information. If a party objects to an IME, the requesting party may go to court for an order—*Order Compelling Independent Medical Examination*—that the exam take place. Conversely, the party who is to be examined may seek a *protective order* from the court, forbidding or limiting the examination. (See Chapter 5, Section VII.)

32. If I am ordered to attend an IME, what preparations should I make?

An IME must be limited to the physical or psychological condition in contention in the lawsuit and to the specific procedures stated in the written agreement or court order. Before going to an IME, a client and lawyer should discuss these limits and those aspects of medical history that should *not* be discussed. For example, if the party has a knee or back injury, a doctor does not need to know the party's mental health history. However, a doctor is permitted to ask for the normal kinds of medical background information that a treating physician would need to diagnose the particular condition.

In many jurisdictions, another person may accompany the person being examined.

The party's attorney may want to be there, to make sure the exam stays within the bounds of the agreement or court order. In some jurisdictions, however, lawyers are not allowed. And even if allowed, some lawyers simply prefer to have someone else—a paralegal, investigator or one of the client's friends or relatives—attend the IME, so that person can testify about the examination later in the litigation, if necessary.

Three Is Not a Crowd

Although you may prefer not to involve friends or relatives in your case or have your medical condition discussed in front of someone else, it may be a good idea to have company at an IME. Having someone by your side may simply help you relax. Being examined by a doctor you don't know can be uncomfortable, and the circumstances make it more so—a lot is on the line for you, and a doctor chosen by the other side is often less than supportive. If you are too uncomfortable, you might not provide the clearest or fullest description of your medical condition.

Also, if the examination is superficial or badly handled, someone else will be able to corroborate that fact. Doctors chosen to conduct IMEs, especially for insurance companies defending personal injury law-

suits, are often heavily predisposed not to find a serious injury and so do only perfunctory examinations. If someone can confirm that a doctor took only five minutes both to get a medical history and to perform an examination, that testimony could undermine the doctor's opinion about your physical condition.

Finally, a support person can help you assert your rights if the examination strays into forbidden areas. If the doctor seeks information that is not relevant to the lawsuit or attempts to perform examinations or tests that are not included in the written examination order, you will have someone to help you stop the doctor's excessive probing—and to report to your lawyer what the doctor did and said.

Section IV: Requests for Admissions

This section discusses requests for admissions: written questions one party sends to another asking whether certain facts are true or documents are genuine. Admissions are used to establish basic, sometimes obvious facts so that all sides may move through the lawsuit without wasting time, energy and money trying to prove those facts. Requests for admissions are usually exchanged following the first stages of discovery—after initial interrogatories and perhaps an early deposition—when the outlines of the case are known but crucial depositions have not yet taken place.

Requests for Admissions Rarely Settle Anything Major

Most requests for admissions are intended to eliminate specific matters in a case that no one wants to bother disputing. But admissions rarely settle anything that determines who wins or loses the lawsuit. Lawyers are too cautious to permit a client to admit anything other than small details or obvious facts.

Theoretically, a court can impose sanctions—usually a fine—against a party who fails to admit something that was clear at the time and is later proved at trial to be true. But lawyers can usually find enough ambiguities in even the simplest assertion —The earth isn't actually round, it is "spherically ovoid"—to avoid such penalties, so they tend not to worry about them when instructing their clients to deny a certain fact.

33. What types of issues do requests for admissions resolve?

A request for admissions may ask a party to admit that a statement of fact is true or that a document is genuine. In most jurisdictions, a request may also ask for a party's belief or opinion about some aspect of the dispute.

Some requests are simple to answer: Yes, so-and-so did work for the company on a certain date; Yes, the signature on a certain document is genuine; Yes, the document specified is a true copy of the original in the company's files. But many requests for admissions are difficult to assess and dangerous to answer. For example, a party might be asked to admit that the way it conducted business conformed to the standard practice in that industry. At first it may seem sensible to admit this. However, by denying it, a party can assert later in the lawsuit that company standards were actually higher than those in the industry.

Certain Requests Need Not Be Answered at All

Some jurisdictions restrict what a party can be asked to admit. In some, a request may not ask for the admission of an *ultimate fact*—one that establishes a crucial issue the party needs to establish in order to win the lawsuit. In a few jurisdictions, a request may not include legal admissions, sometimes referred to as *conclusions of law*. For example, a request in one of these jurisdictions could ask whether you admit to driving a specific speed but not whether you broke the speed limit. If a request violates one of these rules, your lawyer should instruct you not to answer it. In place of an answer, the lawyer will provide a written *objection*, which states the legal reason the request is not being answered.

---

34. What is the effect of a party's admission?

If a party admits a particular statement of fact, that party is bound by the "truth" of that fact for the remainder of the case. The party who has admitted the fact will not be permitted to introduce evidence contradicting the fact at any later stage of the litigation. For example, if a business admits that it "employed" someone at a certain time, the business may not later claim that the person was only an independent contractor or subcontractor, facts which might be crucial in deciding whether the business is legally responsible for the employee's actions. Because seemingly insignificant differences in language can have a large impact down the road in a lawsuit, the question of whether or not to admit something must be very carefully considered by client and lawyer together.

 How You Can Help Your Lawyer Answer a Request for Admissions

Because the effect of an admission can be so serious, your lawyer will play the greater role in deciding what should be admitted and what should not. Your lawyer will do so with great caution and a lawyerly talent for quibbling about details.

Even so, your lawyer may not realize that a fairly simple "fact" to be admitted is actually somewhat tricky. You should carefully review every request for admission and do a little "lawyering" yourself. That is, try to think of any way in which the request might be complicated or ambiguous. Make a note of your ideas and discuss them with your lawyer before your reply is sent to the other side.

35. Can I take back an admission?

In some narrow circumstances, it is possible to get out from under an admission that turns out to be incorrect. The admission may be corrected if it resulted from a clerical or other normal human error. An admission may also be retracted if later information turns up that proves the admission was made in error. An admission may not be withdrawn, however, simply because a party realizes that it was damaging, even if there is good reason that a denial would be just as valid an answer. Nor is a party permitted to withdraw an admission based upon new information if a reasonable search of that party's files or documents, or discussion with others within a business or organization, would have disclosed the information before the admission was made.

If there might be a valid legal basis for correcting an erroneous admission, the admitting party's lawyer may file court papers called *Motion for Leave to Amend/Withdraw Admission* or *Motion for Relief From Admission*. A judge will then decide if there is good cause to reverse the mistake.

36. How should I respond if I am asked to admit something that is partly true and partly false, or is unclear?

If a request for admission is mostly but not completely true, or if the answering party is not entirely certain whether it is true, generally it should be denied. This is not merely a tactic to avoid making life easier for the other side. Because it's so difficult to take back an admission, a party cannot be too cautious in responding to these requests.

For example, a business might be asked to admit that it checked the status of a subcontractor's license before hiring that subcontractor. If the business had indeed checked to see that the subcontractor had a current license, it might seem that the fact should be admitted. But checking the "status" of a license might also be construed—once the lawyers start playing with words—to mean that the business had checked with the license bureau to see if there had been any complaints against this subcontractor, rather than merely seeing if the license was currently valid. If one of the issues in the case is this subcontractor's history of shoddy work, the way this request for admission is answered could be important.

Have It Both Ways and Save Some Money. In those instances when a statement of fact in a request for admissions is mostly but not completely true, you can admit the parts that are true and briefly explain what is not true rather than denying the statement entirely. This answer with an explanation may be better for both you and the requesting party. If you deny the entire statement, the other side might engage in lengthy discovery to get to the bottom of things, which would also require a lot of unnecessary and expensive work by your lawyer.

37. What if I don't know how to answer a request for admissions?

Often, a responding party simply does not know one way or the other about the "fact" at issue in a request for admission. Or the responding party may not have enough information either to admit or to deny a particular statement of fact. A responding party is obligated to make reasonable efforts to investigate the matter. However, if those efforts do not provide the answer, the responding party is permitted to deny the "fact" and state that the denial is based upon insufficient information.

Section V: Depositions

This section explains depositions: the face-to-face questioning of a party or witness by lawyers. Although depositions take place out of court, the witness—called a *deponent*— answers under oath and the entire proceeding is recorded and transcribed. Depositions are the most expensive and explosive of all discovery procedures. Generally, they are

also the most useful to the lawyers and most important to the litigants.

38. What is a deposition?

A deposition is a less-formal version of courtroom testimony. Typically in a lawyer's office rather than a courtroom, one party's lawyer questions a witness (with an opposing lawyer sometimes objecting), the witness answers under oath and the lawyer follows up with more questions. Then the opposing lawyer gets a chance to ask questions. This goes back and forth until all the lawyers have asked all their questions.

A deposition witness (deponent) may be anyone, party or not, who might have information about any aspect of the case. The deponent typically must answer a wide range of questions regarding his or her personal and business history and virtually anything about the dispute and its consequences. A deposition serves to pin down each deponent's story so that it cannot significantly change later on. It also gives the lawyers a chance to experience what a deponent looks, sounds and acts like—a preview of what a jury would see and hear if the deponent became a witness at trial. The deponent's responses and reactions under pressure give the lawyers a good idea not only of what a witness would say at a trial but also of whether a jury would believe it.

As compared with the carefully limited written answers the lawyer receives from interrogatories (Section II) or requests for admissions (Section IV), a deposition gives lawyers the opportunity to explore broadly what a witness knows. In a deposition, a lawyer will ask not only planned questions but also follow-up questions suggested by a previous answer. This chance to follow up on the spontaneous responses of a deponent is the element of a deposition that sets it apart from all other types of discovery. This spontaneity not only permits the lawyer to probe deeply and broadly into important lawsuit matters but also often reveals new facts and issues that the lawyer can then explore further.

 Multimedia Show. The traditional way to record a deposition is to have a stenographer—called a court reporter—take down everything said, transcribe it and bind it into a booklet. The booklet is then corrected and signed by the deponent and becomes the official record of the deposition. In recent years,

however, lawyers have become enamored of audio and video recordings of depositions. In addition to adding voice and/or picture to the record, audio or video recording has the potential advantage of being cheaper than a stenographer's fees. However, many lawyers only use audio and video recording as a supplement to the court reporter, thereby adding cost rather than saving. Even if audio and video recording is the only method used, the cost-saving may turn out to be illusory—to use an audio or video deposition record for arbitration or trial, a transcript has to be made anyway.

In many jurisdictions, the lawyer arranging the deposition has a choice among stenographic, audio or video recording. A notice or subpoena for the deposition must indicate which recording method(s) will be used. But any other party may choose to record the deposition in a different way, as long as that party notifies everyone and provides and pays for the extra recording method. Whatever

method is used, all parties have a right to a copy of each record, paying for the copy themselves.

Computers have also entered the deposition recording scene. Some court reporters have digital equipment that produces a transcript of the testimony as the reporter records it. The transcript can be transferred immediately to lawyers' laptop computers, making the testimony available for immediate review—as another lawyer questions the witness, during breaks and immediately after the deposition (instead of waiting days or weeks for the reporter to prepare a transcript). Because this technology is new, reporters have recently invested in the equipment and so may charge higher rates for its use. If a lawyer plans to use these other forms of recording, he or she should consult with the client to go over any extra costs involved and the benefits of using the procedure.

39. Who attends a deposition?

In addition to the deponent, each party to the lawsuit has a lawyer present. Not every lawyer asks questions, however. If the witness being deposed has nothing to say that affects a particular party in the lawsuit, that party's lawyer might merely observe the deposition. On some occasions in a multi-party lawsuit, one party's lawyer might not even bother to attend the deposition of a witness whose testimony does not affect that lawyer's client.

The parties themselves also have a right to attend all depositions, though usually they do not. If both a party and the party's lawyer are there, only the lawyer is permitted to ask questions. If a party has no lawyer, then the party may do his or her own questioning.

The deponent may also have a lawyer present to protect his or her interests during questioning. A party being deposed always has a lawyer present but a non-party witness rarely does.

 For more information on the deposition process, see *Nolo's Deposition Handbook,* by Attorneys Paul Bergman & Albert Moore (Nolo).

How You Can Help Your Lawyer With Depositions

Before your lawyer takes the deposition of any witness personally known to you, you should tell your lawyer what you know of that person's personal history, connection to the case—particularly the role the person plays in a business—and relation to other parties and witnesses. Your lawyer may already know much of this from answers to interrogatories and documents, but you may be able to add useful details.

You also have a right to be present during every deposition. But lawyers often prefer to conduct some depositions without their clients present. Lawyers might be concerned that a client's presence might intimidate or greatly agitate certain deponents—particularly an opposing party—which might prevent the witness from opening up and saying as much as possible.

There are times, however, when it may be useful for you to attend a deposition. This is particularly true if there are non-legal, technical aspects to the case that you may understand more thoroughly than your lawyer. You may be able to help your lawyer with these issues during the questioning. It may also be useful for you to attend at least one deposition as preparation for your own deposition. There is nothing like seeing the real thing to prepare you for the grilling that lies ahead during your own testimony.

40. How does a deposition proceed?

A deposition begins with some preliminaries, including a discussion of ground rules and of how long the questioning is expected to take. Then the witness is sworn in—takes an oath to tell the truth under penalty of perjury—by the court reporter, and the questioning commences.

Direct examination. The first segment of a deposition is called *direct examination*: questioning by the lawyer who has scheduled the deposition. Direct examination may cover any subject that relates to the lawsuit, including the personal and business background of the witness. Direct examination continues as long as the scheduling lawyer wants to keep asking questions.

Cross-examination. After the lawyer who scheduled the deposition is finished questioning the deponent, one lawyer for each of the other parties has an opportu-

nity to ask questions in what is called *cross-examination*. Technically, a cross-examining lawyer is not permitted to ask questions on any subject that hasn't been covered in the direct examination; lawyers refer to these questions as "beyond the scope" of direct examination. But this rule is only loosely followed in depositions. The subjects covered in direct examination are usually quite broad, so few questions are clearly beyond their scope. Also, deponents' answers sometimes open up subjects that were not included in the questions themselves. So cross-examination questions are objectionable as beyond the scope of direct examination only when they refer to subjects that were obviously and entirely untouched during the direct examination.

Redirect and Re-cross-examination. After the first round of questioning by each party's lawyer, each of the lawyers is permitted another round, called *redirect examination* and *re-cross-examination*. A lawyer's re-examination is supposed to be confined to those subjects raised by questions and answers that followed that lawyer's original questioning. In other words, the lawyer is not supposed to go over the same ground he or she covered in the previous round. It is often difficult to say, however, exactly when a new matter has been raised rather than merely a different aspect of a subject previously discussed. Commonly, the lawyers' exhaustion ends the questioning before application of this rule does.

Breaks in the Official Record

A deposition begins when the court reporter administers an oath to the deponent, under penalty of perjury, that his or her answers will be true. From this oath onward, every audible sound anyone in the room utters is supposed to be recorded until the lawyer who scheduled the deposition officially ends it. That is, the record is *supposed* to include every word. But in practice, lawyers sometimes go "off the record," a time when the reporter stops recording. Some of this is quite routine: conversation during coffee, bathroom, lunch and telephone breaks or discussion among the lawyers about other business in the case. Other routine occasions have to do with settling technical matters—how to mark documents, for example, or the order in which to proceed—about which the lawyers agree to speak informally, without recording.

Other breaks in the record, however common, are not exactly routine. The lawyers sometimes argue so vehemently over a point that they ask to go off the record to avoid their embarrassing spat being preserved for posterity. And if one of the parties is being deposed, the deponent's lawyer may refuse to permit the deposition to continue until he or she has had a chance to speak with the witness in private about how the deponent should respond to a question. In that case, the deposition may halt for some time while the lawyer and deponent/client huddle outside for a lengthy and important discussion that nonetheless is off the record.

41. Do lawyers object to deposition questions the same way they do in court?

Deposition questioning is frequently interrupted by lawyers' objections to certain questions and by disagreements among the lawyers about those objections. It is not unusual for these disagreements to become heated arguments. The resulting disruptions, combined with the wide scope of questions permitted, cause depositions to drag on. Any lawyer may object to any question. But the frequency and vehemence of objections is markedly increased when it is a party who is being deposed—that party's lawyer is much more protective of his or her client than any of the lawyers tends to be with independent, non-party witnesses.

The purpose of most objections is to clarify the question asked so that the answer can be clear. And lawyers for deponents sometimes object in order to maintain their clients' privacy or other privileged information. But lawyers also object—particularly if the lawyer makes a little speech explaining the objection—in order to hint to the witness what the lawyer thinks the answer should be. This is technically improper, but it goes on all the time. It happens most often when the deponent is a party and his or her own lawyer is objecting.

42. What happens when a lawyer objects to a question?

When a lawyer makes an objection, all the lawyers present discuss whether the objection is legally correct. Often the objection is to the form of a question; the lawyer who asked the question will usually respond by asking it again in a different way, which lawyers call "rephrasing" the question. But a lawyer might also object to the subject matter of a question. For example, a lawyer might object that a cross-examination or re-direct question is beyond the scope of what has been asked before, that a question is completely unrelated to the lawsuit or that a question delves into private or otherwise privileged matters. See Section VI.

What happens when the lawyers cannot agree whether a question is proper? That depends on how significant or intrusive the question is and whether the deponent is a party to the lawsuit. A non-party deponent usually must answer every question despite any objections. And party-deponents, too, usually answer most questions even if their lawyer objects. The objection is merely stated "for the record"—the lawyer is preserving the objection for later argument in court over whether the question and

answer may be used as evidence in the case. If the lawyer is merely objecting for the record, the lawyer follows the objections by telling the party-deponent that he or she may answer the question.

Occasionally, however, the lawyer for a party-deponent does not think the question should be answered at all. The question might intrude into privileged or confidential matters, seek the party-deponent's opinion or ask the deponent to speculate about something. Or, the question may simply be the final straw in a long line of questions heading too far afield from proper issues in the case—at some point, the lawyer simply decides to draw the line at a particular question.

Whatever the reason, the lawyer representing the party-deponent may formally "instruct" the deponent not to answer the question. This formal instruction from the lawyer takes the burden off the deponent, who is then legally permitted not to answer. It also makes clear to a judge, if the matter later comes up in court, that it was the lawyer's professional judgment that led to the refusal to answer and not merely the witness's personal opinion or orneriness. If the questioning lawyer believes that the objection was legally invalid, that lawyer may go to court for a judge's order that the question be answered, and perhaps for monetary sanctions against the opposing party who would not answer or against the lawyer who gave the instruction not to answer. See Chapter 5, Section VII.

Depositions Can Get Wild and Woolly

Depositions often create a lot of unpleasant fireworks among lawyers, clients and deponents—lengthy arguments and hostile remarks between lawyers; rambling, balking and angry answers by witnesses; even threats by one side or the other to get up and leave. In part, these melodramatics occur because of pressure on the lawyers and deponents: usually, only one deposition per witness is permitted in a case and that deposition may be crucial to winning or losing the lawsuit.

Depositions are also so fractious because they take place in person rather than through an exchange of papers and because their course cannot be predicted or fully controlled by the lawyers. All the lawyers are together in one room, with opposing sides sometimes trying to get the deponent to say completely different things. Also, most deponents dislike getting grilled by lawyers, particularly if it is their own lawsuit on the line. Witnesses feel especially put out because legal rules permit the questioning to wander far and wide into a deponent's personal and business life. And all of this happens with no judge around to keep a lid on things.

43. How and when do depositions get scheduled?

In most jurisdictions, depositions may not begin until about 30 days after the Defendant has been served with the Complaint, in order to give the Defendant time to hire a lawyer and get up to speed on the case. In the first month or two of a case, lawyers might take the deposition of one key member of a business or other organization in order to get an overall picture of how that organization works. An early deposition might also be scheduled if a lawyer feels a particular deponent may forget valuable information, die, disappear or move outside the court's jurisdiction.

Otherwise, the heaviest concentration of depositions is usually in the three to six months before the trial date, after the other forms of discovery have been completed. Depositions may be scheduled up to a specific cut-off date some two to four weeks before the date set for arbitration or trial. The final depositions are usually of experts, if any, who have been hired to assist each side in presenting its case.

The Dating Game

As a practical matter, lawyers often agree among themselves on dates for depositions. This saves the hassle of one lawyer picking a date and then having to change it to accommodate the schedules of the other lawyers or parties. This is particularly useful when there are several parties and lawyers in the case, since all lawyers have a right to be present at any deposition.

Unfortunately, by the time depositions roll around, lawyers may have descended into the bickering and gamesmanship that so often plague discovery. As a result, they may set deposition dates without first checking with the other side, then use the inconvenience to the other side as a bargaining chip to try to win some other concession.

One of the results of this game-playing over dates is that the depositions them-selves keep getting pushed further and further away, delaying the progress of the entire case. If you want your case to keep moving, these delays can become extremely irritating. If this kind of tit-for-tat reschedul-ing seems to be happening in your case, ask your lawyer to avoid contributing to it. And ask that your lawyer establish a firm date—lawyers call it a "date certain"—for your own deposition.

44. How is deposition testimony used?

Informally, deposition testimony lets every-one in the case know what a witness has to say—indeed, has now committed to under oath—on both large issues and small details in the case. It also lets the lawyers see a witness's demeanor—that is, how be-lievable and appealing the witness is. Once the lawyers and parties have considered the testimony from important depositions, they may alter their assessment of the likelihood of winning at trial, or of the amount of compensation that might be awarded, which often brings them closer to settling the case.

Formally, deposition testimony may be used when a lawyer asks a judge to decide important issues, and even the entire case, before trial. (See Chapter 5, Section VIII.) At arbitration, deposition testimony often is used instead of live testimony. (See Chapter 7). At trial, deposition testimony may be used in a couple of ways. First, if a witness at trial contradicts something he or she said at deposition, the deposition testimony may be used to *"impeach" the witness.* That is, the deposition testimony can be read to the judge or jury to show that the witness had previously said something different. (See Chapter 9, Question 48.) Also, all the important parts of a deposition may be read to judge or jury in the case of an *un-available witness*—someone who has died, is physically unable to appear at trial, can-not be located or lives beyond the court's jurisdiction.

Controlling Deposition Costs. Depositions can be very expensive. Lawyers for every party take part and some depositions go on for days. It takes time for attorneys to prepare for depositions, and later to review the transcripts of what was said. If a deponent lives far from the lawyer's office, there is the cost of the lawyer's travel. Non-party deponents must be paid witness fees and travel costs. And there are considerable expenses for recording the deposition and preparing transcripts.

For all these reasons, if your lawyer schedules more depositions than are necessary, costs will quickly mount, particularly if you are paying the lawyer by the hour. It is difficult to control depositions taken by the other side, but you can ask how many depositions your own lawyer intends to schedule and talk about whether those depositions are necessary. You can raise the possibility of waiting for the other side to schedule some independent witness depositions, so that the other side and not you must bear the witness fees and the cost of the court reporter. And you can ask the lawyer to use less expensive discovery devices when practical.

However, bear in mind how important depositions can be and resist the temptation to be deposition-wise and case-foolish. If, after your discussion, your lawyer still believes a particular deposition is necessary, it probably is.

45. Must a deposition always be face-to-face?

Not always. A money-saving but rarely used alternative to the standard deposition is the *Deposition Upon Written Questions.* Instead of traveling some distance to depose a non-party witness, lawyers prepare written questions that the deponent answers orally, under oath, before a court reporter. The lawyer who schedules the deposition writes up an initial set of questions, which are sent to all the other lawyers. The other lawyers add their own questions, and all the questions are sent to a court reporter where the deponent lives.

If the deponent is within the court's jurisdiction, he or she will be legally obligated to appear to answer these questions. If not, the witness may appear voluntarily. If and when the deponent does appear, the court reporter reads the questions to the deponent and records the deponent's answers.

The advantage of this process is purely economic. The lawyers don't have to travel to and spend time in a deposition. But the disadvantages may be significant. The lawyer has no opportunity to see and hear the witness or ask spontaneous questions. A deponent's answer that suggests follow-up questions will just sit there silently as the next scripted question is read. Despite these drawbacks, if you are paying your lawyer by the hour, a Deposition Upon Written Questions could be used for a witness from whom only limited details need to be gathered—especially if the witness's answers are not likely to be evasive or misleading in favor of the other side.

46. Do I have any control over the scheduling of my own deposition?

The other side in a lawsuit will decide when they take an opposing party's deposition. When a party's lawyer receives notice that the opposing side intends to take the party's deposition on a certain date, the party has several possible responses:

- **Accept the date.** One choice is simply to accept the inevitable, agree to the date the other side has chosen and begin to prepare for the deposition.
- **Informally request changes.** If the date the other side has chosen presents a scheduling conflict for either the client or the lawyer, the lawyer may informally request a new date from the other side. When several lawyers are involved, finding a date convenient for everyone can be tricky business. Nonetheless, scheduling conflicts are common, so a request to reschedule is not usually met with much resistance unless the date has been changed before.
- **Make a formal objection.** More complicated problems with the deposition notice may require more formal responses. If there is a substantive problem that cannot be worked out—for example, if the deponent is asked to bring documents to the deposition

which the deponent's lawyer believes should not be produced—the deponent's lawyer may seek a court order to have the terms of the deposition changed or the deposition cancelled. (See Chapter 5, Section VII.)

47. How important is my own deposition?

The most stressful and significant part of the discovery process—indeed, of the entire case short of trial—is a litigant's own deposition. It is probably the first time the litigant will be face-to-face with lawyers on the other side, and also perhaps with the opposing party. The litigant must answer difficult questions in a tense atmosphere often made downright hostile because of bickering among the lawyers.

The importance of a party's own deposition varies with the circumstances of the case. If the dispute involves the party-deponent's own personal conduct—such as an automobile accident case in which the deponent was the driver—then the deposition might be crucial. On the other hand, if there is little question who was at fault for the accident and the only real question is the extent of someone else's injuries, the deponent's testimony might not be of great significance. Similarly, if the deponent actively engaged in business that is the subject of the lawsuit, or was a witness to how someone else performed key business tasks, the deposition testimony may be crucial. But if the main issue in the dispute is someone else's performance about which the deponent knows little or a technical matter about which the deponent has no expertise, then the litigant's own deposition might be less important.

 How You Can Help Your Lawyer By Preparing for Your Own Deposition

If your deposition testimony may be crucial to your case, your lawyer should thoroughly prepare you for it. However, as with many other things in litigation, the extent of that preparation may depend on what you can afford. That is, if you are paying the lawyer by the hour, your finances might limit the time your lawyer spends on this particular aspect of the case. If your lawyer is being paid on a contingency fee basis, or is being paid by an insurance company, the amount of time your lawyer spends helping you prepare will depend on whether your testimony will be crucial to the case.

Regardless of how much time your lawyer can put into your preparation, there are a number of things you can do to prepare yourself, including:

- **Highlight special areas of concern.** Perhaps the first thing to do in preparing for your deposition is to alert your lawyer to any concerns you have about your privacy or other privileged or sensitive information. (See Section VI.) Your lawyer can then advise you about the extent to which these matters must be disclosed, and you and your lawyer can discuss how to handle deposition questions

about these subjects if they come up. Raising these concerns will also remind the lawyer to prepare legal arguments to protect this information.

- **Review results from previous discovery.** You should go over any information—documents, answers to interrogatories and responses to requests for admissions—you have already provided during discovery. Your lawyer can also provide you with key documents or witness testimony received from the other side. And you should gather and review any documents you are to bring to the deposition. These reviews will help you focus on the subjects of questioning to come and remember what you have already sworn in writing.

After you have reviewed this material, you and your lawyer might want to go over some of it together, to discuss any special areas of concern. Of course, how this is done—a long session in person, a written summary of concerns sent to your lawyer and a meeting in response, or just a phone call—might depend not only on the importance of your testimony but also on how the lawyer is being paid and how much you can afford.

- **Practice deposition.** If there is time to arrange it and it is affordable for you, your lawyer or another lawyer in the same office might put you through a practice deposition. This gets you used to the questioning process itself and familiarizes you with how your lawyer can help out during the deposition through the use of objections, digressions and breaks for consultation.

Who conducts this practice deposition and how extensive it is will depend on what you can afford. Preferably, your lawyer can "play" himself or herself during the practice run while someone else in the same firm plays the role of the lawyer from the other side. This can help get you used to answering questions posed by someone unfamiliar—as well as to your own lawyer's interventions and interruptions. Even if hourly billing presents a financial pinch, it is almost always worth doing at least a brief dry run, just to get the feel of things.

- **Attend or view other depositions.** Another thing you might do is attend another deposition in the case. This can give you a sense of the process and a feel for the particular style of the opposing lawyers who will question you. Alternatively, it may be possible to view a deposition on videotape. A videotaped deposition in the same case would provide the best preparation—same lawyers, same issues and some of the same questions. If there are no videotaped depositions from the same case, your lawyer might have videotape copies of depositions in other cases. This will at least give you a sense of the deposition process in general and also, if your lawyer was involved, how he or she operates.

- **Agree on ground rules.** At a deposition, questions and objections can come

pretty thick and fast. It is sometimes as important to know when *not* to answer a question as how to answer. If you blurt out an answer before your lawyer has a chance to object to the question, your answer will stand—and you might be forced to answer more questions on the same subject. (See Section VI.) Before your deposition, try to get a feel for how your lawyer will let you know when to immediately stop speaking—a bark to "Stop!," a kick to the shins, a raised hand. You should also ask your lawyer how to stop the questioning yourself in order to consult with the lawyer, if a question poses a particular problem for you.

Section VI: Discovery Limits

As explained in Section I, virtually any bit of information that might have even a slight connection to the lawsuit is fair game for discovery. But this enormous latitude sometimes leads to abuse. Lawyers pry into subjects that seem to have no legitimate significance for the lawsuit, or that are private and confidential, serving only to annoy or embarrass the parties. Fortunately, there are some legal limits on this kind of probing, and some protections against public disclosure for material that must be revealed. This section discusses the kinds of information a party or other witness may refuse to disclose during discovery.

48. Do I have to reveal my personal or business finances?

In certain cases. The kind of financial information a witness has to reveal depends on the type of case and the person from whom the information is sought.

You May Be Able to Prevent the Other Side From Revealing Material You Disclose

Even if you are required to disclose certain information to the opposing side in a lawsuit, you may be able to keep them from revealing it to anyone else. Some information crucial to the other side in the lawsuit might be embarrassing to you or damaging to your personal or business reputation. Or, it might be confidential information that business rivals could use to their advantage, sometimes referred to as "trade secrets."

In such situations, you may be able to have a judge require the opposing side to keep the information strictly to themselves —that is, to the other party, opposing lawyer and people working on the case for the other lawyer—and not reveal it to anyone else. If you believe information heading to the other side should be kept confidential, alert your lawyer and ask the lawyer to seek protection for the information. The procedure for obtaining such a *Protective Order* or *Order Sealing Matters Produced Upon Discovery* is discussed in Chapter 5, Section VII.

Plaintiff's finances. If an individual or business Plaintiff claims lost income as a result of the Defendant's conduct, the Plaintiff's recent income history is fair game in discovery. This includes information about any specific lost business or business opportunities, as well as earnings and related information for the previous five or so years (because average earnings over time are often used to determine potential earnings during the "lost" period). Similarly, if a Plaintiff claims that property has been damaged, information pertaining to the value of the property is discoverable.

Defendant's finances. The Defendant in a lawsuit generally does not have to reveal financial information to the Plaintiff. There are three standard exceptions to this general rule. First, if the lawsuit seeks *punitive damages*—an amount calculated to punish the Defendant for especially bad behavior —the Defendant's financial information might be relevant to the amount of these damages. For this reason, a Defendant's lawyer should attempt to have a punitive damages request thrown out of the lawsuit as early in the case as possible, before discovery gets rolling. A Defendant is usually also required to reveal any insurance coverage that might pay for damages. Disclosing insurance information is intended to promote settlement because it gives the Plaintiff a realistic picture of the Defendant's financial backing. And a Defendant's business records may be subject to discovery if the Complaint alleges that the Defendant deceived a Plaintiff partner, shareholder or investor by "cooking the books."

Non-party's finances. A witness who is not a party to the litigation is not usually required to reveal any personal or business financial information, except the existence and nature of any financial relationship with any of the parties to the lawsuit. Such a relationship is discoverable because it might influence the witness's credibility— the ability and willingness to provide complete, accurate and unbiased information.

You Waive It, You Lose It

This Section discusses the subjects you may protect from inquiries during discovery. However, if you respond to a discovery question or request without your lawyer raising a legal objection, you might lose your right not to reveal this information. Your answer cannot be withdrawn after the fact. You might also have to answer other inquiries into the same general subject for the remainder of the lawsuit. This failure to assert your right not to answer is known as *waiving a privilege*, or simply *waiver*.

Because of this problem of waiver, you must alert your lawyer as soon as you believe that a question or request might be heading toward protected information. And before your own deposition, make sure to discuss with your lawyer the subjects that might need protection, when they might arise and how you and your lawyer will communicate if these issues come up.

Your lawyer will probably be aware of the areas where this protection might be needed. But you may know confidential details that the lawyer does not, or you may have a particularly strong feeling of privacy about a certain matter. In these circumstances, protect your own privacy rather than waiting for your lawyer to speak up—it may make the difference between keeping the matter to yourself and opening it up to everyone involved in the lawsuit.

49. Can I keep my private communications confidential?

AHHH...

Sometimes. Communications between people engaged in certain relationships are given a special legal protection known as *privilege*. Courts and legislatures have decided that the free flow of confidential information in these relationships is so important that it must be protected, even if that information might be important to others in a lawsuit. Under the law, no one need disclose any information, verbal or written, that was confidentially exchanged within the following relationships:

- **Spouses.** Confidential communications between spouses are privileged. A party or other witness need not divulge the contents of any conversation or other communication with his or her spouse, and can prevent the spouse from disclosing a communication even against the spouse's wishes. If a couple divorces, the privilege still applies to communications made during the marriage, though not to those made after its dissolution. The spousal privilege is not usually available to either spouse in family law cases (divorce, child custody and visitation) or lawsuits in which spouses are suing each other. And in most jurisdictions, the spousal privilege is not available to couples who are not legally married.
- **Doctor-patient.** A patient has a right to have a medical doctor, or anyone employed by the doctor, keep private any information confidentially disclosed in connection with medical diagnosis or treatment. In some jurisdictions this privilege is limited to M.D.s only; in other jurisdictions, the privilege is extended to some non-M.D. medical and mental health practitioners and clinical social workers. A Plaintiff who is suing for personal injuries may not claim this privilege for communications with a doctor who has diagnosed or treated those or related injuries.
- **Religious counsel.** Sometimes referred to as the *priest-penitent* privilege, this protects confidential communications between a member of the clergy and someone seeking spiritual counsel. Most courts only include within this privilege clergy who are members of mainstream religions. A client who received counsel on subjects pertaining to the lawsuit from a spiritual adviser who is not a member of a traditional clergy should alert the lawyer to this

fact as early as possible in the lawsuit. This will allow the lawyer time to prepare a legal argument to support the claim of privilege, if one might exist.

Privilege Applies Only If Communication Was Confidential

This section explains types of communications that need not be disclosed during discovery. But in order for any of these communications to be protected, they must have been made in confidence. That is, they must have been made with the expectation that no one else would hear or read them. If they were not made in complete confidence, they are not protected. For example, if you and your spouse discuss sensitive personal matters but friends or relatives are in on the conversation, the spousal privilege might not apply. Or, if you and your doctor are at a party and you discuss your medical condition while others listen in, the conversation might not be protected. Similarly, if you write a letter to your clergy about personal problems but also send it to a lay counselor or to elders in the church, the letter might not be protected.

- **Lawyer-client.** All communications with a lawyer from whom legal advice is sought are privileged, whether or not the person seeking advice actually hires

the lawyer. This includes communications between representatives of a business or organization and a lawyer, made in confidence for the purpose of obtaining legal advice. The privilege also applies to communications with someone working for a lawyer, such as a paralegal or investigator. However, the attorney-client privilege only applies to communications with lawyers in which the client is seeking legal advice. For example, many lawyers are directly involved in business and finance matters (by, for example, serving as board members of a corporation) and others give business and financial counsel that has nothing to do with legal advice. Communications with them about non-legal business matters are not protected. Also, a person's communication with a lawyer who was representing someone else's interests at the time is not privileged. Normally, a lawyer will recognize more quickly than the client when to raise the attorney-client privilege in discovery matters. But if there are written communications with other lawyers in business files, the client should alert the current lawyer to that fact. Also, if other people within a business have communicated with lawyers on behalf of the business, those people should be identified for the current lawyer so that steps can be taken to ensure that those people do not divulge confidential material.

Attorney Work-Product Privilege May Protect Your Work, Too

The attorney-client privilege protects communications between lawyer and client. A separate rule protects work done to prepare for or conduct litigation. This *work-product* protection, as it is called, includes work done by those employed by an attorney, such as law clerks, paralegals and investigators. In some jurisdictions, it also protects work the client does to assist with or prepare for the litigation, even if that work is not given or communicated to the lawyer. This may include such things as summaries of events, time-lines, notes and questions, if you made them to help with the litigation and not as part of regular personal or business records. If you have prepared any such notes or other writings, let your lawyer know so that the lawyer may prepare to protect them from the other side's prying.

50. How far into my private life is the other side allowed to pry?

In recent years, courts have increasingly recognized that some aspects of personal life should remain private, beyond the reach even of lawyers. But the *right to privacy* is a fairly recent and still-developing notion. There is no clear definition of what it covers, and the extent of its protection varies considerably from state to state. Nonetheless, familiarity with some privacy basics can prepare a litigant at least to alert his or her lawyer when privacy rights might be threatened.

Roughly, the right to privacy protects those matters a person would not normally discuss or reveal to anyone outside of immediate family—and almost certainly protects those matters a person would not reveal to anyone other than a spouse, intimate partner or physician—unless they are obviously relevant to the lawsuit. These generally include issues such as:

- the body or health
- sexuality
- spiritual or religious beliefs, and
- immediate family relationships.

51. What should I do if the other side tries to obtain private information?

If a discovery request or question asks a party to reveal information on any of the subjects listed in Question 50 and the party wants the information to remain private, the party should discuss the matter fully with his or her lawyer before deciding how to respond. If a privacy-violating question is posed during a deposition and the deponent's lawyer fails to object, the deponent should not immediately answer but instead should ask to discuss the matter privately with the attorney.

52. How do discovery disputes over privacy get resolved?

If a party makes a privacy objection to a discovery inquiry, the objecting party and the lawyers on both sides—and ultimately a judge, if disagreement over the matter winds up in court—must decide how much intrusion into private matters seems fair in the particular circumstances of the case. This means balancing the amount of intrusion into privacy against the importance of the information to the lawsuit. In general, the more sensitive the private matter, the more protection it is given. Conversely, the more important the matter is to the lawsuit, the more likely the party will have to divulge it.

This kind of balancing is often required regarding the medical history of someone whose lawsuit claims a physical or emotional injury. If a Plaintiff claims physical or emotional damage, the right of privacy may not be used to completely block the other side from learning the details of the Plaintiff's medical or psychological condition. In lawyer's parlance, the Plaintiff has put his or her condition "in issue." On the other hand, the fact that someone has sustained a back or knee injury does not allow the other side in a lawsuit to obtain records of the injured person's psychological counseling sessions or to ask about the Plaintiff's sex life—unless Plaintiff has claimed that the injury had psychological or sexual consequences. Similarly, if a Plaintiff claims sexual harassment, he or she will probably have to go into explicit detail about the precise nature of the harassment, regardless of how personal and embarrassing that is.

A Delicate Balance Can Sometimes Be Struck

The balancing act between protecting and disclosing sensitive private information is often difficult. Both sides may have legitimate concerns and interests, so a solution that requires either full disclosure or complete protection of information may do injustice to one side or the other. But these decisions do not always have to be all or nothing. Instead, partial disclosures can sometimes be worked out, either by carefully limiting the subject to be discussed or by censoring—lawyers call it "redacting" —documents to protect certain information while revealing the rest. For example, if a letter discusses both business decisions and personal matters, it may be possible to cut out those portions relating to personal matters while leaving the business discussion.

Such compromises may be arranged between lawyers, with the advice and consent of the client. Or, a judge may fashion a compromise if the matter winds up in court. If your lawyer advises you that you run a serious risk of being forced to disclose extremely sensitive information, you may want to support a compromise that protects as much of that information as possible.

53. Does the right against self-incrimination apply in a civil case?

Yes. A party to a civil lawsuit may invoke the constitutional right against self-incrimination if the information being sought might be used as evidence against that party in a criminal prosecution. This is true even if a criminal prosecution has not actually been initiated. In civil litigation, this situation might arise if someone is accused of fraud, embezzlement or breach of fiduciary duty, or when there has been a physical injury that resulted from an assault or reckless behavior, such as driving under the influence of alcohol or drugs. Once a criminal case against a party or witness has ended, however, the right no longer applies.

54. Can my lawyer object if the other side's discovery requests ask for too much information?

Yes. Certain discovery requests may be rejected because they are just too big a pain in the neck. If the amount of searching a party is asked to do seems to far exceed the value of the information sought to the other side, the party should check with his or her lawyer to see if one of the following objections would be proper:

- **Cumulative.** Many lawyers fail to keep good track of what they receive through various discovery processes. As a result, they sometimes ask for information that has already been provided. For example, an interrogatory might ask for a description of medical treatment received from a certain doctor even though medical records of that treatment have already been provided. Such duplicate requests may be objected to as cumulative.

- **Equally available.** Sometimes one side in a lawsuit asks the other to produce information to which both sides have access. For example, in a lawsuit between two feuding former business partners, a request for production of documents from one partner might ask that the other produce all records of their joint business venture. If both partners have access to the same business records, however, one side might not have to do the work of gathering that information for the other.

- **Excessively burdensome.** This catch-all category refers to requests that are far too much work for the minimal useful information they might produce. Courts try to strike a balance between the amount of work it takes to produce the information and the likely benefit to the side making the request. If a discovery request is challenged as too burdensome, a judge will consider the importance of the information sought to a fair resolution of the case, the amount of damages claimed (the bigger the case, the more discovery is permitted) and the parties' resources. A judge is more likely to require a government agency or a big corporation with plenty of resources to respond to a request for data than an individual. Similarly, a party who has computer access to records is more likely to be forced to produce those records than a party who would have to search and gather records by hand. For example, a request for a small business to name all the people with whom it has done any business in the past ten years might be considered excessively burdensome. On the other hand, a request for a city government to produce records of all the accidents at a given intersection over the past ten years is probably not too much to ask. ■

Chapter 5

Motions and Other Court Proceedings Before Trial

How You Can Help Your Lawyer

M ore than 95% of all lawsuits end without ever going to trial. In most, the parties reach a compromise settlement. (See Chapter 8.) But many litigants will not move toward compromise until they are pushed. A significant factor in changing the parties' views of their case—and therefore their willingness to compromise—is the outcome of pretrial court proceedings in which a judge makes decisions that affect the shape of the lawsuit. A pretrial court ruling might even make compromise unnecessary—in some instances, a judge declares one side the winner without a trial ever taking place. These rulings are generally based on motions (requests) made by either party.

Section I of this chapter explains the general procedures for bringing pre-trial motions. The remaining sections explain the most common and important specific pretrial motions.

Section I: Motion Procedures

When a lawyer for any party wants a judge to decide a litigation dispute—in legal parlance, to *rule on a motion* or *make a ruling*—the lawyer must follow certain procedures, which include:

- setting a time for the parties to be in court
- filing a written notice and legal arguments—known as *moving papers*—and sending them to the other parties
- replying to the other side's opposition papers
- appearing in court to argue the matter, and
- preparing a written order that reflects the judge's decision.

Whoever makes a motion is known—for that procedure only—as the *moving party*. Whoever opposes a motion is called the *opposing party*. The opposing party also files written arguments—called *opposing papers*—presenting reasons why the judge should not grant the motion.

You Can Appeal Any Motion That Ends the Lawsuit

Several motions discussed in this chapter may lead to a final Judgment for one party or the other: in other words, an end to the lawsuit. A Motion for Default Judgment may end the lawsuit in favor of the Plaintiff, a Motion for Dismissal may lead to Judgment for Defendant and a Motion for Summary Judgment may end the lawsuit in favor of either side. A Judgment following one of these motions has the same legal effect as a victory after trial.

Once any Judgment—including a Judgment following a motion—is entered, the losing party has the right to appeal to a higher court. However, that appeal must be filed within a set time limit. When and how to file an appeal, and some tips on choosing the right appellate lawyer, are discussed in Chapter 10, Section II.

1. When may a party schedule a court hearing on a pretrial motion?

The moving party must give the opposing party adequate time to prepare for a hearing and, if the party desires, to file responsive papers. Each court can set its own time limits for motions. Usually, a court hearing must be scheduled no less than 15-20 days after the date the moving papers are "served" on the opposing party (see Question 4). The moving party need not consult the opposing party as to the date for the hearing. Many lawyers do, however, since legitimate prior commitments on the part of the opposing lawyer would probably result in the hearing being rescheduled by the court.

Lawyers Must "Meet and Confer" Before Heading to Court

Many courts have a rule that, before filing a motion, a lawyer must *meet and confer* with the lawyer on the other side to see if they can resolve the matter between themselves. The idea is to get lawyers to settle small wrangles rather than always taking the most antagonizing, time-consuming and expensive route of asking a judge to decide them. In some courts, the meet-and-confer requirement applies to all motions. In other courts, it applies only to squabbles over discovery. (See Chapter 4.) The "meeting" itself can be merely a phone call during which one lawyer tells the other about the motion that is planned, and the lawyers discuss whether they can reach a compromise.

2. How is a court date selected for a pretrial motion?

In some courts, a lawyer may pick any date at all for a hearing, as long as it gives the other side the required minimum time to respond. However, in busy courts, the motion may not be heard until the court has an available date—which might be later than the moving party would prefer. And in many courts, certain kinds of motions are only heard in certain courtrooms, and only on certain days of the week.

Delays May Drive You Nuts

Three little words make many clients see red—"It was continued." A *continuance* is the postponement of a scheduled court proceeding. Continuances are common and occur for a variety of reasons, including illness, unavoidable conflicts with other scheduled court cases or even because the judge is tied up with other matters. Most continuances are unavoidable. However, some occur because one attorney finds the date inconvenient and the other attorney agrees to a continuance out of courtesy. If the word continuance is becoming too common in your case, raise the matter with your lawyer. Knowing how you feel may stiffen your lawyer's attitude towards any future requests for a continuance.

3. Can a motion be heard on very short notice?

Sometimes the normal 15-20 days notice required for a motion hearing may harm a client's case. For example, a lawyer may need a judge's ruling on whether the other side must produce a key document before an upcoming deposition. (See Chapter 4.) In this and innumerable other situations, a lawyer may go to court and ask for permission—called an *Order Shortening Time*—to schedule a motion sooner than the normal waiting period would allow. To obtain such a court order, the lawyer must:

- prepare an *Application for Order Shortening Time*, which explains why the shorter period is necessary
- notify the other parties of this request, and of when the lawyer will go to court to seek a judge's permission, and
- make a special trip to court to explain to a judge the need for the shorter notice time.

A judge might permit the shorter time if there is "good cause," meaning a likelihood of some harm to the requesting party's case if the normal waiting period is required. But the judge will also consider whether a shorter time period would be unfair to the other side. And the judge will consider who created the emergency. If the rush was caused by the requesting lawyer's or client's failure to do something in a timely manner, the Order Shortening Time is less likely to be granted.

 Who Pays for Seeking an Order Shortening Time? If you are paying hourly legal fees and you are billed for hours spent seeking an Order Shortening Time, you may want to find out why. If the lawyer had to prepare extra papers and make a special trip to court just to make up for the lawyer's own tardiness or commitment to other cases, you rightly may ask why you should have to pay for it. On the other hand, if it is simply the result of an unexpected but all-too-common twist and turn of litigation, you will just have to accept it as another reason lawsuits cost so much.

4. How does the moving party notify the court and the other side about the motion?

A party starts the process of obtaining a court hearing by filing a *Notice of Motion* or an *Application for Order* (in some courts, it is referred to as the motion itself). For example, to have a judge rule on whether to dismiss the Complaint, a Defendant would file a "Notice of Motion to Dismiss Plaintiff's Complaint." To ask a judge to force the other side to answer interrogatory questions, a party would file a "Notice of Motion to Compel Defendant's Response to Interrogatories." To ask a judge to stop the other side from harassing a party, an "Application for Protective Order" would be filed.

The notice or application tells when and where—date, time and courtroom—the court hearing will be held. It also briefly describes what the lawyer is requesting. However, the notice or application doesn't go into detail: that is done in other documents filed with the court at the same time as the notice (see Question 5).

5. How does a party present its legal reasons for bringing or opposing a motion?

A lawyer who files a notice of motion or application also must file what is officially called a *Memorandum of Points and Authorities*. A lawyer opposing a motion also files a Memorandum of Points and Authorities.

The "points" in Points and Authorities are the legal arguments that a lawyer makes in support of his or her side. For example, a request by a Defendant that Plaintiff turn over income records would be supported in the Points and Authorities by an argument about why the information was needed.

The term "authorities" refers to specific laws—federal and state statutes, county and city ordinances, administrative regulations and local rules—and prior court decisions that support the "points." So, the Defendant seeking Plaintiff's income records would include in the Points and Authorities specific reference to the laws and cases that support a Defendant's right to see the Plaintiff's financial records.

The lawyer for the party opposing the motion would file a responsive Memorandum of Points and Authorities, citing different laws and court decisions that restrict or prohibit financial disclosure or protect certain personal financial information.

 Researching and Preparing Written Legal Arguments Can Get Expensive. Sometimes, a lawyer can bang out in an hour a short, simple Memorandum of Points and Authorities in support of a pretrial motion. Many issues—relating to discovery, for example—come up repeatedly in a lawyer's litigation practice. Writing a Memorandum on these issues may be a simple matter of cutting and pasting from Memoranda used in earlier cases. But sometimes writing a good Memorandum on an important matter in the case takes time and effort—to organize facts, research laws and write a clear and persuasive argument. Although a carefully prepared Memorandum can generate substantial legal fees, it can also be among the most effective uses of a lawyer's time and a client's money.

If you are paying hourly attorney fees, you and your lawyer should discuss ahead of time any motion that will require lots of research and writing. Together, you can then balance the cost of that work against the odds and potential benefit of winning the motion. If the odds of winning the motion or the benefits of winning are slight, your lawyer may be able to do the motion with less extensive, and thus less expensive, research and writing.

6. How are the facts of a case presented to a judge?

A Memorandum of Points and Authorities in support of a motion (see Question 5) argues that, based on certain facts and rules, a judge should make a particular ruling or decision. The judge has law books to check on the rules. But how does the judge know the facts of the case that pertain to the motion? That is the role of the *declaration* or *affidavit.*

A declaration or affidavit is a sworn written statement. The person making the statement—known as a *declarant* or *affiant*—states under oath that the information contained in it is true. At trial, such a sworn statement usually may not be used in place of live testimony. But for a pretrial motion, a sworn statement is the legal equivalent of a witness's testimony in court.

A Sworn Statement Is Not Necessarily Acceptable Evidence

Putting information in a sworn statement does not guarantee that the information will be accepted as evidence. An opposing party may object that the information, in the form presented, violates some legal rule. The judge deciding the motion must then determine if the information qualifies as proper evidence. For example, a declarant might claim in a declaration that someone else "knew" something on a particular date. But such a claim violates a legal rule prohibiting speculation about someone else's "state of mind," and so would not be considered as evidence.

If a judge finds that certain information in a declaration or affidavit is not admissible evidence, that does not disqualify the entire declaration, nor does it necessarily doom the motion. Instead, the judge considers whatever valid evidence there is in the declaration, along with other proper evidence presented, in deciding whether to grant the pretrial motion.

Often, the declaration or affidavit is made by one of the lawyers in the case. For instance, it might be used to tell a judge about what one of the lawyers has or has not done, such as failing to confer with the other side before filing the motion or refusing to produce Answers to Interrogatories or other discovery (see Chapter 4).

Sometimes a lawyer prepares a declaration or affidavit for his or her client to sign. A party's own sworn statement might be needed to describe or identify something the party has seen, heard or done—for example, to identify a contract, letter or other document the party had signed or received. A sworn statement may also be made by a third party: an independent witness, lawyer's investigator or expert, for example.

Your Sworn Statement Is a Permanent Commitment

Once you sign a declaration or affidavit and your lawyer files it with the court, it becomes a permanent part of the case. For the rest of the lawsuit, what you said in the statement will be considered your word on the matter, just as if you had spoken from the witness stand in open court. For that reason, you must be careful about what you put in a declaration or affidavit. If you have any question about the accuracy of what you are writing in such a statement (or what your lawyer has written for you), be sure to go over it with your lawyer and explain your concerns before you sign it.

7. Are there other ways to get facts before a judge regarding a motion?

Facts to support a pretrial motion can almost always be established by declarations and affidavits, and by the documents to which they refer. For example, a party

seeking to compel more complete answers to discovery might attach the other party's responses to interrogatories to show that the original answers were incomplete. In some rare circumstances, a judge will ask or permit a witness to testify in person at the pretrial court hearing. (See Question 16.)

Sometimes, there are facts that no one disputes but that would be very difficult or expensive to prove. For example, it might be necessary in an accident case to establish that Main Street and Broadway intersect at a certain point. But proving it would require time and money.

Fortunately, the courts have created a simple procedure for proving this type of fact. It is called *judicial notice*, and it permits a judge simply to officially declare— "notice"—that a fact is proven. In order to have a judge "take" judicial notice of a fact, a lawyer must file a *Request for Judicial Notice* setting out exactly what the court is being asked to officially recognize and some basis for recognizing it. The categories of facts that may be judicially noticed vary a bit from state to state, but generally include:

- the contents of government rules, regulations and files (not the *truth* of what a document states but only that it is part of a particular official file)
- universally accepted truths about the physical world (the sun has long set by 9:00 p.m. in December), and
- general knowledge about local conditions (1st Street and 2nd Street run parallel to each other).

8. How must the notice of motion and accompanying documents be delivered to the other party?

Once the hearing date is scheduled and the moving papers are prepared, the lawyer for the moving party files those papers with the court and delivers copies to lawyers for all the other parties. All parties must be given the notice, even if the motion or application is directed at only one other party. Copies do not have to be delivered to the parties themselves, unless they have no lawyer. And delivery itself is simple. Once a party is officially part of a case (see Chapter 3), legal papers may be served on that party's lawyer by regular mail, and in some states by fax.

The Moving Party Has the Final Word

The party opposing a motion has the opportunity to file a written argument against it, usually up to five days before the hearing date. The lawyer who filed the motion then has a last shot, a written *Reply to Opposition* in which the points raised by the other side may be countered. This reply is not supposed to introduce new legal arguments that were not in the original motion—it can only reply to what the opposition has argued.

9. How do my lawyer and I decide whether to compromise or fight a motion?

When one party files a motion or application, the other side has two choices. The lawyer for the other side may try to settle the matter—not the whole lawsuit, necessarily, but the specific litigation dispute involved in this motion—before and instead of going to court over it. Alternatively, the lawyer may formally oppose the motion or application by filing responsive papers and arguing the matter in court.

Most often, lawyers simultaneously pursue both paths, preparing a written opposition in the event a compromise is not reached. In deciding whether to compromise—and how much to concede in doing so—the opposing lawyer and client must consider a number of factors:

- **Likelihood of getting a good decision from a judge.** Obviously, the better the chance of winning, the less likely the opposing side is to compromise a motion. However, there is almost always at least some small chance of a judge ruling in an unexpected way. If a compromise would be simple, cost much less than going to court and cause no harm to the client's case, the lawyer and client may want to consider it despite good odds of winning in court.
- **Wanting to show capacity to litigate.** On the opposite extreme of willingness to compromise in the face of victory is willingness to fight in the face of defeat. Particularly early in a case, when each side is still feeling out the other, it may be worth fighting the other side's motion simply to show the capacity and will to put up a court fight if necessary. Forcing the moving party to spend time and money on a court hearing might demonstrate that the opposing party will not merely roll over every time the other side threatens to go to court. And that may make the other side more willing to

compromise when other disputes arise—and eventually more willing to settle the entire case.
- **Possibility of compromise.** No matter how much one side is willing to compromise, nothing will come of it unless the other side will bend a bit, too. On some matters, there may be plenty of room to maneuver. For instance, one side may be able to give the other much of what it wants without hurting its own case, and may also get concessions in return. On the other hand, sometimes a motion leaves little room for compromise. A motion to dismiss the entire lawsuit, for example, might offer no option other than settlement of the whole case.
- **Cost of fighting the motion.** Opposing a motion can be expensive. If the motion is not particularly important and a painless compromise would be easy to reach, it may not make sense to spend lawyer hours and expenses to fight the motion—even if there is a good chance of winning. Particularly if the client is paying by the hour, whether and how hard to fight the other side's small-time motions may be a financial question rather than a legal one. Cost may be the deciding factor for motions regarding compliance with discovery requests (see Chapter 4) and those concerning the scheduling, rather than the substance,

of proceedings. If the client is paying by the hour, it is particularly important for client and lawyer to consult before the lawyer plunges ahead with a full-blown opposition to a motion filed by the other side.

- **Delay caused by going to court.** Sometimes fighting a motion is just not worth the delay it causes. For example, there might be a dispute over which documents are to be brought to an upcoming important deposition. If the parties fight that all the way to court, the deposition may have to be rescheduled, perhaps months later. And that delay may reverberate through the entire case by setting the whole discovery schedule back.

10. How soon after receiving notice of a pretrial motion must the opposing side decide whether to fight or to compromise?

Negotiations to compromise may continue right up to the moment the motion is called in court. A moving party that seemed unwilling to compromise when it filed its motion might soften after seeing the other side's written opposition. Or, the opposing lawyer may be more (or less) willing to compromise after researching the legal issues involved.

Your Lawyer May Need Extra Time to Respond

Normally, a client does not like to hear that a court hearing or other procedure has been postponed. But sometimes it's in your interest for your lawyer to obtain a *continuance*. Often a motion from the other side comes as a surprise, or is scheduled for a time when your lawyer is committed to other work, on vacation or out sick. If so, the normal time to prepare a response—15 to 20 days—may not be enough to do a good job. Your lawyer may and should try to have the court date postponed, providing more time to prepare an opposition. The moving party might agree to the postponement. If not, a judge will probably grant it if the reasons seem sound.

11. What documents does a lawyer prepare to oppose a motion?

To respond to a motion, a lawyer files a *Memorandum of Points and Authorities in Opposition*. This document takes the same form as the Points and Authorities filed in support of the motion. (See Question 5.) The opposition memorandum might oppose the motion on technical grounds—for example, it might argue that the motion was filed late or is incomplete. It also may oppose the motion *on the merits*, that is, argue that the facts, laws and prior court decisions do not support the motion. As with the Memorandum of Points and Authorities in support of the motion, the opposition memorandum may introduce facts through declarations and affidavits.

12. What happens to a motion if the lawyers agree to compromise?

If the lawyers for both sides work out a compromise, they will prepare documents that memorialize the agreement. This may simply be a letter from one lawyer to the other—known as a *letter agreement*—spelling out the terms of the compromise. If either side fails to live up to the bargain as the lawsuit continues, the other side may ask the court to enforce the agreement.

In some situations, the lawyers do not rely on an informal letter agreement. Instead, they draw up a paper called a *stipulation*, which spells out the compromise. Unlike a letter agreement, a stipulation is immediately filed with the court. A stipulation might be used when the agreement involves important rights or when the lawyers just don't trust each other.

Once the compromise has been put on paper, the lawyer for the moving party contacts the court and asks that the hearing be taken *off calendar*, which means that the motion won't be heard as scheduled. Taking the motion off calendar does not preclude the lawyer from filing it again, if for some reason the compromise falls apart.

13. What judge conducts the court hearing on a motion?

The judge who hears and decides a motion or application may not be the same judge who would preside over the trial, if there is one. In what are called *direct calendar courts* (including most federal courts), one judge is assigned to a case at the outset. That judge hears all matters in the case, including pretrial motions and trial.

In what are called *master calendar courts*, however, certain judges are specially assigned to hear all pretrial motions for all cases. These judges do nothing but hear pretrial motions, in a courtroom usually called the "law and motion" department. In a master calendar court, a lawyer must schedule a pretrial court hearing according to the particular calendar of the law and motion court. If a lawsuit winds up going to trial in a master calendar court system, a different judge would then preside.

14. Are the parties stuck with the judge who is assigned to hear the motion?

Two mechanisms permit a party to ask that a particular judge be removed from the case—a *challenge for cause* and a *peremptory challenge*. A challenge for cause is available any time, in any court, whenever information about, or comments or conduct by, a judge indicates that the judge may not be entirely impartial. However, it's not wise to accuse a judge of bias unless there is strong proof of it. A judge who is unsuccessfully challenged may be resentful. As the old saying goes, "If you shoot at the Emperor, don't miss."

Some jurisdictions also permit a party to make a peremptory challenge, in which a party does *not* need to give any reason for asking that a judge be removed. The mere challenge is enough to have the hearing transferred to another judge. A peremptory challenge against a specific judge must be exercised as soon as that judge is assigned to hear any part of the case. A party may not wait to see how a judge acts in the case before exercising a peremptory challenge. And if it is permitted at all, only one peremptory challenge per case is allowed per party. So in master calendar jurisdictions, lawyers usually reserve their one peremptory challenge for the judge assigned to hear the trial, if needed, rather than for a judge hearing less important pretrial matters.

Pretrial Disputes May Be Decided by Court Personnel Other Than Judges

In large court systems, many pretrial disputes are referred for hearing to judicial officers whose position is slightly lower than judge. These court officials may be called *magistrates, court commissioners, referees, special masters* or the like. They most often handle routine but time-consuming pretrial matters, especially disputes over discovery. (See Chapter 4.) Although these officials may not have the experience and expertise of a judge, they are experts in the small areas of law with which they deal every day. And they are more likely than judges to listen at length to in-person argument from lawyers.

15. Is it always necessary to wait until the hearing on the motion to learn of the judge's decision?

In some courts, a judge may make a preliminary decision, called a *tentative ruling*, regarding a pretrial motion. These rulings are issued a day or so before the hearing date, based solely on the papers filed by both sides. The lawyers can call a special court telephone number to hear if there is a tentative ruling for their case. Increasingly, lawyers can also find tentative rulings on the court's website. The purpose of these tentative rulings is to save court and lawyer time—the lawyers might skip the hearing unless one of them has something extra to tell the judge that was not included in the papers already filed.

If neither side chooses to go to court for the hearing, the judge's tentative ruling will become final on the hearing day. However, either side may choose to argue the matter in person before the judge. If either lawyer decides to appear in court after a tentative ruling, that lawyer must notify all other parties, and the court itself, of the intent to show up for the hearing. In that case, the tentative ruling may not become final until the judge hears from the lawyers in person.

Should My Lawyer Insist on a Hearing?

If a tentative ruling on a pretrial motion is completely in your favor, there is no reason for your lawyer to show up if the other side doesn't intend to go. If the other side does decide to argue its case, however, your lawyer should be there to argue in support of the tentative ruling.

If the tentative ruling goes against you, your lawyer shouldn't contest it unless there is some likelihood of winning. Especially if you pay by the hour, you don't want your lawyer to go sit around the courthouse for no good purpose while the attorney-fee meter is running. Even a simple one-minute appearance before a judge can use up half a day of attorney time—there are often many cases set for the same time in any given courtroom, and your lawyer might not be able to tell exactly when your case will be called.

On the other hand, even if the judge isn't likely to entirely reverse the decision, there may be some room for modifying it slightly in your favor. So, your lawyer must decide whether there is enough chance of a change to justify appearing at the hearing. That decision will depend on several circumstances:

- the tentative ruling might indicate that the judge misunderstood something about the motion, which your lawyer might be able to straighten out in person
- the tentative ruling might indicate that the judge is willing to hear more from the lawyers on a certain point, or that a certain part of the ruling is incomplete or may be modified
- the subject of the judge's ruling might be so important that any possibility of changing the judge's mind is worth the effort
- the ruling might not be important enough to justify the added attorney time (and fees), or
- your lawyer may know that the particular judge who is hearing the case rarely—or frequently—changes his or her tentative rulings.

16. What is the procedure at a pretrial court hearing?

The exact procedure for a hearing on a pretrial motion usually is determined by a combination of statewide Rules of Court, supplementary rules of the local court and, importantly, the habits of the particular judge who conducts it. Some judges run their courtrooms informally; others have very strict rules. Some judges like to give lawyers an opportunity to argue their cases. Other judges want to hear as little argument as possible. In crowded urban courtrooms, a hearing might be one of dozens scheduled for the same time. A lawyer may have to wait hours before actually getting to speak, then the argument may be limited by the judge to a minute or two. In less crowded courtrooms, or those in which each hearing is given a precise time, a lawyer might know exactly when to appear, be given a full opportunity to argue the case and be in and out of court in less than an hour.

Should You Appear at a Pretrial Hearing?

You have a right to be present at any court proceeding in your case. But do you want to bother? The answer is mostly a matter of time and taste. If you don't mind traveling to court and perhaps sitting around for hours, only to hear the lawyers and judge speak legal mumbo jumbo for a minute or two, then it may be worth it to you. You may see how your lawyer performs, how the other lawyers act and how a judge views your case. But the likelihood of seeing or hearing something useful to you— that is, more than what your lawyer could explain—is probably small. On the other hand, some court hearings may be so important that you want to be there to see and hear whatever happens.

Whatever the local rules and the courtroom quirks of particular judges, most hearings involve the same few basic steps. The moving party is usually given an opportunity to speak first. Then the opposing lawyer has a chance to respond. The argument is usually brief; judges do not want lawyers to repeat what was in the written papers. In addition to the lawyers' initial remarks, the judge might ask them questions about the law or facts. The process tends to be quicker if there has been a tentative ruling (see Question 15). In that case, the lawyer for the party who lost the tentative ruling will start the proceedings by explaining why the judge should change his or her mind; the other lawyer may not need to speak at all. When the issue being decided will have a major impact on the lawsuit, judges tend to give the lawyers more time to argue.

Only the Lawyers Are Heard From

In the vast majority of pretrial hearings, the judge only considers the evidence that was included with the papers that request or oppose the motion. No party or other witness testifies in person. In a few exceptional situations, however, a judge will permit, or ask for, in-person testimony at a pretrial hearing. Because such a special *evidentiary hearing*, as it is called, takes longer than other hearings, it is specially scheduled for a time when the judge is free to hear it. If this is going to happen in your case, you will know about it ahead of time.

Evidentiary hearings are most often held when the judge's ruling might affect a party's conduct beyond the lawsuit itself, such as with an Application for a Temporary Restraining Order or Preliminary Injunction. (See Section II.) They are also used on occasion to settle technical matters that are difficult to assess through documents alone, and in which a judge wants a chance to ask direct questions. For example, a judge might want to hear the testimony of an expert about whether certain crucial but fragile evidence could be safely tested.

17. How does a judge inform the parties of the decision?

Following the lawyers' argument at a pretrial motion hearing, one of several things might happen. The judge might want to hear more from the lawyers before issuing a decision, in additional written arguments, documents or even a further hearing. More often, the judge issues a decision immediately, ruling *from the bench* (meaning in the courtroom, immediately following the lawyers' arguments). Typically the decision will be that the motion is *granted, denied,* or *granted in part and denied in part.* In a few courts, a judge might read from the bench a written decision—called an *intended ruling*—that has been prepared ahead of time but is subject to modification before it becomes final. (See Questions 18 and 19.) The judge might invite the lawyers to submit written proposed modifications to the intended ruling, some of which the judge might incorporate in the final version.

Rather than announce the decision in the courtroom, the judge may delay the decision to consider the matter further. This is called taking a matter *under submission.* If the judge takes the motion under submission, the decision will come later in the form of a judge's *Notice of Ruling.* In a very few unusual or complicated matters in federal court, a judge might also issue a written *Opinion,* in which the reasons for the decision are explained.

18. Is there any way to get a judge to change the decision announced at the hearing?

Before a judge's ruling becomes final (see Question 19), and in some courts for a certain period after it has become final, a party may ask the judge to change the decision. This is done by filing a document called a *Motion (or Request) for Reconsideration* or a *Motion for Rehearing*. The same judge who made the initial decision also decides this motion.

Reconsideration is rare: judges tend not to change their minds soon after making a decision. However, a Motion for Reconsideration has some small chance of success if a party comes up with new facts that might have affected the judge's decision had they been presented in the original motion. The facts must have been discovered *after* the original papers were filed, and the failure to have previously discovered them must not be the fault of the party asking for the reconsideration.

Do Judges Ever Admit Their Mistakes?

On rare occasions, a judge may reconsider a decision if a party shows that the judge clearly made a mistake regarding rules, laws or controlling court decisions, or about a clearly established fact in the case. However, this happens *only* if the judge based the decision on an obvious factual or legal error, not merely because the losing side thinks the judge should have reached a different conclusion.

19. When does a judge's pretrial decision become final?

Regardless of how a judge announces a pretrial ruling, it must be reduced to writing and signed by the judge before it becomes an official court *order*. In most courts, the moving party will have submitted a proposed court order along with all the other motion papers. If the judge's ruling is exactly what the moving party requested, the judge may simply sign the proposed order, which then becomes final. A judge may also modify the proposed order—often handwriting minor changes right on the document—before signing it.

If the judge's final decision varies significantly from the proposed order, another order must be prepared after the hearing. This order, which must reflect exactly what the judge has ruled, is drawn up by whichever side won the motion. In many courts, the party preparing the order must show it to the other side for review, to make sure it conforms precisely to what the judge decided, before it may be submitted to the judge for signature. Once the judge has signed the order, the party who won the motion files it with the court and sends copies to the lawyers for all parties in the case.

20. If my pretrial motion is denied, can I file it again?

With some motions or applications, losing once does not necessarily mean losing for all time. A motion might be denied because not enough information has yet been developed in the case for the judge to grant the request. Or, the judge might consider the motion premature, meaning there is not yet good reason for the court to step in. Often, a judge includes in the ruling a specific statement that the motion is *denied without prejudice*, meaning that the judge might be willing to view the matter differently if circumstances change.

In these situations, the party who lost the previous motion may make a *renewed motion*. This motion repeats the earlier request, but must explain the circumstances—new evidence, for example, or an inability to work things out without the court's help—that have changed since the last time a judge heard the matter. In master calendar courts, any judge may hear the renewed motion—not just the one who previously heard it.

21. Is it possible to appeal right away to a higher court about a ruling on a pretrial motion?

If a party loses an important pretrial motion, the party can sometimes ask a higher court —usually called the *Court of Appeals* or *Appellate Court*—to intervene immediately to reverse the decision. Although an appeals court normally will not consider any aspect of a case until the entire lawsuit is over, it will, in rare instances, step into the middle of a case to correct a lower court's decision. A party asks a higher court to intervene by filing an *Application for a Writ (of Mandamus* or *Prohibition)*, an *Extraordinary Writ* or an *Interlocutory Appeal*.

Parties do not request writs routinely. The process is time-consuming and expensive. Transcripts of the motion proceedings and extensive legal briefs must be prepared. And the odds of winning are slight. An appeals court will intervene only if the decision of the lower court is blatantly incorrect *and* it significantly alters the lawsuit or changes the position of the parties while the lawsuit is pending. For example, an appeals court might step in to correct a decision to dismiss a Complaint against one Defendant in a lawsuit. The Plaintiff might be willing to file a writ in this situation if the dismissed Defendant is the only one who could pay a Judgment. An appeals court might also step in if a judge has ruled out an important Cause of Action for a Plaintiff or an entire line of defense for a Defendant.

Your Fee Agreement Might Not Cover a Writ

Following a serious legal blow by a judge, you and your lawyer might agree that filing a petition for a writ is worth the effort and expense. But your retainer agreement with the lawyer might not cover such a writ.

If you are paying by the hour and your lawyer can and will prepare the writ, your lawyer might agree to do the writ for the same hourly rate. However, you and your lawyer may negotiate with each other for a higher or lower rate for work on the writ.

If your lawyer is handling your case on a contingency fee basis, your agreement almost certainly will not include the handling of a writ. You and your lawyer will have to agree on separate terms for the writ—either an hourly fee or some modification of the original contingency fee percentage.

Finally, it may be that your lawyer cannot handle the writ. Your lawyer might not have sufficient experience with writs. Or the lawyer may simply be too busy to handle the continuing lawsuit and the writ at the same time. If so, the lawyer will refer you to another lawyer to handle the writ. And you and that other lawyer will negotiate a fee specifically for work on the writ.

---

22. If an appeals court agrees to review a pretrial decision, does the lawsuit continue while the appeals court considers the case?

When an appeals court considers an Application for a Writ, the court may put a temporary halt to all proceedings in the lawsuit. This *Stay of Proceedings* might be very important. An appeals court could take months to reach its decision; without a stay, the parties would continue discovery and other pretrial maneuvers without knowing whether the lower court's ruling will stand, or instead be overturned or altered by the appellate court. The party that has asked the appellate court to intervene often asks for such a stay.

If a stay is granted, everyone in the case must wait for the appeals court decision before continuing with any formal proceedings in the lawsuit. This can delay the case for many months. But such a delay might be better than the alternative. If no stay is granted and the appeals court eventually overturns the lower court's decision, some important procedures in the lawsuit might have to be done all over again.

Section II: Restraining Orders and Injunctions

Only street repair right outside the window seems to take as long as a lawsuit. Until a case is over—in a year, two years or three—the Plaintiff gets no money or other compensation and the Defendant is not forced to do—or to stop doing—anything. Sometimes, though, waiting to the end of a lawsuit can cause serious harm to the Plaintiff that cannot be undone by a final victory in the case. For example, if the Plaintiff's partner is siphoning off assets and running their business into the ground, Plaintiff needs the court's help *right now*—winning the lawsuit years later could be meaningless if the business is ruined in the meantime. Or, someone who has an expensive sailboat, in which Plaintiff claims an interest, might be preparing to sail it off to the Bahamas, beyond Plaintiff's reach and that of the court.

In such situations, a Plaintiff may ask the court to take immediate action to prevent harm or loss—in legal parlance, to *preserve the status quo*—until a permanent resolution is reached through the more thorough but much slower regular lawsuit process. These immediate court actions, usually requested by a Plaintiff at or near the very beginning of a lawsuit, are known as *Temporary Restraining Orders (TROs)* and *Preliminary Injunctions.*

These measures provide a Plaintiff with only temporary relief. A judge may change one of these court orders, or end it altogether, at any time during the lawsuit. Moreover, granting one of these temporary orders has no formal effect—though it may exert strong informal pressure—on which party ultimately prevails in the lawsuit.

23. When do courts issue restraining orders and injunctions?

TROs and Preliminary Injunctions are most commonly used:

- to halt damage to, alterations in or removal of property, or the spending of assets that are related to the lawsuit dispute
- to prevent destruction or alteration of evidence
- to stop a change in title to, or imposition of a lien on, real estate that is the subject of the lawsuit
- to stop harassment, intimidation or civil rights violations
- to halt what the law calls a "nuisance," such as excessive noise, pollution or a health hazard
- to stop any kind of behavior that is likely to cause what the law calls "irreparable injury": injury that could not be easily measured and remedied by economic compensation at the end of the case. Examples of "irreparable injury" might be trademark or copyright infringement or unfair business competition.

If a Plaintiff believes that a Defendant—or anyone who works for or is directed by the Defendant—is engaging in acts that fit any of these categories, the Plaintiff may request a Temporary Restraining Order and/or Preliminary Injunction. (A Defendant who is countersuing the Plaintiff can also seek a TRO or Preliminary Injunction.) These costly procedures should be used only in true emergencies, however. A court is unlikely to step in unless there is a serious and immediate problem.

24. What is a Temporary Restraining Order (TRO)?

A Temporary Restraining Order is a sort of legal emergency brake—a temporary response to a crisis situation, imposed by a judge only when necessary to prevent serious, irreparable harm and only when there is no other immediate solution to the problem. A TRO is an order by a judge that the Defendant immediately stop (be "restrained" from) doing something, or immediately take certain action, to prevent imminent harm to the Plaintiff or property. The Plaintiff usually seeks a TRO at the very beginning of a lawsuit, though it may be requested at any time.

Unlike most court rulings during a law-suit, a TRO does not address how the litigation itself will be conducted. Rather, a judge issues a TRO to halt, alter or require actions by the Defendant beyond the law-suit process—out in the "real world"—if those actions are related to the subject of the lawsuit.

25. How does a judge decide whether to issue a TRO?

Judges do not grant TROs lightly. A judge will use a TRO to get involved in a Defen-

dant's business outside the courtroom only to the *least* extent necessary, and only if three conditions exist:

- The Plaintiff has no other lawful way to prevent the harm
- The harm to Plaintiff is both likely and imminent, and
- The harm Plaintiff would suffer would be irreparable (meaning that it would be impossible to calculate the damage and compensate Plaintiff for it at the end of the case).

A judge must balance the potential harm to Plaintiff if the restraining order is not issued against the possible harm to Defendant of meddling in Defendant's affairs. Plaintiff will win only if this balance tips substantially in favor of the Plaintiff; if not, a judge will refuse to issue the TRO. Even if the TRO is denied, however, a Plaintiff can sometimes seek a judge's protection in the form of a Preliminary Injunction. (Preliminary Injunctions are discussed in Questions 28-34.)

When balancing the pros and cons of issuing a TRO, a judge pays little attention to which side is likely to win the lawsuit. A judge will check the Complaint and Answer to see if there is any basis at all for Plaintiff's claims, but otherwise will not consider who is likely to win the long-term legal struggle. Since requests for a TRO usually come at the very beginning of a case, a judge does not yet have enough information to weigh what lawyers call *the merits* of the lawsuit. And because a TRO usually is intended to last only a very short time, such consider-ations can safely wait until the next step in the proceedings, a hearing for a Preliminary Injunction.

26. What is the process for obtaining a TRO?

When a Plaintiff asks a judge to issue a TRO, usual court procedures are set aside. Because a TRO is sought only in an emergency situation, the process is streamlined and less formal than most court proceedings.

Short notice. Plaintiff's lawyer need not give Defendant the standard notification time required for most motions—usually 15 to 20 days before the court date. Instead, the court hearing for a TRO may be set for only a day or two—even hours, in extreme emergencies—after Defendant is notified, orally or in writing, of the hearing.

Limited paperwork. Plaintiff's lawyer can arrange for a TRO court hearing merely by filing a simple paper (*Application for Temporary Restraining Order*) stating in non-technical terms what Plaintiff wants the judge to do and why. Accompanying this application is a sworn statement (a Declaration or Affidavit) by Plaintiff's lawyer, Plaintiff and/or other witnesses to Defendant's conduct or Plaintiff's harm. These statements explain the emergency and the likely damage that Plaintiff will suffer if the judge doesn't act immediately. These papers must be delivered to the Defendant as far ahead as possible of the time Plaintiff will appear in court to ask for the order. If the TRO is sought at the same time the Complaint is being filed,

the Complaint and Summons, along with the TRO papers, must be personally served on Defendant. (For an explanation of "personal service," see Chapter 3, Section I.)

If for any reason the TRO papers cannot be personally delivered to the Defendant, Plaintiff's lawyer must at least try to inform the Defendant by phone of the date and time of the hearing and the substance of the TRO request. In extreme emergencies, Plaintiff and Plaintiff's lawyer can skip the papers altogether and simply go speak to a judge in person. In these rare situations, Plaintiff's lawyer must at least have tried to notify the Defendant of the plans to see a judge.

Informal court hearing. Before deciding on the TRO request, a judge will read the Plaintiff's paperwork and any written arguments and documents Defendant or Defendant's lawyer can manage to pull together before the court hearing. If Defendant has had only a day or two to respond, the judge will probably accept papers handed in at the court appearance itself. Because of the limited paperwork, a judge may decide to personally question the Plaintiff or Defendant.

In the gravest emergencies, a judge may issue a TRO even if the Defendant does not appear in court—what lawyers call issuing an order *ex parte*. Judges are extremely reluctant to do this, however. A judge must be convinced that Plaintiff's lawyer contacted the Defendant, or did everything possible to do so, and that the order sought is absolutely necessary.

How You Can Help Your Lawyer Seek a TRO

If your lawyer seeks a TRO, it will probably be at the very beginning of the lawsuit, before any information has been formally exchanged through the discovery process. (See Chapter 4.) The only evidence your lawyer will have to present to a judge will come directly from you in a sworn statement about the emergency situation, plus any supporting documentation you may have.

The procedure for obtaining a TRO is quick and rather hectic. If there is any doubt in a judge's mind about whether a TRO is necessary, the judge will probably deny it.

Your lawyer's ability to present a coherent and convincing picture to the judge may depend on how well you assist your lawyer by:

- providing a complete and honest description of the situation—incomplete or inconsistent information may scuttle your lawyer's chances
- coming up with written support or witnesses to back up your version of events
- anticipating Defendant's side of the story—if your own description can be easily clouded or contradicted by the Defendant, a judge is unlikely to issue a TRO, and
- remaining available when the lawyer goes to court seeking the TRO, in case the judge wants to question you directly or get more information about the problem.

27. How long does a TRO last?

Unlike most other types of court orders, which last for the entire lawsuit, a TRO usually lasts only a few days or weeks. Sometimes a judge orders that the TRO will expire automatically on a certain date. Or the TRO may continue until a more extensive hearing is held in conjunction with Plaintiff's Application for a Preliminary Injunction, which seeks to have the restraint continue for the duration of the lawsuit. (For a discussion of Preliminary Injunctions, see Questions 28-34.)

Occasionally, a TRO will stay in effect for a longer time even though the Plaintiff does not seek an injunction. If the TRO prevents a party from transferring disputed property, for example, a judge may order that it continue until the conclusion of the lawsuit.

If a judge issues a TRO without having heard from the Defendant, the order may last only as long as it takes the Defendant to get into court after receiving notice. And a Defendant may request at any time that a TRO be ended ("lifted" or "dissolved," lawyers say) in a *Motion to Dissolve Temporary Restraining Order*. If restraining certain conduct will likely have a serious impact on the Defendant, a judge will make the TRO as brief and as limited as possible.

28. What is a Preliminary Injunction?

A Preliminary Injunction is a judge's order that the Defendant do, or not do, something out in the "real world" while the lawsuit is being contested. The conduct to be controlled must be related to the subject(s) Plaintiff has raised in the lawsuit. A judge usually issues a Preliminary Injunction early in the lawsuit, well before all the facts are in, as an interim decision. The Injunction does not necessarily cover all issues raised or relief sought in the Complaint. It may end at any time if the judge decides it is no longer needed or justified.

An *Application for Preliminary Injunction* is often filed with, or immediately following, a request for a TRO. But in many cases a Plaintiff requests a Preliminary Injunction without having bothered to seek a TRO. Requesting a TRO can be time-consuming and costly—and the likelihood of success is slim. If the situation to be addressed is not an emergency, a Plaintiff frequently chooses to forego the extra work of a TRO application and instead focus on the request for a Preliminary Injunction.

29. When is a Preliminary Injunction appropriate?

A judge issues a Preliminary Injunction to prevent the Defendant from taking actions, or to require the Defendant to take certain actions, for the duration of the lawsuit or until the judge ends the injunction. The general purpose of a Preliminary Injunction is the same as a TRO: to halt conduct during the litigation that could not be easily undone or compensated for at the end of

the case—referred to as "irreparable harm." Plaintiffs who seek a Preliminary Injunction often also seek a Permanent Injunction against the same conduct by the Defendant. (For a discussion of Permanent Injunctions, see Chapter 3, Section I).

Preliminary injunctions may be issued in any case in which Defendant's ongoing conduct is a subject of the lawsuit. They are most often sought by Plaintiffs—or by Cross-Complainants (see Chapter 3, Section III)—in lawsuits that involve:

- a property or business dispute in which the Defendant's conduct during the lawsuit could do irreparable harm to Plaintiff's business or property
- a dispute with a state or local government or other public entity, in which Plaintiff is trying to 1) prevent the public entity from taking action that could not be easily remedied (for instance, knocking down a building or constructing a road) or 2) prevent the entity from enforcing a law against Plaintiff (for example, a new health law that would require a restaurant to close its outside patio)
- a complaint about corporate or other organizational discrimination or harassment, in which Plaintiff wants not only to receive compensation for the harm done but also to stop the questionable conduct while the lawsuit proceeds (for example, a company's policy of searching its employee's lockers or using discriminatory hiring practices).

30. How does a judge decide whether to issue a Preliminary Injunction?

A judge reviewing an Application for a Preliminary Injunction first considers the likelihood that Defendant's actions—or lack of action—will cause the Plaintiff imminent and serious harm. Is the harm certain to occur or continue? Is it likely to occur in the immediate future? Can that harm definitely be traced to Defendant's conduct or lack of it? How serious is the harm? And could the Plaintiff take simple steps to temporarily prevent the harm without enjoining the Defendant?

The judge then balances the likely harm to Plaintiff against the harm an Injunction would cause the Defendant. Would forcing the Defendant to stop certain conduct seriously or permanently harm the Defendant's business? Would the cost to Defendant be significant?

Finally, the judge considers whether the Plaintiff is likely to win the entire lawsuit and therefore be able permanently enjoin the Defendant's conduct. Unless Plaintiff is likely to prevail in the end, a judge will not issue a Preliminary Injunction.

For example, a Plaintiff might seek an injunction ordering a Defendant to halt removal of a drainage culvert that had directed rainwater runoff away from Plaintiff's neighboring hillside property. The judge must determine whether:

- removing the culvert would increase the risk of flooding

- a landslide is more likely if the culvert is removed
- there is a similar or greater danger to the Defendant's property if the culvert is not immediately removed
- there are temporary steps Plaintiff or Defendant could take to avoid that danger while the lawsuit proceeds and
- any runoff damage to Plaintiff's property—if the culvert were to be removed—would be Defendant's legal responsibility.

31. Does the granting of a Preliminary Injunction indicate what a judge's final decision in a case would be?

While the issuance of a Preliminary Injunction indicates that a judge believes the Plaintiff is likely to win, it does not necessarily predict or affect the judge's final decision in the case. A judge hears only a portion of the total evidence in the case during a hearing for a Preliminary Injunction. At trial, the judge renders a final judgment based on all the evidence both sides present, using standards that are different from those applied in a Preliminary Injunction hearing. The judge may have a change of heart once all the evidence is in or all legal arguments have been heard.

Nonetheless, a Preliminary Injunction can have a profound practical effect on a lawsuit—which may justify the large expenditure of lawyer and client time and money required to put the application together. If an Injunction forces an end (for the foreseeable future) to activity important to the Defendant or indefinitely delays the start of some project, it may put significant financial or other pressure on the Defendant to settle the lawsuit. The judge's preliminary ruling in favor of Plaintiff—which includes the judge's determination that Plaintiff is "likely" to win at trial—may also force Defendant to seriously consider the possibility of losing the entire case. This, too, may increase the Defendant's willingness to settle the case.

32. Are there any protections for the Defendant in case it turns out that the injunction was improperly issued?

A preliminary injunction forces a Defendant to temporarily alter his or her conduct before the Plaintiff has proved at a trial that the Defendant should be permanently required to do so. But what if the Plaintiff is unable to prove Defendant's legal responsibility at trial? What if the Plaintiff simply drops the lawsuit after the preliminary injunction has been in effect for awhile? Does the Plaintiff owe the Defendant anything for having hampered the Defendant while the preliminary injunction was in place?

The answer is sometimes yes, sometimes no. A judge may order, as a condition of granting a preliminary injunction, that the Plaintiff post a bond—a sum of money to be held in trust by the court while the

injunction is in effect. A Defendant who faces a Request for Preliminary Injunction should ask a judge to require such a bond. If the Plaintiff fails to win a permanent injunction against the Defendant, some or all of that bond money may be forfeited to the Defendant to compensate for what the Defendant lost while the preliminary injunction was in effect. Judges most often require such bonds when the Defendant will suffer direct economic loss as a result of the preliminary injunction—for example, if the injunction prohibits a business from selling a product or starting a lucrative project.

33. How does the procedure used for Preliminary Injunctions compare with that used for TROs?

Unlike the hurry-up, emergency process of seeking a TRO, the procedure for requesting a Preliminary Injunction is more formal and orderly. It requires the preparation of all the papers normally included with any motion (see Section I) and the standard advance notification period (15-20 days) to give the Defendant time to respond.

In addition to the written legal arguments that accompany all motions, an Application for (and Opposition to) Preliminary Injunction are usually accompanied by extensive evidence in the form of sworn statements (affidavits or declarations) from the parties and other witnesses and documents that support each side's position. In some courts, the judge may even conduct a trial-like hearing in which witnesses testify in open court, often with the judge asking many of the questions. Because of the preparation required for all this, a request for a Preliminary Injunction can be very time-consuming and expensive.

34. Once it is in place, is there any way for a Defendant to get out from under a Preliminary Injunction?

Any time after a judge issues a Preliminary Injunction, the Defendant may ask the judge to end it (lawyers say "lift" or "dissolve"). To end the Injunction, a Defendant must demonstrate to a judge that circumstances have changed, or that new evidence has become available that shows:

- the Injunction is no longer necessary to protect the Plaintiff
- the negative effect of the Injunction on Defendant is considerably greater than anticipated, or
- Plaintiff is not, in fact, likely to win at trial.

Section III: Motions to Secure Assets: Lis Pendens, Attachments and Receiverships

State courts only have jurisdiction—legal authority—over people and property within the state's boundaries. But people move freely from state to state. In the modern world, some people spend time in several places and do business in many others. This mobility can sometimes make it difficult to get fair resolution of a dispute. For instance, a Plaintiff might not be able to force an out-of-state Defendant into court. Even a Defendant who has shown up in court may move assets out of state if the litigation starts to go badly, leaving the Plaintiff with nothing from which to collect a Judgment. In response to such problems, courts have developed several procedures that put a hold on the Defendant's assets while the litigation is pending. These are known as "lis pendens," "attachment" and "receiverships."

35. What is a *lis pendens*?

Defendant might own real estate in the jurisdiction where the lawsuit is proceeding but have few other assets with which to pay Plaintiff an award. If so, Plaintiff may be permitted to place a special lien on the local property, preventing Defendant from selling that property while the litigation is pending. In most jurisdictions, Plaintiff's lawyer may impose this lien—called a *lis pendens*—without a judge's permission. Importantly, the property itself need not have any connection to the dispute between the Plaintiff and Defendant. In some jurisdictions, a lis pendens is not permitted if the property is the Defendant's principal place of residence.

36. What is an Attachment?

Attachment is the temporary seizure by the court, at the very beginning of a lawsuit, of assets belonging to the Defendant. The court attaches—takes legal control of—the assets until the case is resolved. If the Plaintiff wins money damages against the Defendant, the Plaintiff may collect those damages out of the value of the assets. The assets themselves need not bear any relation to the dispute. They need only be assets in which the Defendant has an ownership interest. (In some states, however, Defendant's primary residence—the home in which the Defendant lives—may not be attached. "Homestead" laws in those states prevent Defendant from being forced to sell or mortgage the home to pay damages.)

In some states, Attachments are authorized any time the Complaint charges Defendant with fraudulent conduct. In most states, however, Plaintiff must present evidence to a judge that the Defendant is likely to dispose of or hide the assets or move them beyond the jurisdiction of the court. To prove such intent, a Plaintiff must usually present evidence of an actual attempt by Defendant to sell or move assets in response to the dispute underlying the lawsuit.

37. What is a Receivership *pendente lite*?

The most common form of Receivership is used for businesses on the verge of bank-

ruptcy. In that type of Receivership, creditors ask a bankruptcy court to appoint an outside overseer to ensure that at least some assets of the failing business are saved to pay the creditors. A similar sort of Receivership is sometimes available at the beginning of a lawsuit involving an ongoing business.

In a lawsuit involving a business or property, either side may ask a judge to place the business or property in Receivership if there is evidence that someone is seriously damaging the business, wasting its assets or planning to destroy or remove valuable property. If the request is granted, the judge appoints a third party—the Receiver—to take over and run the business or property *"pendente lite"* (until the lawsuit is resolved).

38. How does a Receivership *pendente lite* work?

The appointment of a Receiver is a big step for several reasons. It may be very expensive, requiring an extensive and complex court hearing about the state of the business or property, with evidence from accountants and other experts. The court-appointed Receiver, who is often highly compensated, will have to be paid for as long as the business remains in Receivership. A judge appointing a Receiver will determine who pays the Receiver's fees, the most likely source being the business itself.

If a Receivership is granted, the Receiver will control the property or business. That is, the business or other asset is taken out of *both* parties' hands for the duration of the lawsuit. The success of the business, or protection of the asset, then depends on the abilities of the Receiver. Finally, a judge must approve all significant actions by the Receiver. This requires continued expensive participation by the lawyers for both sides, in addition to their ongoing work on the lawsuit itself.

Section IV: Motions to Expand, Narrow or Move a Lawsuit

In several common situations, a party may ask a judge to change the shape of the lawsuit. For instance, someone who is a party in two or more related lawsuits may request that the separate cases be joined into one. Or, if a lawsuit includes multiple disputes among several parties, a party might request that the disputes be separated into two or more different lawsuits. And someone sued in a court distant from that Defendant's residence or principal place of business may ask a judge to transfer the case closer to home.

39. What does it mean to consolidate lawsuits?

When at least one person, business or organization is a party in two or more

lawsuits that have something in common, *any* party in any of the related cases may ask the court to join the separate lawsuits into one. This request is called a *Motion to Consolidate* or *Motion to Coordinate.*

40. When can a judge order consolidation?

The basic purpose of consolidating separate cases is simply convenience, both for the parties and the court. If two different cases involve some of the same facts or legal issues, the parties can save time and energy by consolidating the cases into one set of legal proceedings rather than duplicating efforts—particularly discovery procedures.

On the other hand, courts don't want to force parties into a single lawsuit if the disputes have only minor facts or tangential legal issues in common. A court will order consolidation only if common facts or legal issues are central to both cases. For example, if two businesses have separately sued a third company because of that third business's fraudulent billing practices, the way the third company did its billing is a set of facts crucial to both cases. Similarly, if a poorly designed drain system has caused flooding in several different buildings, separate lawsuits filed by the owners of the flooded buildings might very well be consolidated into one lawsuit.

In deciding whether consolidation is appropriate, a judge balances the convenience of the parties requesting it, and of the court itself, against any difficulty consolidation might present to any other party. For example, it might be unfair to a party whose lawsuit is set for trial in a few months to consolidate that case with a case that would not be ready for trial for over a year. It might also be unfair to drag an individual or small business with a simple lawsuit into a complex, multi-party lawsuit just because consolidation would be more convenient for one of the other parties.

41. When may a party request that lawsuits be consolidated?

A judge may order consolidation at any point in any of the lawsuits. However, consolidation usually isn't ordered until all parties have completed their pleadings (see Chapter 3) and some initial discovery (see Chapter 4). By then, a judge will have enough factual information to determine if the connection between the cases justifies consolidation. Although judges usually coordinate cases in the early to middle stages of litigation, cases may also be consolidated for trial only.

42. If lawsuits are consolidated, is there just one trial?

When lawsuits are consolidated, all proceedings thereafter are generally held jointly, including trial. But a judge may order cases consolidated for all pretrial proceedings and then separated again for trial. Separate trials might be ordered if:

- a joint trial would be too long or too complicated for one jury, or
- a party's chance of a fair trial in one case might be threatened if trials were consolidated. This might happen if a co-party is accused of serious misconduct in another dispute.

A judge may also order a consolidated trial of only those issues common to both cases, leaving the issues unique to each case to be tried separately. For example, one jury might decide whether a Defendant business sold a defective product to a group of Plaintiffs. Then, issues unique to each Plaintiff—whether the Plaintiff was harmed by the product, whether the Defendant was responsible for that harm and the extent of any injuries—could be decided by separate juries.

Would Consolidation Be Good for Your Case?

The question of consolidation can arise in two ways. You and your lawyer might consider asking to consolidate your lawsuit with another case. Or a party in another case might seek to consolidate with your lawsuit. In either situation, you and your lawyer must consider several basic questions:

- Would your lawyer save work—and you save attorney fees—by sharing the load with other lawyers on the same "side" of a consolidated lawsuit?
- Would joining the cases speed or slow the pretrial process?
- Would joining your lawsuit with another put you in a better settlement bargaining position? (For instance, going to trial alongside other parties might make your case appear stronger or weaker in the eyes of a jury, depending on how the other parties' cases look and sound.)
- If trying both cases together seems a bad idea, is it advisable to request (or agree to) pretrial consolidation and separate trials?

43. What is a Motion to Sever?

Frequently, a Plaintiff includes numerous claims against different Defendants in a single lawsuit. Defendants might add several counterclaims to the mix, not only against Plaintiffs but also against entirely new Cross-Defendants. The resulting branches of a single lawsuit can sometimes resemble a polygamist's family tree. The proceedings in such a multi-party lawsuit can easily become unmanageable. If the case gets to trial, it might need the Ringling Brothers rather than a judge.

Sometimes, one party in a lawsuit simply does not want to be associated in the eyes of the jury with another party who is technically on the same "side."

For either of these reasons, a judge has the authority to separate a lawsuit into two or more cases. Any party may ask for such a separation by filing a *Motion to Sever*. If the Motion to Sever is granted, the part of the case that is severed becomes a separate case of its own. From that point forward, the two cases have separate fates—separate schedules, separate proceedings and separate trials.

44. What sorts of cases are likely to be severed?

Several different disputes might be combined in a single lawsuit because one party is involved in all of them. Except for that one connecting party, however, the other parties and legal issues might easily divide into two or more separate, unrelated cases. If the case remains one big lawsuit, all the parties are forced to go through litigation procedures that have nothing to do with them. There is also the risk that a jury might be confused by a complicated trial involving unrelated parties and legal issues.

For example, several employees sue their employer for unlawful employment discrimination. The company counter-sues against one of those employees and against a rival business—with no connection to the discrimination claim—for unfair competition. In this situation, there are really two entirely separate sets of legal issues and parties, except for the one employee involved in both. If the case is not split, the employees suing for discrimination will be forced to wait for all the legal maneuvers that are connected to the unfair business practices claim. And the rival business will have to wait for all the litigation pertaining to the discrimination claims. In such circumstances, a judge might agree to split the case in two.

Severance might also be appropriate if some Defendants have to travel to a distant locale for trial. If the facts and legal issues involving the "distant" Defendants are not crucial to proving the case against the "local" Defendants, a judge might sever the case, forcing Plaintiff to pursue separate lawsuits in each district. For example, a company doing business in many parts of a large state might sue several of its distributors for unpaid accounts. But unless the com-

pany contends that the different distributors conspired with one another, a judge might agree that there is no good reason to make a Defendant in one end of the state travel to the other end simply for the convenience of the company suing.

45. Can the conduct of a party justify severing its case from other parties?

Sometimes one party or set of parties has been much nastier, or otherwise presents a much uglier face, than other parties on the same side of the case. If so, a judge might split the case in order to separate the good and bad apples before the jury looks into the barrel. In the situation described in Question 44, for example, one of the employees might be counter-sued by the company for embezzlement and fraud. In that situation, a judge might split the case to spare the other employees charging discrimination from being tainted, in the eyes of a jury, with evidence of such deceitful conduct committed by their co-worker.

46. What is venue and how can it be changed?

As explained in Chapter 3, Section I, a Plaintiff sometimes has a choice of *venue*— a county or other judicial district—in which to file a lawsuit. If Defendants reside or do business in different counties, and the activities that underlie the Complaint occurred in still other districts, the lawsuit may be filed in any of those locales.

The Plaintiff's initial decision about where to file the Complaint, however, does not permanently cement the lawsuit to that court. The lawsuit location might be extremely inconvenient for some Defendants. If a more convenient court in the state would also have been proper for Plaintiff's lawsuit, a Defendant may ask the judge to move the case there. In federal court, a case may be moved to any other federal district in which the lawsuit could properly have been filed. The procedure for requesting such a move is called a *Motion for Change of Venue*.

YOUR COURT OR MINE?

Whose Venue Really Matters, Yours or Your Lawyer's?

If you are a Defendant in a lawsuit outside of the county where you reside, you and your lawyer may want to discuss requesting a change of venue. This motion is relatively simple and inexpensive to bring, unless it is based on unfavorable pretrial publicity (which sometimes calls for hiring a public opinion sampling company to determine the effect of the publicity on potential jurors).

In deciding whether to make the motion, consider your lawyer as well as yourself. If your lawyer's office is far from the court, it may be convenient and cost saving to move the case so the lawyer will not have to travel far to get to court. Your lawyer may also be more familiar with court procedures and judges in the local district. If, on the other hand, your lawyer's office is close to where the lawsuit is filed—and you don't want to switch lawyers—you may not want to change venue, even if the court's location is inconvenient for you.

47. What factors does a judge consider when deciding whether to order a change of venue?

Judges decide change of venue requests by comparing and balancing the convenience of all the parties. If most of the parties in a multi-party lawsuit reside in one county or district but a Plaintiff has filed the lawsuit elsewhere, a judge might move the case to the county or district nearest to where most of the parties reside.

A judge might also consider a change of venue if all the important witnesses live outside the court's judicial district. If the distances are substantial, it might be inconvenient and unnecessarily expensive to have the lawyers travel to take the witnesses' depositions (see Chapter 4, Section V) and later to bring all the witnesses to the court where the trial is held.

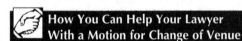

How You Can Help Your Lawyer With a Motion for Change of Venue

If you and your lawyer believe that a change of venue would be beneficial, you may be able to provide information for the motion. The motion will probably be made early in the case, when your lawyer may not know all the players in the dispute. Because the geographic location of witnesses is usually the key to a judge's decision regarding change of venue, you should give your lawyer a comprehensive list of everyone who might be a witness in the case. This must include people who will be key witnesses for the other side. Give their business and/or home location, relationship to the parties or their businesses and the subject of the testimony they are likely to give in the case.

In a change of venue motion based on pretrial publicity, you may be able to provide your lawyer with evidence that the dispute has been publicized—such as newspaper or magazine articles, online sites that have

discussed the dispute, local radio and television coverage of the dispute (with the dates of reports or discussions, if known) and any public meetings concerning the dispute.

48. At what point in a case is a judge likely to grant a change of venue?

A judge may agree to change venue any time after all Defendants have filed their Answers. However, the earlier a Motion for Change of Venue is made, the more likely it is to be granted. Each court has its own scheduling rules and lawsuit procedures. So, a judge will be reluctant to move a case if a number of procedures have already been completed and might have to be repeated if the case were moved to another court.

49. Can publicity about a dispute justify a change of venue?

It is one of the basic tenets of the judicial system that matters of local concern should be litigated in local courts and tried by local juries. Occasionally, however, local publicity about a particular dispute has been so sustained and inflammatory that it might be difficult to find an unbiased local jury to hear the case. (This happens more frequently in criminal cases than in civil lawsuits.) Courts usually deal with the problem of pretrial publicity by simply delaying trial until media exposure and public interest have died down. But sometimes the media hype in a civil case has been so extreme, and has painted one party so unfavorably, that moving the case to another part of the state where there has been little publicity is the safest route to a fair trial.

A change in venue on these grounds usually is granted in a civil case only when the dispute involves or affects a wider community than just the specific litigants. For example, if a lawsuit involved the possible contamination of a town's ground water by a refinery or gas works, continuing public concern about the issue might make it difficult to pick an unbiased jury. Similarly, if a group of parents in a town or a small city were suing a school district over

injuries to their children sustained in a school bus accident, the school district might successfully move the case to a court some distance away.

50. Is it possible to move a lawsuit to another state?

Change of venue in a state court lawsuit moves the case from one county or district within the state to another. In rare cases, however, a state court lawsuit may be moved to another state entirely. Some lawsuits are filed in one state but could also have been filed in another. (See Chapter 3, Section I.) If it would be considerably more practical to litigate the case in the other state instead, a judge may invoke the legal doctrine of *forum non conveniens* (meaning "inconvenient location") to dismiss the case, forcing Plaintiff to file it anew in the other state.

The guidelines for a judge to dismiss a case under *forum non conveniens* are roughly the same as for a change of venue. (See Questions 46-49.) But a Defendant who wants to move the case to another state must work a much stronger argument. If the Plaintiff is a resident of the state where the case is originally filed, a judge almost certainly will not dismiss the case under *forum non conveniens*.

A judge sometimes waits to dismiss the case until Plaintiff has actually filed a new lawsuit in the other state and Defendant has filed an Answer. This ensures that the

Defendant submits to the jurisdiction—legal authority—of the other state's courts and does not use *forum non conveniens* to slip out of the lawsuit entirely.

Section V: Plaintiff's Motions for Default

Under certain circumstances, a judge may enter a final *Judgment* for the Plaintiff if the Defendant fails to properly respond to the Complaint within the time limits set by law.

51. Can Plaintiff win a Judgment if the Defendant fails to respond to the Complaint?

Not every person named as a Defendant actively defends against the lawsuit. A Defendant might fail to defend—by not filing responsive documents within the allotted time at the beginning of the case—for various reasons:

- the Defendant might not dispute the facts in the Complaint and see no point spending time or money to defend
- the Defendant might have few assets to lose and little money to spend on litigation
- one Defendant might believe that his or her Co-Defendants will adequately defend the case for all the Defendants or will pay any damages won by a Plaintiff

- the Defendant might hope that Plaintiff filed the Complaint merely as a threat and will not seriously pursue the lawsuit, or
- the Defendant might just procrastinate too long and miss the deadline to respond.

Whatever the reason, if the Defendant fails to file a responsive pleading within the time allowed by law, the Plaintiff may ask the court to grant a *Default Judgment*. A Default Judgment declares that the lawsuit is over and that the Plaintiff has won everything the Complaint requested from this particular Defendant. It does not, however, affect any other Defendants.

52. How does the Plaintiff go about getting a Default Judgment?

In most courts, obtaining a Default Judgment is a two-step process. First, once the time for Defendant to file a response to the Complaint has expired, Plaintiff's lawyer asks a judge to order that the Defendant's *Default* be entered. In some courts, Plaintiff's lawyer goes directly to the court clerk to officially enter the Defendant's Default in the case file. This is done by filing a simple form called something like *Request for Entry of Default*. Plaintiff's lawyer must send a copy of the Default to the Defendant and then wait a certain prescribed time—usually 14 to 30 days—before taking the second step of requesting a Default Judgment.

53. How might the Defendant escape a Default Judgment?

During the 14-30 day waiting period after Plaintiff serves the *Request for Entry of Default*, Defendant may file an opposition, sometimes called a *Motion to Set Aside Default,* detailing the reasons why the Defendant failed to respond in time.

Judges usually look favorably on a Motion to Set Aside Default. There is a strong preference in the court system for deciding cases "on the merits"—the substance of the dispute—rather than on a procedural foul-up. A Default is usually denied or set aside if the Defendant's non-response was due to almost any normal human failing, such as a mix-up with paperwork, an illness to the Defendant or a close family member or Defendant's misunderstanding of the law.

Default is more likely to be denied or set aside if the Defendant was *not* represented by a lawyer when a response to the Complaint was due. And the sooner a Defendant asks for a Default to be set aside, the more likely a judge is to do so.

54. If a Defendant's Default is not set aside by a judge, how does it become a final Judgment for Plaintiff?

If a Plaintiff obtains ("takes") a Defendant's Default and the Defendant fails to have the Default set aside, Plaintiff's lawyer must file a *Motion for Entry of Default Judgment*. If

the amount of damages Plaintiff claims from this Defendant can be precisely calculated, Plaintiff might be able to obtain a Default Judgment simply by submitting sworn declarations or affidavits (and documents to which they refer) spelling out the exact amount of damages. For example, if the Complaint asked for only a specific, certain sum, such as the amount of money owing on a note or contract, Plaintiff need only present evidence of the agreement to prove how much the Judgment should be.

However, Plaintiff's lawyer might have to file extensive documents establishing the amount of Plaintiff's damages if the Complaint asks for:

- compensation for intangibles such as pain and suffering or other "general damages"
- emotional damages
- the value of a business, or
- the loss of potential future income.

And written proof alone might not be enough. Instead, a judge might require a court hearing, with testimony and arguments about how much should be awarded for damages, costs and fees.

55. Once a Default Judgment has been entered against a particular Defendant, is the case over for that Defendant?

Even when a Default Judgment has been entered, a Defendant may ask the court for another chance to fight the case by filing a

Motion to Set Aside Default Judgment. If a Defendant did not actually receive either the Complaint or the Notice of the Default in time, a judge will consider setting aside the Default Judgment and permitting the Defendant to file a response to the Complaint. A judge might also be favorably disposed toward the Motion to Set Aside Default Judgment if serious illness or other significant incapacity prevented the Defendant from responding in time. And judges are more sympathetic to a Defendant who was not represented by a lawyer at the time the Complaint was served and the Default Judgment entered.

56. If a Defendant files an Answer but later fails to respond to legal procedures, may the Plaintiff obtain a Judgment without going to trial?

Sometimes, a Defendant files an Answer to the Complaint and begins to litigate the case, but later stops participating in the lawsuit process, refusing to comply with discovery or respond to pretrial motions by Plaintiff.

In these circumstances, a judge may enter what is called a *Penalty Default Judgment.* A judge takes this extreme step only if the Defendant fails continuously—over many months—to participate in any litigation or cooperate in a critical part of the case (such as answering key questions at Defendant's own deposition or turning over crucial documents once production has been ordered by a judge).

Section VI: Defendant's Motions to Dismiss

57. When might a judge dismiss the Plaintiff's case prior to trial?

Some Plaintiffs file a lawsuit merely to pressure the Defendant to settle their dispute, without intending actually to litigate the case. Other Plaintiffs file a lawsuit with full intent to pursue it, engage in a certain amount of litigation, then stop pursuing the case. Some Plaintiffs might decide that they just do not want to continue spending lawyer fees and litigation expenses. Others might realize that their case is weak or futile. Still others might simply lose the will to litigate once it becomes clear that the Defendant is willing and able to put up a legal fight.

In any of these situations, the Plaintiff's failure to pursue the lawsuit leaves the Defendant hanging. As long as the lawsuit technically remains open in the court's files, the Defendant cannot be sure if and when the litigation might someday erupt again. The Defendant cannot securely plan a business or personal life, since the threat of a lawsuit, attorney fees and potential compensation to the Plaintiff has not been entirely eliminated. Also, a pending lawsuit might compromise Defendant's personal or business financial and credit records.

Because of the harm to a Defendant who is left in this legal limbo, court rules permit a Defendant to ask a judge to dismiss the case if Plaintiff fails to litigate.

58. How can a Defendant get a dormant lawsuit dismissed?

When a Plaintiff fails to pursue a lawsuit, there is a simple procedure to ask for dismissal. The Defendant's lawyer files a *Motion to Dismiss for Lack of Prosecution*, along with a declaration or affidavit that summarizes Plaintiff's disappearing act: how long it has been since Plaintiff initiated any legal proceedings, whether Plaintiff has failed to respond to Defendant's litigation procedures and how little Plaintiff has done in the case. Of course, the Plaintiff may oppose such a Motion to Dismiss, offering excuses for failing to actively pursue the lawsuit.

If the judge agrees to dismiss the case for lack of prosecution, the *Order of Dismissal* is usually made "with prejudice." This means that the Plaintiff may never again file a lawsuit against that Defendant based on the same dispute. The judge may also order that the Plaintiff pay the Defendant's court costs, and in some cases the Defendant's attorney fees.

Following an Order of Dismissal, a bit more paperwork might be required to finally close the case. In some courts, Defendant's lawyer must file a form—sometimes called a *Notice of Entry of Dismissal*—that instructs the court clerk to enter the Dismissal in the court's records. Then the Defendant's lawyer finalizes the Dismissal by having the judge sign a *Judgment of Dismissal*. A

Judgment is the final step in any case. The Defendant might need a Judgment to prove to other courts, creditors and financial institutions that the case is completely finished and that the Defendant has prevailed.

59. What factors does a judge consider when deciding whether to dismiss a lawsuit for failure to prosecute?

A judge is more likely to dismiss a lawsuit for lack of prosecution if:

- Plaintiff has taken few or no steps in the case since filing the Complaint
- months have passed since Plaintiff last took any action on the case
- no lawsuit proceedings are presently scheduled, and
- the Plaintiff or Plaintiff's lawyer has failed to respond to legal proceedings the Defendant has initiated, or to correspondence or telephone calls.

Most judges are reluctant to take the serious step of dismissing a case merely for failing to keep up a steady litigation pace. The Defendant usually needs to show several of the above-listed factors before a judge will agree to dismiss. A single failure by a Plaintiff to respond to a proceeding, or a period of inactivity lasting only a few months, is probably not sufficient to justify dismissal—particularly if Plaintiff has no attorney or is in the process of looking for a new one.

You May Want to Drop Your Own Lawsuit

You may find yourself in the awkward position of having initiated a lawsuit that you are unable or unwilling to pursue. Perhaps it's become too expensive, your chances of winning seem slim or you simply have lost the will to do more legal battle. If so, you may want to consider *Voluntary Dismissal* of the case.

There can be some significant advantages to seeking a Voluntary Dismissal rather than waiting for the Defendant to request Dismissal. First, you may voluntarily file a *Dismissal Without Prejudice*, which means that you could possibly file the lawsuit again, at a later date. Voluntary Dismissal may also allow you to avoid paying the Defendant's litigation costs and perhaps attorney fees, which you might have to pay if the Defendant is forced to file a Motion to Dismiss. You can also avoid having an adverse Judgment appear on your credit records or business history.

In some courts, the Plaintiff may voluntarily dismiss the case, without asking the court's permission, any time before the start of trial.

In other courts, however, a Plaintiff must obtain the court's permission to dismiss without prejudice once the Defendant has filed an Answer. The court usually gives permission unless the case is close to trial. But the farther the case has progressed, the more likely a judge is to force Plaintiff to pay Defendant's litigation costs and perhaps attorney fees as the price of dismissal without prejudice. If you are willing to file a voluntary *Dismissal With Prejudice*—meaning you may never file a lawsuit about the same dispute again against this same Defendant—you do not need a judge's permission in most courts.

If you need a judge's approval for a *Dismissal Without Prejudice*, it may be a good idea for your lawyer to negotiate the terms of the Dismissal with the Defendant *before* going to court. Defendant may be so relieved to have the case dismissed that he or she will agree to give up any request that the judge award costs or attorney fees, or at least negotiate a lower amount than a judge might otherwise order.

Section VII: Discovery Motions

Although most of discovery takes place outside of court, judges do get involved in the process at various times. There may be a regularly scheduled conference at which a judge oversees the entire discovery process and takes steps necessary to ensure its progress. Lawyers may go to court on their own initiative for permission to engage in special types of discovery, or to extend discovery beyond its normal time limits. Lawyers also go to court if an opposing party fails to respond to a discovery request or responds insufficiently. And lawyers go to court to seek protection for their clients against improper or excessive intrusions by opposing parties. This section discusses each of these occasions when lawyers wind up in court over discovery.

60. Do judges regularly monitor discovery?

At some point during the long road toward trial, some courts require all the lawyers in a case to attend a conference with a judge to discuss discovery. The timing and scope of these conferences vary. Each state and federal court district has its own rules, and each individual judge determines informally what is covered in a conference. During these conferences, a judge might review what has gone on so far in discovery, set boundaries for upcoming procedures and attempt to resolve disputes the parties have not been willing or able to work out themselves. These conferences require lawyer preparation and a court appearance, but they usually solve discovery problems that would cost much more time and money if left for the lawyers to battle out on their own.

Depending on the rules of the court in which a lawsuit is to be tried, one or more (though not all) of the following conferences may come up in a case. At any of these conferences, a judge might consider certain discovery issues.

- **Scheduling Conference.** A scheduling conference may be held within the first two to three months of a lawsuit. At this conference, the judge may establish a schedule for discovery as well as other pretrial proceedings. A lawyer who anticipates problems with discovery can ask the scheduling conference judge to set some groundrules for certain procedures.
- **Discovery Conference.** Some judges schedule a separate discovery conference for each case, usually within the first six months of the litigation. Here, a judge focuses exclusively on discovery, reviewing the status of ongoing procedures, handling problems that have cropped up and trying to ensure that discovery will be finished in a timely manner.
- **Status Conference.** Somewhere in the middle to latter part of the case, a court may schedule a status conference.

This conference permits a judge to make sure the case is moving along steadily. Often a judge uses a status conference to set deadlines for completion of discovery.

- **Settlement Conference.** If the lawsuit has not settled or otherwise been disposed of as it nears a trial date, the parties and lawyers will be required to go to court for a settlement conference. There, a judge will try to maneuver everyone into a settlement. (See Chapter 8, Section II.) If the entire case is not settled during this conference, the judge may settle lingering discovery disputes.
- **Pretrial Conference.** A few days or weeks before trial, the judge may call the parties into court to sort out procedural and evidentiary issues that might arise during trial. If any discovery disputes remain unresolved, the judge can address these issues as well.

61. Does a lawyer have to get court permission to use certain discovery procedures?

Lawyers initiate most discovery procedures without specific permission from a judge. However, in some courts a few types of discovery may only be conducted with a judge's prior written order. The most common of these procedures requiring court approval include:

- conducting any type of discovery earlier than is permitted by normal rules, for which a lawyer must file a request called a *Motion to Initiate Early Discovery*
- conducting discovery after the normal period of discovery has ended, for which a lawyer files a *Motion to Extend Discovery Cut-Off* or a *Motion to Reopen Discovery,* and
- obtaining a physical or mental examination of one of the parties (in a court that requires prior judicial approval), for which a lawyer files a *Motion for Physical (or Mental) Examination.*

62. Can my lawyer ask a judge to protect me from the other side's overreaching discovery requests?

Sometimes, one side goes too far in a discovery request, repeatedly asking for information that need not be revealed. For example, a party might seek discovery of information that is privileged or otherwise confidential, make unreasonably broad discovery requests or ask questions at a deposition that are needlessly embarrassing or inflammatory. Most disputes over discovery limits are settled through informal wrangling between the lawyers. But sometimes, no compromise is possible—or the other attorney simply won't stop. In such situations, the lawyer may go immediately to court to ask for protection against the other side's improper request, question or other discovery. The lawyer may file a *Motion for Protective Order*, which seeks protection from a specific discovery request, or a *Motion to Quash*, which seeks to cancel an entire discovery procedure.

A lawyer might also ask the court to prevent the other side from publicizing the information provided in discovery. Ordinarily, information produced during a lawsuit is a matter of public record. But if there is good cause—for instance, if a party has produced confidential commercial information or personal information that would be embarrassing if publicly revealed—a judge may order that the information be "sealed." If the judge grants this *Motion for Protective Order* or *Motion to Seal Matters Produced Upon Discovery*, the other side can use the information for the lawsuit but cannot divulge it to anyone else.

63. Can my lawyer go to court to force the other side to provide more or better information?

Most discovery disputes are about the sufficiency of a response. Is an answer evasive or incomplete? Has the party done a thorough search of its records? Are an objection and refusal to answer legally proper? Is a delay in responding, beyond the regular time limit, legitimate?

If there has been no response from the other side, or the response appears to be insufficient, a lawyer may file a motion to compel a full answer. Each side files papers giving its version of what has been requested and why the response is or is not sufficient. The judge or special *discovery commissioner* (a lower level judge who only presides over discovery disputes) then holds a court hearing to listen to each party's arguments.

These discovery motions include:

- *Motion to Compel Answers to Interrogatories*, if a party failed to answer an interrogatory or gave an insufficient answer
- *Motion to Compel Production of Documents* or *Motion to Compel Inspection of Property*, if a party has produced some documents but refused to produce others or has set improper limits on inspection of property
- *Motion to Determine Sufficiency of Response to Request for Admissions*, if a party's response appears to dodge the question rather than answer it
- *Motion to Compel Answers to Deposition Questions*, if an opposing party has refused to answer certain questions at a deposition, and
- *Motion to Compel Physical Examination*, if the other party refuses to submit to a physical examination (in a case in which it is appropriate) or sets unacceptable limits on the exam.

Stop and Consider Before Heading for Court. Courtroom battles over discovery can significantly increase the cost and aggravation of a lawsuit. This is particularly true if you are paying your lawyer an hourly fee. Even without hourly bills, however, court fights over discovery may increase tensions, distract the lawyers from more important work, delay progress and run up expenses. And you may have to pay sanctions if you lose. (See Question 65.) For these reasons, you should ask your lawyer to notify you before filing any discovery motion, particularly if you are paying by the hour.

When you and your lawyer discuss the advisability of going to court over a particular discovery matter, consider the following:

- How important is the information your lawyer is seeking?
- How important is it to you personally, or to the success of your case, to protect information the other side is seeking?
- How much is a court fight likely to cost?
- How likely is it that you will prevail in court?
- Is going to court a tactical decision? If so, will it be worth the expense?
- Is there a compromise that might avoid a court fight? Could you provide only some of the information sought or seek the other side's information in a different way?
- What is the likelihood that the other side will have to pay your costs and attorneys' fees if you win the court fight?
- What is the likelihood that you will have to pay sanctions if you lose?

64. Can someone be held in "contempt of court" for dodging a legitimate discovery request?

"Contempt of court" is one of those legal animals that everyone has heard of but few have actually seen. The popular image usually includes a wild outburst in a courtroom by a party or lawyer. However, contempt findings are more common for failure to abide by a court order, frequently regarding a discovery matter. This kind of discovery contempt arises in several situations. An opposing party may fail to respond at all to a legitimate discovery request. A party or other witness might fail to properly respond to a discovery request that was made by subpoena rather than simply by notice. Or a party may fail to provide a discovery response that was ordered by a judge after a previous motion to compel discovery.

In any of these situations, the party who requested the information may file an *Order to Show Cause re Contempt* (OSC). Both sides give written arguments detailing what has happened with the discovery request, then appear in court. If there was no good excuse for failing to respond to the discovery request—particularly if the party has ignored a court order—a judge may hold the party in *contempt of court*. However, this kind of contempt of court does not result in the sort of drastic action —"Bailiff, take him away!"—that many people associate with the term. Rather, a judge decides how to respond to a party's or other witness's discovery shortcomings—whether or not they're technically in "contempt of court"—based on the seriousness of the offense and the importance of the information sought. (See Question 65.)

65. How can a court punish a party for abusing the discovery process?

As part of the ongoing discovery wars, lawyers often ask judges to impose penalties called *sanctions* on the other side for failing to provide what has been requested, requesting something to which they are not entitled or otherwise conducting discovery in an abusive manner. Judges have wide discretion to impose sanctions for unreasonable conduct during discovery. The frequency and severity of sanctions vary widely from court to court and from judge to judge, but they may include the following:

- **Costs and fees.** A judge may order a party who loses a discovery motion to pay the other party's costs and attorney fees for preparing and filing the papers and for appearing in court.
- **Monetary sanctions.** In addition to attorney fees, a judge may also add a penalty amount, known as a monetary sanction. Such an additional amount is more frequently added when a lawyer or party has been held in contempt of court or when a judge feels his or her conduct has been obviously and exceedingly unreasonable.

- **"Merit" sanctions.** In cases of serious abuse of the discovery process or repeated refusal to produce discovery ordered by the court, judges have the authority to make rulings about the use of the information sought in discovery. These rulings can directly affect a party's ability to win the case. *Merit sanctions* are tailored specifically to the nature and importance of the discovery and the degree of misconduct in refusing to provide it. Merit sanctions may include a) prohibiting a party from using at trial any information that has improperly been withheld, b) excluding a witness—including a party—from testifying if the witness's identity was improperly withheld or the witness was uncooperative in some major way, c) instructing the jury to accept certain facts as true if information about them was improperly withheld and d) throwing out an entire claim or defense, or the case itself, for truly serious discovery abuse (for example, the destruction of crucial evidence).

 Who Pays Sanctions, Client or Attorney?
Judges may impose discovery sanctions against either the client or the lawyer. If you have stubbornly refused to provide information despite your lawyer's advice to the contrary, then you should pay the sanctions. But if information is not produced because your lawyer refuses to hand it over, or has advised you not to provide it, then the judge should

impose any sanctions against your lawyer personally. However, judges sometimes cannot tell who was responsible for failing to provide discovery.

In such cases, you should have a clear agreement with your lawyer about who will pay sanctions, which may include considerable attorney fees for the other side. If your lawyer advises you to resist producing certain information, discuss who will pay possible sanctions if you continue to resist all the way to court. Your lawyer might offer personally to take the risk, might insist that you pay or might suggest splitting the risk. Whatever agreement you reach, you and your lawyer should put it in writing.

Section VIII: Motions for Summary Judgment and Summary Adjudication

In the American judicial system, judges and juries have different roles. Before trial, a judge makes decisions concerning procedural rules and other legal matters but does not decide the facts of the dispute—the questions of who, what, when, where, why and how. Those questions must wait for the trial where a jury, or a judge if there is no jury, decides which party's version of the facts is true. In a Motion for Summary Judgment, however, a judge may decide the facts and end the case without trial.

66. What is Summary Judgment and when is it appropriate?

In a Summary Judgment Motion, the moving party presents a judge with the crucial, clearly established facts in the case, called *undisputed facts, uncontradicted facts, uncontroverted facts* or *facts without substantial controversy*. The moving party argues in its supporting papers that these facts show "as a matter of law" that the moving party *must* win the case, and therefore is entitled immediately to a Judgment in its favor. To succeed, the moving party must satisfy the judge not only that the parties agree on these crucial facts but also that the laws applied to those facts are subject to only one interpretation—that the moving party wins the case.

For example, an employer who is sued by an employee for accidental injuries might be able to demonstrate facts that conclusively prove the employee was injured on the job. If so, the employee might not have the right to sue the employer, but might instead be required to file a Workers' Compensation claim—an employee's exclusive remedy for on-the-job injuries. The employer's Motion for Summary Judgment would present facts showing that the employee was injured while performing work-related duties. If those facts were uncontradicted, a judge could grant Summary Judgment for the employer, without hearing any facts about how the accident happened or who was at fault. The employee's task in opposing this motion would be to contradict the facts that indicate the accident was work-related. Or the employee could offer legal arguments that the Workers' Compensation laws don't apply in this case. If the party opposing a Summary Judgment can show either that the facts are in dispute (and therefore must be decided by a jury) or that the law is on his or her side, the motion should be denied.

In another example, suppose Plaintiff was badly injured when Plaintiff's and Defendant's cars collided in an intersection. The state's driving laws state that a left-turning vehicle must always yield the right-of-way to on-coming traffic. The Defendant might win a Motion for Summary Judgment by showing beyond any dispute that the Plaintiff was making a left turn while Defendant was going straight. However, if the Plaintiff can show that the Defendant might have contributed to the accident by breaking another traffic law—by speeding or driving without headlights after dark, for ex-ample—the Summary Judgment Motion might not be granted.

67. Who is permitted to make a Summary Judgment Motion?

A Summary Judgment Motion may be brought by:

- any Plaintiff, seeking to win a final Judgment against any one or all Defendants named in the Complaint
- any Defendant, seeking to win Judg-ment against any one or all Plaintiffs

- any Counterclaimant or Cross-Defen-dant seeking to win Judgment on a Counterclaim or Cross-Complaint by any opposing party.

If there is more than one party on the other side of the lawsuit, a Summary Judg-ment Motion may address one opposing party or all parties. If there are multiple "Causes of Action" in the lawsuit (see Chapter 3), a Motion for Summary Judgment must present facts and arguments that attempt to dispose of all of them. A related procedure is available to knock some but not all Causes of Action out of the lawsuit. (See Questions 73-75.)

68. When may a Summary Judgment Motion be made?

A Motion for Summary Judgment may be brought almost anytime before trial. How-ever, Summary Judgment Motions are most often made, and are most likely to be granted, when discovery is nearly complete. (See Chapter 4.) To win a Motion for Summary Judgment, the moving party must convince a judge that the case's crucial facts have been established beyond doubt or dispute. The discovery process is the way most information is nailed down in a lawsuit—including whether there is more than one version of any particular "fact." Only when most discovery is completed can any party successfully assert, and a judge confidently decide, that a crucial fact is undisputed.

Should You Move for Summary Judgment?

In deciding whether to make a Motion for Summary Judgment, you and your lawyer must consider a number of factors. The positive factors begin with the obvious—it's a chance to win the entire case without having to go through a trial. On the other hand, most judges prefer not to decide an entire case without allowing both sides a trial, so they will only grant a Summary Judgment Motion in the most obvious and overwhelming circumstances.

Summary Judgment Motions can be both expensive and time-consuming. Those most likely to succeed present a few simple, clearly undisputed facts on which an unequivocal legal decision—often applying a technical legal rule—can be based. Other types of Summary Judgment Motions are usually bad bets. For example, a motion that asks a judge to decide whose witnesses are telling the truth, or which version of complicated facts makes most sense, stands little chance. (One general rule lawyers use is that the more "uncontested" facts needed to support the motion, the tougher it is to win.) Similarly, Summary Judgment is highly unlikely if it depends on a judge deciding on a party's or other person's state of mind—what someone intended, understood, was aware of or expected. And Summary Judgment is rarely granted if the motion relies on the opinions of expert witnesses. The other side can almost always come up with at least one expert of its own whose opinion will dispute some crucial aspect of your experts' opinions.

There are other reasons to hesitate before filing a Motion for Summary Judgment. Filing the motion may delay the whole case for months. Your lawyer is unlikely to do much else on the case while working on Summary Judgment. And once the motion is pending, no other litigation proceedings are usually scheduled. Also, a Summary Judgment Motion often prompts a similar motion from the other side, meaning your lawyer will have to spend time, energy and money to oppose it. Unless there is a good chance of winning the motion, all this may be too high a price to pay.

On the other hand, your lawyer may know that the court or particular judge hearing your case grants Summary Judgment Motions more often than other courts. Particularly in crowded court systems, certain judges like to use Summary Judgment motions as a way of clearing cases off their calendars. If so, you may want to file a motion even if the odds of winning in another court might not be strong.

Also, merely filing a Motion for Summary Judgment may produce some positive results even if the chances of winning are only so-so. By forcing a detailed response to the facts you contend are undisputed, your lawyer might induce the other side to reveal the evidence and legal theories they will rely on for trial. A strong Motion for Summary Judgment might push the other side toward a more favorable settlement of the case. Fear of losing the motion, and therefore the entire case, may prompt a change in settlement position. And having to spend lots of time and money opposing the motion may nudge the other side to consider settlement.

69. How does a party present a Summary Judgment Motion to a judge?

In addition to the documents filed with any standard type of motion (see Section I, above), in most courts the moving party has to set out in a separate document—called something like *Statement of Undisputed Facts* or *Statement of Uncontroverted Facts*—those facts it contends are undisputed. These must be *material* facts: each must help to establish the legal basis for the moving party to win the entire lawsuit. Attached to this document are sworn declarations or affidavits that include or refer to evidence that proves each crucial fact. This evidence might be records or other documents, statements by parties or witnesses, testimony from depositions, a party's admissions or answers to interrogatories. (See Chapter 4.)

For example, suppose a seller sues a buyer for refusing to pay for the seller's products. The buyer contends that the seller delivered different, more expensive products than were described in the parties' contract; the seller contends that the buyer agreed in writing to accept the different products, thereby modifying their contract. If the seller brought a Summary Judgment Motion, he might attach evidence such as correspondence between buyer and seller in which the different products were described and discussed without objection by the buyer; records showing that the buyer

paid the higher price for a period; and deposition testimony from the manager of the buyer's business, stating that he agreed to accept the more expensive items.

Delaying the Other Side's Summary Judgment Motion

As mentioned, a party usually does not make a Summary Judgment Motion until most discovery in the case has been completed. Occasionally, however, a party files a Summary Judgment Motion as soon as one key fact surfaces that seems to deliver a knockout blow. Judges are reluctant to grant Summary Judgment if they believe there is still more important evidence to be developed. If a Summary Judgment Motion has been filed against you when there is more discovery to be done, the judge might postpone the other side's motion until that discovery is completed. And while more discovery is being conducted, your lawyer will know exactly what kind of evidence must be obtained to dispute the facts raised by the other side.

70. How does a party oppose a Summary Judgment Motion?

The party opposing a Motion for Summary Judgment usually files, in addition to the standard Memorandum of Points and

Authorities in Opposition (see Section I), a raft of other documents:

- *Objections to Evidence*, in which some of the evidence presented by the moving party is attacked as legally improper, in an effort to have the judge eliminate that evidence from consideration regarding the motion. For example, the party opposing the motion might object to a contract the other side offered as evidence, arguing that the contract is invalid because it was never signed.

- *Statement of Disputed Facts*, also called a *Statement of Genuine Issues,* in which those facts asserted by the other side as undisputed are contradicted. For example, the moving party's "undisputed" fact that a business manager approved a contract change might be disputed by the fact that the manager was not authorized to make changes to contracts for the company.

- *Statement of Undisputed Facts in Opposition*, in which the opposing party proposes its own uncontested facts to show an overall legal picture different from the one presented by the moving party. In the example discussed above, the opposing party might present facts showing that the manager had never changed any other contract and that the company handbook authorized only its CEO to contract on the company's behalf.

- sworn declarations or affidavits, in which evidence is presented that disputes the other side's "facts" and supports different supposedly undisputed facts. In the contract example, the opposing party might present deposition testimony from the manager and CEO describing the manager's authority, affidavits from other managers stating that they had no authority to change contracts for the company and letters from the other side showing that they knew the manager had no authority to change the contract.

These documents are often highly detailed; they must be prepared with great thoroughness and care. As a result, opposing a Motion for Summary Judgment is often extremely time-consuming. On the other hand, losing a Summary Judgment Motion might mean losing the entire case, so it is not a procedure in which a lawyer should stint on time or energy.

How You Can Help Your Lawyer With a Summary Judgment Motion

There might be little help you can offer on a Motion for Summary Judgment. The motion may be based on a few fairly simple facts and a technical legal argument based on those facts. Whether your lawyer is making or opposing such a motion, the lawyer can easily handle the whole thing without your help. In other cases, there might be more complicated evidence, but you might not know enough about it to help your lawyer out.

On the other hand, making or opposing a Summary Judgment Motion sometimes requires sorting through and organizing a lot of evidence and producing new evidence on specific factual issues. In these cases, there may be a number of things you can do to help your lawyer.

- On any crucial factual point, you may know of documents—whether or not they have already surfaced in the case—that support your side of the argument. You can retrieve these documents for your lawyer.
- You may know of some fact that supports your argument, or counters the other side's, but which has not yet emerged in the case. If so, your lawyer can present this fact to the court in a sworn affidavit by you or another witness.
- You may know of a witness who has not yet testified in the case and has information helpful to your side of the Summary Judgment argument. That witness can make a sworn statement to be presented to the court.
- You may be required to write an affidavit to submit with your motion or opposition. You should find out when your lawyer plans to bring (or anticipates that the other side will bring) the motion, so you can be available to work on your affidavit.

In any of these situations, your first move should be to discuss the matter with your lawyer and ask the lawyer how you should proceed.

71. Who has the last word, the Plaintiff or the Defendant?

After the other side has filed its papers opposing the motion, the moving party files a reply. This reply may include formal *Objections to Evidence* (arguments that some of the other side's evidence is legally improper), factual contentions and a final Memorandum of Points and Authorities that counters the other side's legal arguments.

72. What are a judge's options when considering a Motion for Summary Judgment?

A judge may do one of several things in ruling on a Motion for Summary Judgment. The judge may grant the motion, which gives a final Judgment to the moving party and ends the lawsuit between the parties involved in the motion. If the motion is denied, the lawsuit continues as before.

Sometimes, a judge takes an intermediate route. Instead of denying a motion, the judge may "take it off calendar"—delay the decision indefinitely—until the parties complete some more discovery that the judge believes is necessary to decide the motion. A judge might also deny the full Summary Judgment but grant what is called a *Partial Summary Judgment*, also known as a *Summary Adjudication of Issues*. This partial ruling declares some portion of the case—a legal issue, cause of action, set of facts—decided in favor of the moving party but does not end the case entirely. (Partial Summary Judgment, or Summary Adjudication of Issues, is explained in Questions 73-75.)

73. May a judge declare one party to have won certain issues in a case without deciding the whole case?

Often, a lawyer believes that some portion of the other side's case—either part of Plaintiff's Complaint, or of Defendant's Answer or Counterclaim—is legally insupportable even though the lawsuit as a whole presents a legitimate dispute. If so, the lawyer may ask a judge to throw out that specific portion of the other side's case without asking that the entire lawsuit be ended. This type of request is called a *Motion for Partial Summary Judgment* or *Motion for Summary Adjudication of Issues.*

74. How does the procedure for a Partial Summary Judgment (Summary Adjudication of Issues) compare with a motion requesting full Summary Judgment?

The procedure for a Partial Summary Judgment Motion is virtually the same as for a Motion for full Summary Judgment. The motion must include a Statement of Undisputed Facts, supporting evidence and legal arguments. The only difference is that the

facts, evidence and legal arguments are directed at limited, specific issues rather than the entire case.

75. Why file a Partial Summary Judgment Motion if the lawsuit will continue anyway?

A Motion for Summary Adjudication of Issues or Partial Summary Judgment can greatly simplify trial, and therefore reduce the time, energy and expense needed to prepare and conduct it. For example, there might be clear evidence that a Defendant is legally responsible for injuries Plaintiff suffered, but a genuine dispute about how badly Plaintiff is injured and therefore how much compensation Plaintiff should be awarded. A Motion for Summary Adjudication of Issues or Partial Summary Judgment in that case might request that a judge declare as a matter of law that the Defendant is responsible for the accident. If the motion is granted, Plaintiff's lawyer would be saved the time and expense of proving the Defendant's legal responsibility at trial and would instead be able to concentrate entirely on proving Plaintiff's damages.

A party might file a Motion for Summary Adjudication to ask the court to decide any important issue before trial, such as whether one state's laws govern a dispute between residents of different states, whether a contract was in effect or whether someone was acting as an employee at the time of certain misconduct.

Summary Adjudication of Issues or Partial Summary Judgment can also be used to reduce the risk a party faces at trial. For example, a Complaint may claim that the Defendant not only owes the Plaintiff money but also violated a law that would permit the Plaintiff to collect attorney fees from the Defendant if Plaintiff wins the lawsuit. (See Chapter 3, Section I.) In that situation, a Defendant might try to convince a judge to rule in advance that the Defendant has not violated that particular law, to eliminate the attorney fees claim. A Defendant might also use a Motion for Partial Summary Judgment to try to knock out a cause of action, like fraud, that would allow the Plaintiff to seek punitive damages. (See Chapter 3, Section I.) Proving or eliminating certain aspects of the case before trial frequently changes the relative strength of the parties' bargaining positions. This can be a significant spur to settlement. ■

Chapter 6

Mediation

At some point during the course of a lawsuit—when costs and fees threaten the litigants' solvency, the drain of time and energy threatens their personal life and work capacity and the stress and nightmares threaten their sanity —the parties may find themselves asking "How did I get into this?" And then, "How do I get out?"

Eventually, both sides are likely to ask these questions at the same time. (In fact, one side may have been asking these questions from the very beginning.) If and when both parties reach this point, there are several ways they can step back from the litigation process and try to resolve their dispute. This Chapter and the two that follow discuss some of these methods: mediation, arbitration (Chapter 7) and negotiated settlements (Chapter 8).

The parties may try mediation, which seeks a resolution of the dispute that works for everyone rather than an adjudication of a winner and a loser. If the mediation is unsuccessful, the parties simply resume their lawsuit.

This Chapter discusses mediation—what it is and how it works to resolve disputes without a judge, jury or arbitrator. Although mediation is essentially an informal, non-legal process for resolving disputes, this Chapter also explains how a client may make use of his or her lawyer to initiate mediation, prepare for mediation and finalize any agreement the parties reach.

Alternative Dispute Resolution (ADR)

You may have heard, or will hear during your lawsuit, the term *Alternative Dispute Resolution* (ADR). ADR refers generally to several processes—mediation, arbitration and private judging—that may be used instead of litigation to resolve a dispute. However, different people and court systems use the term ADR in different ways. In some states, ADR refers to one particular system of arbitration or mediation set up by the court. In other places, the term means any kind of alternative to litigation, whether set up and controlled by the court or run by private services.

In this book, the term ADR is not used to refer to any one particular process. Instead, each kind of alternative dispute resolution is referred to and explained under its own separate category—mediation, arbitration, neutral evaluation, court-directed settlement conferences and private judging.

1. What is mediation?

All too often, lawsuits come to resemble the dilemma of the sorcerer's apprentice. In that tale, a magician's assistant overheard and repeated his master's magic words to set buckets and mops in motion to do the apprentice's job of cleaning the sorcerer's laboratory. However, the apprentice did not know the words to stop the brooms and buckets, and soon the laboratory was not merely cleaned but completely flooded.

Lawsuits may follow a similar path. After months of litigation, a party often finds that, instead of moving the dispute toward a resolution, the lawsuit has driven the two sides farther apart—and closer to the poor house—than they were when the case started. While it may have been easy enough to utter the magic words "Sue the bastards!" finding the formula to stop the lawsuit can be much more difficult. That's where mediation might come in.

Mediation is a process by which the parties try to reach a mutual resolution of the dispute with the help of a trained facilitator. If the mediation fails to produce an agreement between the parties, the lawsuit can continue as before. Mediation works especially well in disputes involving only a few people, and disputes among individuals or small businesses, rather than larger companies or organizations. Mediation is particularly helpful if the parties will carry on a relationship after the dispute is over, such as with business associates, employers and employees, a landlord and tenant or neighbors.

Where to Find a Complete Guide to Mediation

Because mediation is entirely different from litigation, this book provides only an introduction. This Chapter will help you understand mediation and decide whether it might be useful to you. If the discussion here leads you to believe that mediation might be a sensible alternative in your case, you may want to read *How to Mediate Your Dispute* by Peter Lovenheim (Nolo), a comprehensive, easy-to-use guide to the entire mediation process, from deciding whether your case might be right for mediation to choosing a mediator, preparing for and going through the mediation itself and turning your mediation settlement into a workable, binding agreement.

2. How is mediation different from litigation and arbitration?

In litigation and arbitration, each party's goal is to obtain a decision by a judge or arbitrator that favors that party's position. (Arbitration is covered in Chapter 7.) Mediation, on the other hand, involves no decision maker. Rather, mediation encourages the parties to mutually craft their own "decision." Some unique features of mediation are:

- all litigation proceedings are put on hold during the mediation process, allowing the mediation to take place without the heat and noise of adversary maneuvering
- the parties may choose to speak for themselves in mediation sessions, rather than relying entirely on the lawyers
- mediation focuses on ways for the opposing parties to agree, rather than harping on who was right or wrong
- mediation offers the assistance of a neutral third party, the mediator, who provides a calming presence that lawyers usually do not
- the mediator employs a set of specific skills designed to foster negotiations between the parties, skills that lawyers and judges frequently lack, and
- mediation is informal, requiring little technical legal preparation, so it is usually completed quickly and inexpensively.

3. What is the basic structure of mediation?

In mediation, the parties sit down together to discuss the dispute with an independent third party, the mediator. Depending on the type of dispute, the mediator may ask the lawyers to present each party's legal position. However, the mediator will focus on how the parties themselves see the dispute, as it is they who will ultimately have to agree to any settlement that is reached. Sometimes the parties will be speaking directly to each other; other times, each party may talk with the mediator separately in what's known as a "caucus."

The mediator has no authority to order either side to do or say anything. However, the mediator will set and enforce certain ground rules for the mediation sessions, to ensure that they proceed in a calm and orderly way. And a mediator makes no final ruling or decision, gives no opinion about who was right or wrong, declares neither party victorious. Rather than setting up a win-or-lose scenario, a mediator encourages both parties to get things off their chests and offers suggestions about how the two sides might come to a resolution of the dispute.

Sometimes the parties use mediation to arrive at a dollar settlement figure. Other times, however, parties use mediation to consider how their relationship might continue in the future—how two businesses might again work together without similar disputes erupting, how a landlord might respond to tenant complaints, how an employer and employee might structure their work relationship to minimize conflicts or how neighbors might jointly maintain property that affects them both.

If the parties reach a mediated agreement, they memorialize it in settlement documents that end the lawsuit. (See Chapter 8.) If mediation does not resolve the dispute, the parties return to the litigation just where they left it.

change each party's view of the prospects for winning (or losing) if the litigation were to continue. If the dispute is about more than just dollars and cents, the mediator is trained to propose innovative solutions that the lawyers likely have not considered.

4. Can mediation work if our previous efforts to settle the case have failed?

Yes. Mediation often works because it is so different from the adversary process of litigation. Because parties may speak for themselves in mediation, they can give voice to creative ideas, personal feelings and practical solutions that litigation might discourage. (The confidentiality of everything said in mediation is discussed below.) By the same token, each party gets to hear directly from the horse's mouth what is most important to the other side, instead of relying on a third-hand version each lawyer reports from the other party's lawyer.

Also, during mediation the parties might at least partly escape the full force of the lawyers' approach to the lawsuit. Litigation lawyers are skilled primarily at finding a way to win. Sometimes, they focus so intently on doing battle that they lose sight of opportunities for resolution that include repairing the parties' relationship. In mediation, however, the parties get to hear a different, impartial voice. The mediator may point out, in different terms than the lawyers would use, the strengths and weaknesses of each side's position. This may, in turn, help

5. What kinds of cases are best suited to mediation?

Mediation isn't helpful in every lawsuit. It might be most useful—instead of normal settlement negotiations between the parties' lawyers (see Chapter 8)—in cases where the primary consideration is something more than how much money one side should pay the other, particularly when the parties have an ongoing business or personal relationship to consider. In fact, mediators sometimes are the first to notice that something other than money is important to the parties; until trying mediation, the parties and lawyers themselves may have only fought over who pays how much to whom.

Mediation is less common in disputes over responsibility for a single incident—an accident causing injury or damage, for example, or an isolated business deal gone bad. In such cases, a mediator has little room to change the parties' thinking or fashion an innovative solution. Nevertheless, in some of these cases a mediator might help by acting as a referee in a settlement negotiation session among lawyers and parties.

Mediation Is Common in Divorce and Custody Disputes

In the past couple of decades, many courts have made mediation readily available to divorcing and divorced spouses to help settle the difficult, emotional problems raised by separating lives and households while continuing to share children. Indeed, many courts have made mediation mandatory for all divorcing or divorced couples with disputes relating to their children. For more information on mediating domestic relations disputes, see *Using Divorce Mediation* by Attorney-Mediator Katherine E. Stoner (Nolo).

Mediation tends to work best in these types of lawsuits:

- Lawsuits involving only two parties. The more people directly involved in the lawsuit, the more difficult it is for everyone to agree on a resolution through mediation.
- Disputes in which the parties are more or less equal in terms of bargaining strength. Mediation doesn't work as well if one party has far more experience or bargaining strength than the other—for example, if an individual goes up against a large employer or other corporate opponent.
- Cases in which both parties are at least a little uncertain about the outcome. Mediation is less likely to succeed if either side believes it has

an iron-clad legal basis for winning the lawsuit. Mediation requires each side to consider the other's position carefully; that is far less likely if one side strongly believes it is certain to win in court.

6. At what point in a lawsuit is mediation appropriate?

The opposing sides in a lawsuit may arrange for mediation on their own, without court permission or involvement, at any time. But there are several key points during litigation at which mediation is most likely to be successful. The first is immediately after the lawsuit has been filed. Having to face the reality, rather than merely the possibility, of long and expensive litigation might shock both parties into accepting mediation as a far better idea. This is also the point when courts might order parties into mediation (in those jurisdictions where mediation is mandatory—see Question 8).

Another moment when mediation might succeed is immediately after a particularly stressful or revealing litigation procedure, such as a party's own deposition or a failed Motion for Summary Judgment. Having just gone through a tense or bruising and expensive experience, the parties may be looking for a saner way out of the mess. Similarly, a party who has been uninterested in mediation might become more amenable to it after a deposition or other legal maneuver has muddied what had previously seemed to be that party's clear legal advantage.

Finally, some parties develop an interest in mediation on the eve of trial. At this point, the parties might realize that litigation has not improved either side's position or disposition, and the prospect of an intense and expensive trial might be decidedly unattractive to both.

You Can Mediate More Than Once

Perhaps you wound up in litigation because prior negotiating efforts failed. You may even have tried mediation before the lawsuit, without success. If you've already tried but failed to settle things face to face, what's the point in again sitting across the table from that unreasonable, hard-headed so-and-so?

It's because the experience of litigation might have made both of you more open to the possibility of a mediated solution. However far apart you and the other party have been in your views of the dispute, you now have something very much in common—the experience of being trapped in a lawsuit. Now that you both have tasted the expense, time and stress of litigation, mediating an agreement might seem much more appealing to both of you than continuing the lawsuit. If mediation otherwise seems to make sense in your case, don't reject the idea just because negotiations or other mediation have failed in the past.

Your Lawyer Might Resist Mediation

Many lawyers understand the advantages of mediation and support their clients' efforts to settle disputes that way. However, other lawyers are uncomfortable with mediation. They believe that clients get in trouble when they speak for themselves. Lawyers are trained in the adversary system, which teaches that battle is the best method for serving a client's interests. Also, many lawyers believe that mediating a solution means a client might be "giving away" legal rights and advantages. As a strategic matter, a lawyer may not want to suggest mediation to the other side, fearing that it might show a lack of faith in the chances of winning the lawsuit. But this fear of signaling "weakness" is also a risk with proposing settlement negotiations, and lawyers find ways to get those discussions moving at almost any point in the case. (See Chapter 8.)

For any of these reasons, your lawyer might not suggest mediation and might be less than enthusiastic if you bring it up. However, if your dispute seems to be a good candidate for mediation, you should insist that your lawyer at least help you investigate the possibility. Ask your lawyer's opinion about mediation for your case and mediation services in your area. (Help in finding mediation services is also available from the Nolo book *How to Mediate Your Dispute* by Peter Lovenheim.) If your lawyer opposes mediation in your case, make sure the reasons are in *your* best interests, not just the lawyer's.

7. What might I gain or lose if the mediation is unsuccessful?

Compared to litigation, mediation is relatively inexpensive. Prices can range from a few hundred dollars to several thousand dollars per party, depending on the complexity of the case and the length of the mediation. And the process is relatively quick. It can be arranged within a few weeks, and the mediation sessions themselves usually last only for a few hours or a single day. If the mediation fails, the parties will not have lost much time out of the litigation process.

Even if no agreement is reached, the mediation sessions might prove to be useful in the long run. Comments and suggested solutions offered by the mediator might become the basis for settlement negotiations down the road. (See Chapter 8.) And what the parties say during mediation might give each of them better insight into what the other is really thinking, which also might make it easier to reach a settlement later on.

But mediation has potential down-sides, too. However reasonable the costs and quick the process, it does use up some time and money. And if a litigant heavily relies on an hourly paid lawyer to help prepare for and sit through mediation, the attorney fees can pile up. Also, mediation may result in the disclosure of a particular weakness in the case that the other side might not otherwise have discovered. And mediation can increase a party's frustration and anger, if the other side doesn't seem to be cooperating in the process. So if the dispute seems *very* unlikely to be resolved in mediation, the added costs and the tactical risks, however slim, might make mediation a shaky investment.

8. How does mediation get started?

Some litigants begin mediation because they are required to do so by the court in which the lawsuit is filed. Certain courts order mediation for certain types of cases—divorce and child custody and visitation, most commonly—and also for any type of dispute if the amount of money demanded

by the Plaintiff is under a certain limit (usually $25,000 to $50,000). If a case is ordered to mediation by court rules, it is usually referred to a mediation service run by or contracted with the court itself.

If a lawsuit is not court-ordered to mediation, the parties may voluntarily—if both agree—enter mediation at any time, and may use any mediation service they choose. Some court-run mediation services are available to litigants who volunteer for it. If a court service is not available, the parties must use a private mediation service or an individual private mediator.

Once the parties have been sent to, or have chosen, a mediation service or individual mediator, they usually enter into a *Mediation Agreement*. This agreement establishes the basics, such as costs, dates and deadlines. It also sets out ground rules for the process, though these are usually very few—mediation succeeds, in part, because of its great flexibility. The rules usually include:

- what kind of written summary of each side's position is to be sent to the mediator in advance of the mediation (and whether that summary will be sent to the other side)
- how documents and other information may be presented to the mediator
- how the mediation sessions will be conducted (see Question 11)
- how the sessions will be kept confidential, and
- the extent to which lawyers or other advisers are expected to participate.

Confidentiality Is Key in Mediation

One of the reasons mediation so often works is that the warring parties are encouraged to fully speak their minds. The parties feel free to do this because whatever they say in mediation is confidential: nothing written in mediation papers or said in a mediation room may be used as evidence in court.

In most states, this confidentiality is established by law or court rule. But to make absolutely sure that nothing you say in mediation can later be used in court if the mediation fails, check to see that confidentiality is spelled out clearly in the mediation agreement. If it is not, have your lawyer ask the mediator to add it to the agreement before you sign.

Bear in mind, however, that while the statements you make during mediation may not be used as evidence in court, the other side is not going to forget what they hear from you during the mediation. What you reveal in the mediation about legal strategy, key witnesses or crucial facts may provide ammunition for the other side that they might not otherwise have had. If the mediation fails, the other party can use this information to plan discovery and trial strategy. For this reason, you should ask your lawyer ahead of time if there is anything that might be best left unsaid during the mediation.

9. How can my lawyer help set up the mediation?

Mediation might be proposed by a lawyer, a client, the opposing side or the court. Once a party decides to mediate, there are several ways a lawyer can help get the process moving.

- **Propose the mediation.** A lawyer can be the one to propose mediation to the other side. The lawyer can informally raise the possibility of mediation with the other side's lawyer, then prepare and send a more formal proposal.
- **Help set up the mediation.** A lawyer can be helpful in several ways before a mediation is actually scheduled. The lawyer can find out whether the court offers mediation for a certain type of case, and if so how that mediation might be started. Or the lawyer can develop information about non-court mediation services, and perhaps individual private mediators.
- **Review the mediation agreement.** The lawyer can review and make suggested changes to the mediation agreement, the written document setting out ground rules that each side usually signs to begin the mediation process. (See Question 8.)

10. Does my lawyer send any paperwork to the mediator?

Mediation is long on talking and short on paperwork. Because it is informal and mostly non-technical, lawyers do not have to prepare the lengthy written legal papers that are so often required in litigation. Nonetheless, a lawyer may still use those lawyerly writing skills by preparing a *Pre-Mediation Memorandum* or *Mediation Brief.* This document summarizes the client's position and introduces the mediator to the client's side of the dispute.

To the extent this document serves to educate the mediator about the client's legal position, the lawyer does the composing. However, the Memorandum is also intended to give the mediator a first impression of the client—a personal, rather than legal, view of the dispute. For this reason, some lawyers devote one section of the Memorandum to the client's personal statement: the client's views and concerns, in the client's own words. Even here, however, the lawyer can remind the client of important points to make. Before the statement goes to the mediator, the lawyer should review it to make sure the client has not left out something important—or included something that might make a bad first impression on the mediator.

11. What are the actual mediation sessions like?

Mediation usually consists of a combination of meetings—joint sessions among the litigants, the lawyers and the mediator, joint sessions with the litigants but not the lawyers, and individual "caucuses" between the mediator and one side only, with or without a lawyer present.

In the joint sessions with lawyers, each party and lawyer has an opportunity to present documents, witness statements and legal arguments. Whether the party or the lawyer does most or all of the talking in these sessions depends on the party's preference and the mediator's questions. The mediator's primary job is to steer the parties toward an agreement, not necessarily to decide whose legal position is stronger. Sometimes, the mediator will try not only to resolve the existing dispute but also to figure out how the parties can reasonably coexist in the future. Consequently, the joint and individual sessions with just the parties are often as useful as those with the lawyers. In these sessions, each party may put in his or her own words the things that are personally—as opposed to legally— most important about the dispute and the other party.

12. How can my lawyer help me prepare for the mediation session?

From litigating the case, a lawyer will be familiar with documents, witness statements and other evidence in the dispute. Because litigation lawyers are trained in organizing such material into a coherent "story," a lawyer can be a great help in preparing the client for the mediation sessions.

Depending on his or her experience with mediation, a lawyer may be able to explain how the process actually works, perhaps communicating better with the client than do the dry mediation service brochures and the written mediation agreement. A lawyer can also help prepare a strategy for mediation, by:

- focusing on what the client most hopes to achieve in the mediation
- gathering and organizing documents and other information to present to the mediator
- alerting the client to things *not* to say, and positions *not* to take, during the mediation sessions, and
- explaining the legal arguments that support the client's case, as well as those the other side might make.

13. If an agreement is reached, does the mediator actually settle the lawsuit?

If the parties reach a mediated agreement, the mediator draws up an outline of its terms while both parties are still in the mediation session. However, while this agreement may set out the basic terms for ending the dispute, settlement of a lawsuit requires certain other, more formal documents that the lawyers prepare. (See Chapter 8, Section V.) Both parties and their lawyers should review the mediator's summary to make sure it accurately reflects the basic terms of the agreement, make any necessary changes, sign the agreement and get a copy.

Your Lawyer Might See Flaws in Certain Mediated Solutions

Lawsuits attempt to determine who was right or wrong in a given dispute, based on the legal rights of the parties. Mediations, in contrast, try to fashion a solution that satisfies both parties, without necessarily deciding who would likely prevail in the lawsuit. Sometimes, a lawyer might think the solution proposed by a mediator compromises a client's legal rights too much, even though that solution might seem reasonable and workable to both the client and the other party.

It is your lawyer's job in such a situation to inform you of any legal rights you might be giving up in accepting a proposed mediated settlement. That includes the lawyer's estimate of how you would fare if the lawsuit continued, and the extent to which your rights would be diminished in the future by any ongoing agreement fashioned by the mediator. Only when you have heard these explanations from your lawyer can you fully judge the benefits and detriments of the mediator's proposal.

Chapter 7

Arbitration

How You Can Help Your Lawyer

Sometimes, the parties reach a point in a lawsuit when they are unable to mediate or negotiate a settlement but have no desire to wage—and fund—a full-fledged trial. If so, the parties might agree to send the case to arbitration. Mutual agreement is not always required for arbitration, however. In some courts, a Plaintiff may send certain types of cases to arbitration without Defendant's permission. And a judge can order certain cases to arbitration even if neither party wants to arbitrate.

This Chapter explains the types of arbitration available to, or required of, parties who are already in a lawsuit—referred to as *judicial arbitration*. The Chapter also explains how to prepare for arbitration, how the hearing process works and—for cases in non-binding arbitration—how to decide whether to accept or reject the arbitrator's decision.

Section I: Arbitration Basics

1. What is arbitration?

Arbitration is an alternative to a courtroom trial, in which the parties present evidence and make legal arguments to an arbitrator rather than a judge or jury. The arbitrator then decides the case just as the judge or jury would in a courtroom: who wins, who loses and how much the loser must pay the winner.

There are two kinds of judicial arbitration. In the vast majority of cases, the parties to a lawsuit choose, or are ordered by the court to use, what is called *non-binding arbitration*. In this form of arbitration, if either party does not like the arbitration result, that party may reject the arbitration decision—by filing what is called a *Request for Trial de Novo*—and resume the lawsuit process in court. However, all parties can agree to submit the case to *binding arbitration*, in which the arbitrator's decision is a final determination of the case. Once the parties agree to binding arbitration, neither party may go back to court to complain about the outcome. Nor may the losing party appeal the arbitration decision to a higher court (except in extraordinary circumstances).

All Court-Ordered Arbitration Is Non-Binding

Binding arbitration replaces a trial. But the right to a full-fledged trial, with a jury in most cases, is a fundamental part of our judicial system. No court can take away that right, even if arbitration seems a more sensible alternative than trial in a particular case. Although a court may require that certain lawsuits be halted for a time while the parties arbitrate, the court may not bind the parties to the result of that arbitration. Each party must be permitted to reject the arbitration decision and litigate the case— all the way through trial, if the party so desires.

Some Disputes Must Be Arbitrated

In some states, certain legal disputes never get to court because they are required, by law or by contract, to be settled by non-judicial binding arbitration. Common examples are disputes about health insurance or HMO decisions. In other disputes, binding arbitration may be required by a written agreement between the parties. For example, uninsured motorist insurance policies, construction contracts and labor contracts frequently include terms requiring binding arbitration instead of litigation.

These binding arbitrations proceed under state arbitration rules or under those of the American Arbitration Association, whichever the law or contract in question requires. In many respects, this non-judicial arbitration is similar to the binding arbitration discussed in this Chapter. To know exactly what procedures apply to your case, however, you and your lawyer must consult the specific rules that govern your non-judicial arbitration.

2. What is the format of judicial arbitration?

An *arbitration hearing* is a kind of informal, non-courtroom trial that delivers a winner and loser in the lawsuit and determines all the issues raised by both sides in the pleadings, just as a regular trial would. The arbitration hearing is conducted by an *arbitrator*—usually a lawyer or retired judge—who decides the case without a jury. Occasionally, an arbitration is conducted by a panel of three arbitrators. The parties and other witnesses may testify, documents and other evidence may be presented and the lawyers for both sides may make all the same legal arguments that they would in a courtroom trial.

Besides the absence of a jury, the major difference between an arbitration and a courtroom trial is that arbitration is conducted without a trial's formality or rigid rules. For example, most witnesses "appear" at an arbitration hearing through their deposition testimony or sworn written statements rather than in person. As a result of this informality, and because there is no jury, arbitration is far quicker and less expensive than a trial. And a case usually can get to an arbitration hearing months or even years sooner than it would come up for trial in the overburdened courts.

3. What happens to the lawsuit while the arbitration process is going on?

Once arbitration has been requested by the parties or ordered by the court, most formal lawsuit proceedings are put on hold. However, discovery procedures (see Chapter 4) usually continue until 15-20 days before the arbitration hearing. And informal work on the case, such as investigation of the facts, consultation with experts, witness interviews and settlement negotiations, may continue throughout the arbitration process.

4. How does a lawsuit end up in arbitration?

There are three ways in which judicial arbitration—arbitration of an active lawsuit —may be initiated:

- by *stipulated arbitration*—arbitration to which both sides agree (stipulated arbitration may be either binding or non-binding, as the parties agree— see Questions 5-7)
- by *Plaintiff's election of arbitration*— non-binding arbitration initiated by the Plaintiff, whether Defendant wants to arbitrate or not (see Questions 8-10), or
- by *mandatory arbitration*—non-binding arbitration which is ordered by the court even if neither party wants it (see Questions 11-13).

Private Judging Is Also Available

After a lawsuit has been filed, there is another shortcut through the litigation process—called *private judging*—in which litigants leave court entirely. Private judging is an almost exact replica of a lawsuit—the same laws apply, and most of the same rules and procedures—but it is conducted by private judges (usually retired regular judges). These private judges work for a commercial judging service that also arranges the physical space and support staff needed for the "trial" and all pre-trial proceedings.

The parties must pay the entire cost of this service and must accept the results as binding. Because the judge and staff are paid directly by the litigants, they give the parties all the time and energy they require. So cases in private judging may get "tried" years faster than they would in regular court. For the same reasons, however, private judging is enormously expensive. It is used mostly in lawsuits between large, well-heeled companies.

5. How does "stipulated arbitration" work?

Stipulated arbitration simply means arbitration to which the opposing parties in a lawsuit have agreed. The agreement, including specific ground rules for the arbitration (see Question 7), is spelled out in a document called a *Stipulation for Arbitration*. The parties file this Stipulation with the court, which then "refers" the case to arbitration. This official referral serves to formally halt all court proceedings until the arbitration is completed.

6. When are the parties most likely to stipulate to arbitration?

Stipulated arbitration most commonly takes place after discovery has been nearly completed. By then, the case is almost ready for trial, and the parties have held enough discussions to know that a negotiated settlement is unlikely. Though this is the usual point for stipulated arbitration, the parties may agree to it almost any time during the lawsuit. (Some local court rules do not permit referral to arbitration in the 30 days before the trial date, but judges may make an exception to these rules in the interest of clearing their court calendars.)

7. What do the parties agree to in a stipulated arbitration?

In a stipulated arbitration, the parties may agree on any limits or procedural ground rules they choose. First and foremost, the litigants must decide that *either*:

- the parties will have the right to *trial de novo* ("a trial from the beginning"), meaning that the arbitration will not be binding and either side may reject the arbitrator's decision and return the case to litigation, or
- the arbitration will be binding, meaning that the parties must accept the arbitrator's decision and may not return to court to continue the litigation or appeal the arbitrator's decision.

In addition, the parties may agree to a dollar limit on the amount either side may win; this is usually done only in binding arbitration. In non-binding arbitration, the parties can agree to limit the right to trial de novo, usually by imposing a penalty on the side that rejects the arbitrator's decision, if that party wins less (or loses more) at trial than the arbitrator would have awarded. The penalty often consists of paying the other side all its costs, and sometimes attorney fees, for the arbitration.

In a stipulated arbitration, the parties may select any arbitration service and any set of arbitration procedural rules. They may use the local court's judicial arbitration system (if it is available for voluntary arbitrations), the American Arbitration Association or any other private arbitration service they choose. Once the procedural rules and other limits have been chosen, the lawyers for the two sides put the agreement into written form—called a *Stipulation to Submit to Arbitration*—and file it with the court.

8. When may the Plaintiff choose arbitration without the Defendant's consent?

In many courts, the Plaintiff has the option to "elect" non-binding arbitration in certain cases, whether or not Defendant wants it. Generally, the Plaintiff can elect arbitration unilaterally only if there are few parties involved and Plaintiff claims damages below a certain limit. Usually, Plaintiff may not elect arbitration until the case is *at issue*, meaning that most discovery and pretrial motions have been completed and the case is ready to be set for trial.

9. How does a Plaintiff elect arbitration?

A Plaintiff may elect arbitration by requesting it in a document called an *At-Issue Memorandum*, *Trial Setting Statement*, *Case Management Conference Statement* or the like. (See Chapter 9, Section I.) In this document, Plaintiff tells the court that the case is ready for trial and provides other information—about the other parties, Plaintiff's claimed damages and the nature of the dispute—necessary for a judge to decide whether an election of arbitration is proper under the court's rules. Some courts require the Plaintiff to request arbitration in a separate document called *Plaintiff's Election of Arbitration*, filed no later than 60 to 90 days before the date set for trial.

10. What are the ground rules for Plaintiff-elected arbitration?

Plaintiff's right to elect arbitration, and the procedures to be used, are determined by each court's own rules. These rules often include a limit on the amount Plaintiff may win in arbitration, usually between $25,000 and $100,000. Also, local rules often provide that certain cases—those in which financial compensation is not the most significant relief requested—may not be eligible at all for Plaintiff-elected arbitration. For example, evictions, domestic relations matters, declaratory relief actions and cases seeking injunctive relief are seldom arbitrated.

Plaintiff-elected arbitration is always non-binding, meaning that either Plaintiff or Defendant may reject the arbitrator's decision and move the case back into litigation if unhappy with the outcome. A party does this by filing a *Request for Trial de Novo*, usually within ten to 30 days of the arbitrator's decision. However, local rules often provide a potential penalty for a Plaintiff who forces arbitration then complains about the result. In these courts, the Plaintiff must pay the other party's entire costs for the arbitration, including attorney fees, if Plaintiff wins lower damages after a trial than the arbitrator would have awarded.

11. How does mandatory, court-ordered arbitration work?

In many courts, a judge can send a case to arbitration even if neither party requests or wants it. Each party retains the right to reject the arbitrator's decision and return the case to litigation after this *mandatory arbitration* is over. Nonetheless, courts still push many smaller cases into arbitration. Some cases end there; for those that don't, the arbitration decision often changes the losing side's view of the case, making the parties more likely to settle out of court.

12. When might a court require the parties to arbitrate?

In courts that use mandatory arbitration, there are two moments in the litigation process when a judge typically orders a lawsuit into arbitration. The first comes near the very beginning of the case, immediately after the Defendant has filed an Answer. A judge will look at the amount of money at stake in the case—and whether there are any issues in the case that make arbitration inappropriate—and immediately refer the case to arbitration if it qualifies under that court's rules.

Judges also might order a case to arbitration later in the process, after each side has filed an *At-Issue Memorandum, Trial Setting Statement, Status Conference Statement, Case Management Conference Statement* or the like, which tells the judge that the lawsuit is ready for trial. (See Chapter 9, Section I.) A judge reviews that document and decides if the case is suitable for mandatory arbitration under that court's local rules. Sometimes the judge makes this decision alone, without consulting with the parties or lawyers. In other courts, the judge holds a conference with the lawyers and the parties—called something like *Arbitration Conference, Case Management Conference* or *Status Conference*—at which the judge listens to reasons why either side thinks the case should or should not be sent to arbitration. The judge makes the final decision, however.

13. What are the usual ground rules for mandatory arbitration?

If a case is sent to mandatory arbitration, court rules usually require that all litigation procedures cease until the arbitration is completed. An exception is made for discovery, which most courts allow to continue until shortly—ten-14 days—before the arbitration hearing. Local rules in many courts also limit the amount of money either party may win in mandatory arbitration.

Once the arbitrator has been chosen (see Question 14), the arbitrator's office notifies both sides of an arbitration hearing date, usually within 30-60 days. As with court dates, it is possible to change the arbitration date if it conflicts with some important event previously scheduled by a lawyer or party. However, if changing the date would delay the arbitration more than a certain time—usually 60 days—after the arbitrator has been selected, the party requesting the change might have to ask the court's permission.

Mandatory arbitration is always non-binding. After the arbitration is over, either party may reject the arbitrator's decision and return the case to normal litigation. However, in some courts a party who wins the arbitration hearing but requests a trial de novo faces a penalty if that party does not do better at trial—which may include paying all of the opposing side's costs and attorney fees for the "wasted" arbitration.

14. How are arbitrators typically selected?

Once the parties have agreed, or been sent, to judicial arbitration, their first task is to select an arbitrator. Under some arbitration rules, certain cases are heard by a panel of three arbitrators rather than only one. The arbitration service—whether run by the court or by a private company—sends to the lawyers for both sides a list of potential arbitrators (usually other lawyers and retired judges). If a single arbitrator will hear the case, the list usually includes three choices. If a panel of three arbitrators will preside, the list usually has five names. If the case involves a highly specialized area of law, the list might include arbitrators with professional experience in that field.

The list usually includes a mix of lawyer-arbitrators who mostly represent Plaintiffs, and others who defend corporate or insurance entities.

After receiving this list, each party's lawyer does a bit of investigating about these potential arbitrators. The lawyers phone other lawyers, check the kind of work each arbitrator's firm does and generally sniff around the legal community to get a sense of whether any of the arbitrators might be slightly predisposed for or against either side of the lawsuit. Then, each side rejects one potential arbitrator from the list.

This decision can be a crapshoot. An arbitrator who does legal work mostly for plaintiffs will not necessarily rule in favor of a Plaintiff in an arbitration, nor will a defense lawyer always find for the defendant. Nonetheless, since some choice has to be made, it usually follows these Plaintiffs' lawyer/Defendants' lawyer lines. When the decision has been made, each side sends a *Notice of Rejection of Arbitrator*—in some systems, just a letter—to the arbitration service and the other party.

When each party has rejected one proposed arbitrator, usually only one arbitrator is left standing. If both sides reject the same arbitrator, the arbitration service chooses one of the remaining two. (If there are to be three arbitrators, the list will include five, and the parties' elimination of two leaves a panel of three.) The arbitration service then sends out a *Notice of Assignment of Arbitrator*.

The Parties May Choose Their Own Arbitrator

Occasionally, the opposing lawyers know someone they agree would be an excellent arbitrator for the case. If the lawyers are from the same city, most likely they know some other lawyers in common. Among these, they may know someone whom they respect as both knowledgeable in the subject of the dispute and absolutely fair. If the parties want to choose that person as their arbitrator without going through an arbitration service, they are usually allowed to do so. If the arbitration is by stipulation, the parties may simply name the arbitrator in their agreement. If the arbitration was initiated by the Plaintiff or ordered by the court, most courts look favorably on a choice both parties endorse, and are likely to grant the parties permission to use an outside arbitrator.

Faster. In today's crowded court systems, it can take anywhere from one to five years from the time a lawsuit is filed until it reaches trial. Even after discovery is completed and the case is considered "at issue" —ready for trial—it may still take another year or two. On the other hand, when a case is referred to arbitration, the hearing is held within months. And the hearing itself may last a day or less, as opposed to many days or even weeks for a jury trial.

Cheaper. The arbitration process usually is much less expensive than a courtroom trial, especially one with a jury. The proceedings have far fewer technical rules than a courtroom trial and so require much less lawyer preparation. (See Section III.) Because the hearing is much simpler and faster, neither attorney fees nor litigation costs are as high as they would be for a trial.

Section II: Arbitration or Trial?

15. What are the advantages of arbitration over trial?

The main advantages of arbitrating a dispute instead of waiting for a regular courtroom trial are speed and reduced cost.

Arbitration Presentations Are Not Permanent Records

One of the reasons lawyers are willing to try non-binding arbitration is that the live testimony presented at the hearing is usually not recorded. Because their testimony is not recorded, the witnesses are not bound by the specific words they utter, which reduces considerably the damage of a "mistake" made at non-binding arbitration. However, in some courts, a written affidavit or declaration submitted in an arbitration may be used later to "impeach" a witness who testifies differently at trial. (See Chapter 9, Question 48.) A lawyer using sworn witness statements in an arbitration must be very careful; those statements may become part of the permanent record in the case.

Nor are the parties tied to the arguments their lawyers make in arbitration. The lawyers are free to change their arguments at trial if they feel that the previous arguments did not work well at the arbitration. In fact, lawyers sometimes use non-binding arbitration primarily as a safe proving ground for a client's side of the story—to see how well the client and the other party perform, how the other side's lawyer presents the case and challenges the client's evidence and how a neutral outsider, the arbitrator, responds to the competing stories.

16. Can I benefit from non-binding arbitration even if the other side rejects the arbitrator's decision and returns the case to litigation?

Yes. Even if a party rejects a non-binding arbitration award and returns the case to litigation, both sides might benefit from the arbitrator's assessment of the case. In the midst of litigation, the people most deeply involved often have trouble seeing the strengths and weaknesses of both sides. The arbitrator's assessment of the case often falls somewhere in between what each of the parties hoped for. And that dose of reality frequently leads both sides to reduce their expectations. Parties are forced to consider that a judge or jury might see the case as the arbitrator did. This reassessment often brings the parties closer together in their expectations, which can lead to a negotiated settlement.

Arbitration may also be useful as a relatively painless dry run through the trial process. Because the lawyers and parties know that the arbitrator's decision may be rejected, they can present their testimony and legal arguments with minimal stress. This dry run permits lawyers to work the kinks out of testimony and arguments, and highlights strengths and weaknesses on both sides.

Whether you receive the same kind of decision from an arbitrator that you might get from a jury depends somewhat on the emotional component of your case. An arbitrator, usually a lawyer, is experienced in hearing all sorts of tales about rotten scoundrels, innocent victims and the related miseries of legal disputes. These hardened veterans of the legal wars will not respond to a case with the emotion and compassion a jury might provide. For example, if you are a Plaintiff who has been seriously injured by the carelessness of a large company, an arbitrator might award you a fair amount of money but not nearly as much as a sympathetic jury might. Conversely, if you are a Defendant who is legally responsible for Plaintiff's damages only because of some hyper-technical legal rule—even though you acted in what most people would consider a reasonable, commonsense way—a jury might sympathize with you more than an arbitrator would.

17. Are there reasons to skip non-binding arbitration?

The greatest single disadvantage of non-binding arbitration is that, if either side rejects the decision, the process might have wasted time and money. Although arbitration requires much less detailed preparation than trial, it still takes a considerable amount of lawyer and client energy. Arbitration costs are not as high as litigation expenses, but they can easily run into many hundreds, if not thousands, of dollars. And if the client is paying the lawyer by the hour, attorney fees for the arbitration can easily run to several thousand dollars over and above other costs. (The potential waste of both energy and money can be reduced somewhat by a low-key approach to the process. See Section III.)

The risk that the arbitration will be a futile, costly exercise often depends on each party's posture before the hearing. Large business and insurance company Defendants tend to reject any arbitration award that is not a substantial victory—they have plenty of money to burn on continued litigation. And if the parties hold widely separate positions—for example, Defendant denies any responsibility for Plaintiff's damages and refuses to offer any settlement, or Plaintiff demands a settlement many times larger than Defendant is prepared to pay—then the losing side in the arbitration almost surely will reject the arbitrator's decision. If, on the other hand, both sides understand that Plaintiff is entitled to some recovery from Defendant and merely disagree on the amount, they are much more likely to accept an arbitrator's decision about damages.

Sometimes, a lawyer believes arbitration would reveal too much about one side's strategy for the trial or highlight certain weaknesses in that side's case. If the lawyer believes that the other side is almost certain to reject any good result the lawyer could obtain in arbitration, the lawyer might counsel the client to skip the arbitration process altogether and save their time and energy for trial.

18. When should I consider binding arbitration?

The great majority of parties who agree to arbitrate their cases choose non-binding arbitration because it offers the chance to return to litigation if they don't like the arbitration outcome. Many lawyers fear an arbitrator's misunderstanding of the facts or incorrect interpretation of the law, from which the losing party in binding arbitration would have no recourse. Binding arbitration lacks the escape hatch of rejecting the arbitrator's unfavorable decision. Moreover, binding arbitration lacks the built-in safeguards of litigation, such as a verbatim record showing the arbitrator's misunderstanding of facts or laws, the right to ask for reconsideration and the right to appeal to a higher court. For all these reasons, lawyers most often advise their clients not to put all the case's eggs in a binding arbitration basket.

Despite these risks, however, it might make good sense for some litigants to choose binding rather than non-binding arbitration, assuming the other side is willing. Binding arbitration can offer these advantages:

- **Saves time and money.** The great advantage of any kind of arbitration is its substantial savings in time and expense over a trial. Yet in non-binding arbitration, a litigant could spend time, energy and money to win an arbitrator's decision, only to have the other side reject the decision and go to trial. This is a particularly serious risk for a party who is paying hourly attorney fees out of pocket. On the other hand, if a party believes an arbitrator would decide the case as favorably as a jury, arbitration offers the great advantage of costing far less and providing an answer far sooner. In binding arbitration, the parties don't have to worry about those advantages being wiped out if the other side is unhappy with the outcome.

- **Avoids involving a jury.** Sometimes a party presents an emotional appeal that is likely to win great sympathy from a jury—for example, a vulnerable individual who seems to have been wronged by an impersonal corporation. On the other hand, a party might present an unfavorable picture to a jury—for example, someone who has taken advantage of business sense or bargaining power to get the best of the opposing party in a business or personal transaction. A party who is likely to appear much less favorably to a jury might do better if the case is decided by a professional arbitrator, who is less likely to be swayed by the case's emotional appeal.

- **Allows for complicated facts or laws.** If a case will require the decision maker to sort out complicated facts, an arbitrator might do a better job than a jury. For technical or otherwise specialized disputes—disputes over construction defects, intellectual property or securities transactions, for example—the parties can choose an arbitrator with expertise in the field. Similarly, if there is a complex set of legal rules that will determine the winner and loser of the lawsuit, an arbitrator is more apt than a jury to apply the rules correctly. So, if one party will rely on a complex set of facts or laws while the opposing side has a simple or emotional appeal, the party with the complicated case might do better in front of an arbitrator.

Section III: Preparing for Arbitration

19. How much energy should my lawyer and I spend on a non-binding arbitration?

There are two basic approaches a party might take to non-binding arbitration. Some parties and lawyers treat non-binding arbitration as a warm-up exercise on which to spend little time, energy or money. They assume that one side or another will reject the arbitration decision and the case will return to litigation. If the arbitrator's decision turns out badly for a party who made little effort, it won't matter much (in this view) because the party can request a trial de novo.

However, some lawyers take the position that it is always important to get the best result possible in arbitration, and that lawyer and client should extensively prepare for the hearing. They believe that a positive result in arbitration might convince the other side to accept the arbitrator's decision rather than spend the time and money to go through a trial which might have the same outcome. A good arbitration result might also move the other side toward a good settlement offer.

There are several reasons why a well-prepared arbitration with a good result might lead the other side to accept the decision or to offer much improved settlement terms:

- It proves to the other side that the lawyer and client can put together a good case and are willing to spend the time and money to do so
- It might shake the other party's stubborn, even irrational confidence in its position (sometimes held against a lawyer's advice), and
- A good arbitration decision might affect how the judge who presides over settlement negotiations views the case. (See Chapter 8.) A settlement judge uses the likely outcome of a trial as a major arguing point to push a reluctant party to settle. The

arbitrator's decision provides the judge with a good indication of what that outcome might be.

20. How does a lawyer prepare for an arbitration hearing?

A lawyer's first task in preparing for an arbitration hearing is to figure out what evidence is needed to present the client's side of the lawsuit "story." Then the lawyer must gather this evidence from material obtained during discovery (deposition testimony, answers to interrogatories and documents produced—see Chapter 4) and from the lawyer's independent investigation.

One of the great cost- and time-saving advantages of arbitration is that testimony from any witness other than a party may be presented in sworn written statements; witnesses do not have to make a personal appearance at the hearing. Each side will already have deposed all the important witnesses, so a lawyer can present a favorable edited version of a witnesses's testimony from the deposition transcript. In practice, both sides usually present most of their evidence through this short-cut—both have an interest in keeping the arbitration process simple and inexpensive.

However, a party may choose to present any witness in person—a good idea if the witness is particularly helpful and persuasive. If a lawyer decides that in-person testimony by friendly witnesses will help the case, the

lawyer will go through the testimony with the witnesses prior to the hearing. A lawyer can also demand that witnesses who work for or are otherwise under the direction of the opposing party appear in person at the arbitration hearing. This might be advisable if the witness is important and makes the other side look bad.

21. What documents does a lawyer prepare for an arbitration hearing?

A lawyer must prepare certain forms to send to the arbitrator(s) and the opposing side, notifying them of the evidence the lawyer intends to introduce at the hearing. One form—usually called something like *Notice of Intent to Introduce Documents*— describes written materials to be presented at the hearing. Usually, it must list every deposition transcript, interrogatory answer, document and sworn statement the lawyer intends to present. This form must be sent to the other side and the arbitrator(s) ten-15 days before the hearing.

A lawyer may also send a *Demand That Witness Appear*. This form notifies the arbitrator(s) and the other side of any witness the lawyer intends to have testify in person at the hearing. If the witness works for or is otherwise under the direction of the opposing party, this form tells the other side to bring the witness to the hearing. For independent witnesses (ones the opposing party does not control), this form asks the arbitration office to issue an official subpoena ordering the witness to appear.

Finally, the lawyer prepares what is called an *Arbitration Statement* or *Arbitration Brief*. See Question 22.

22. What is an Arbitration Statement?

An Arbitration Statement or Arbitration Brief summarizes the entire case. It is the first description of each party's version of the dispute and its legal issues that the arbitrator sees. The Arbitration Statement:

- describes the parties
- explains the background of the dispute
- puts forth the party's version of the facts
- makes arguments that support the party's legal positions
- responds to legal arguments anticipated from the other side, and
- describes the damages suffered (for Plaintiff), or counters the other side's claim of damages (for Defendant).

The Arbitration Statement can be extremely detailed and complex, describing precisely what the evidence will show and arguing all the fine legal points in full. In a non-binding arbitration, however, a lawyer might instead submit only a short, simple description of the case and its legal issues. If the arbitration is non-binding, the party's overall approach to the process will dictate how much time, effort and client's money a lawyer puts into the Arbitration Statement.

23. What tactical considerations might apply to the Arbitration Statement in a non-binding arbitration?

A lawyer might choose not to include certain pieces of evidence or certain arguments in the Arbitration Statement. If the lawyer believes that the non-binding arbitration is unlikely to end the case, it might be prudent not to reveal to the other side exactly how the lawyer would present the case to a jury. The lawyer might hold back evidence more likely to sway a jury than a professional arbitrator—for example, material attacking the other party's credibility—or technical matters, such as the opinion of an expert, about which the lawyer does not yet want to "educate" the other side.

How You Can Help Your Lawyer By Preparing for Arbitration

In an arbitration hearing, you have your first chance to tell your side of the story under the friendly guidance of your own lawyer. With your lawyer's help, you need to prepare that story, developing ways to emphasize its strengths and avoid or explain its weaknesses. You must also prepare for questions from the other side's attorney. By this point, you will probably already have been through your deposition, so the uncomfortable experience of being questioned will already be somewhat familiar. You should review the transcript of that deposition testimony to learn from both its high and low points.

There are several other steps you might take to prepare to testify at the arbitration hearing.

Review any documents with which you might be expected to be familiar. And go over crucial aspects of the testimony of other important witnesses. Your lawyer can help you prepare by:

- identifying documents and testimony for you to review and explaining why each is significant
- going over what your lawyer will ask you when you testify
- discussing how your lawyer hopes you will respond, and
- preparing you for the other lawyer's questions.

If you are entering binding arbitration, this preparation should certainly include an actual dry run of your entire testimony, complete with cross-examination by another lawyer (see the discussion of preparing for your own deposition at Chapter 4, Section V). For non-binding arbitration, the thoroughness and intensity of this preparation depends on how aggressive you and your lawyer have decided to be in the arbitration process.

Keeping Your Cool

An arbitration hearing may be the first time since the case was filed that you come face to face with your lawsuit opponent. It may be the first time you will have to listen to his or her version of events—a version that, at the very least, will conflict with yours and might even infuriate you. To prepare for the hearing, you must get ready to keep your emotions in check and to focus on what you need to say in your own testimony.

You should also be prepared for the remarks you will hear from the opposing lawyer. You might have already felt the lash of this lawyer's cross-examination during your deposition. But the arbitration hearing might be the first time you will hear the lawyer's full argumentative talents describing the case—and perhaps your personal character—in ways that are offensive or even hurtful to you. You must be ready to listen to these remarks without giving an immediate and angry response. To counter the other side's characterization of you and version of events, you must instead rely on the quality of your own testimony, and on the skills and preparation of your lawyer.

Section IV: The Arbitration Hearing and Decision

24. What are the basic mechanics of the arbitration hearing itself?

Informality is the hallmark of most arbitration hearings. This begins with the location. The hearing is usually held in the office of the arbitrator, or at the offices of the arbitration service, rather than in a courtroom. The arbitrator, or panel of arbitrators, conducts the hearing around a table in a conference room or library, or perhaps even in an arbitrator's private office. There is usually no court clerk or stenographer. In fact, there is usually no one present except for the arbitrator(s), the lawyers and the parties.

Unlike court hearings, which operate with stiff legal etiquette and formal rules about how evidence may be presented, arbitrations are fairly simple. Each party's story is presented through the same kind of question-and-answer process with the lawyers as in a deposition or a court hearing, but arbitrators usually are not very concerned about formal objections to the way in which questions are posed or answers given. Most of those rules are intended to prevent impressionable jurors from hearing unreliable things that might improperly affect their perception of the case. For an experienced arbitrator, this is not a problem—arbitrators are well able to sort out proper evidence from improper without the help of objections and interruptions from lawyers. As a result, a party's

testimony is usually much less heated and chaotic, and takes less time, than the party's deposition.

Work Out a Communication System With Your Lawyer

Arbitration hearings tend to fly by quickly. Many are completed in only a couple of hours. There may not be many breaks during which you can consult with your lawyer, give helpful comments about things the other side has said or get help with your own testimony. And because of the close quarters, it may not be easy to speak privately to your lawyer while the hearing is going on. You should work out, ahead of time, a way to let your lawyer know when you have something important to say or to ask about privately. Your lawyer will then immediately know when to take a break to discuss the matter with you.

Because the lawyers submit full written legal arguments before the hearing (in the Arbitration Statement or Arbitration Brief—see Question 22), arbitrators usually limit the lawyers' speaking time. Each lawyer makes an opening statement, often restricted to five minutes or so. An arbitrator already knows what the case is about and does not need the kind of extensive scene-setting that a jury might find useful. At the end of the hearing, each lawyer is permitted a closing argument, which might be restricted to comments about testimony or other evidence produced at the hearing itself.

often limited to questions that directly probe the crucial issues in the case, without the long side roads into background, personal life and other peripheral matters permitted in a deposition.

An Arbitrator Is Not a Mediator

Although arbitration is much less formal than a trial, an arbitrator's role is very much like that of a combined judge and jury. The arbitrator listens to testimony, receives other evidence, controls the proceedings, keeps a harness on the lawyers, considers and rules on legal arguments, then renders a decision. What an arbitrator does *not* do is try to work things out between the parties. Unlike a mediator, whose job is to bring the parties together, or a judge, who may try to forge a settlement, an arbitrator begins the hearing without any preliminary attempts to settle the case.

25. What will it be like when I testify at an arbitration hearing?

A party testifies at an arbitration hearing in the same question-and-answer format as in a deposition. Unlike a deposition, however, the process is likely to begin with friendly questioning from the party's own lawyer, before cross-examination by the lawyer for the other side. Also, an arbitrator or panel of arbitrators is likely to curtail cross-examination. The opposing party's lawyer is

Who's on First?

In a trial, the Plaintiff's side presents its evidence first. But that doesn't always mean that the Plaintiff testifies before the Defendant. In most states, a Plaintiff may call the Defendant to testify at trial before the Plaintiff or any other witness. Many Plaintiffs' lawyers like to put the Defendant on the hot seat before the Defendant has a chance to hear any other evidence. This also allows the Plaintiff to listen to the Defendant before having to give his or her own evidence.

However, arbitrators do not always permit this approach. Each arbitrator decides whether the Plaintiff is allowed to call the Defendant first or must start with Plaintiff's own evidence. If you are the Defendant, have your lawyer find out from the arbitrator(s) before the hearing what the witness order will be. If you will have to begin your testimony under hostile questioning by the Plaintiff's lawyer, your own lawyer should prepare you for it. Ask your lawyer what points to make and pitfalls to avoid during that hostile questioning, as well as what to hold back, if possible, until your own lawyer asks the questions.

Often, the most important aspect of the hearing is the arbitrator's impression of the parties' testimony. In many cases, an arbitrator must determine which party's personal version of crucial facts seems more likely. As a part of this determination, an arbitrator may question the parties directly. If an arbitrator asks a question, the answer is probably important. Even if the question seems minor, the way in which the party answers could be significant—when an arbitrator asks a question directly, he or she is likely to pay particularly close attention to the fullness and honesty of the reply.

26. How long does an arbitrator take to make a decision?

An arbitrator usually decides the case very soon after the hearing, usually within ten days. If there has been a panel of arbitrators, it might take a bit longer for the different arbitrators to consider and coordinate their decision.

27. What is typically included in an arbitration decision?

Arbitration decisions usually come in the form of a document called an *Arbitration Award*, a copy of which is sent to lawyers for both parties. The Award will indicate:

- which party won
- how much money, if any, the losing party is to pay

- what other relief—for example, the return of property or the termination of a lease or contract—has been granted, and
- whether the losing party is to pay any of the winning party's attorney fees, or the costs of litigation or arbitration.

In the Arbitration Award, the arbitrator(s) may briefly explain how and why the particular decision was reached. However, an arbitrator is not under any obligation to explain the decision; many Arbitration Awards contain only bare-bones statements of who won and how much.

28. How do I decide whether to accept or reject a non-binding arbitration decision?

The parties usually have only a short time —15 to 30 days—to decide whether to accept or reject a non-binding arbitration decision. In some cases, the decision is obvious. If the award is completely, or very heavily, in one side's favor, the other side immediately rejects it. However, if the award is not so clear cut—for example, if the decision goes in Plaintiff's favor but not nearly in the amount Plaintiff sought—then both parties face a decision. In these situations, lawyer and client must consider several factors:

- **Likelihood of doing better at trial.** Lawyer and client need to have a heart-to-heart discussion about whether they are likely to do much better at trial than they have in arbitration. They should realistically assess the client's testimony and that of other important witnesses. Can it improve? How will it play in front of a jury? Will other witnesses seem better or worse in person than in their written testimony presented at the arbitration? Can the lawyer do more at trial? Will the other side be able to repair mistakes made at arbitration and present a stronger case at trial?

- **Costs and benefits.** Trials are expensive. And if the client is paying the lawyer by the hour, attorney fees will rise dramatically. Even if the lawyer is paid on a contingency fee basis, the lawyer's percentage may go up sharply as the trial approaches. (See Chapter 1, Section III.) A client must consider whether the added expenses and fees are likely to offset any added compensation that might be won (Plaintiff), or reduced damages that might have to be paid (Defendant), after a trial.

- **Risk of paying the other side's costs and attorney fees.** If one party has made a claim for the other side to pay its attorney fees, lawyer and client must consider whether the court is likely to grant this request. They must also consider the possibility of having to pay the other side's litigation costs, which will rise sharply if the case is tried. If the arbitration award ordered payment of the other side's attorney fees, the party faces a serious risk that a judge or jury will make the same decision about fees (which by then will be much higher).

- **Risk of penalty for not doing better.** In some courts, a party who requests trial de novo and wins less at trial than at the arbitration must pay a penalty: the other side's attorney fees for the arbitration, or the trial, or both (depending on each court's rules). Because this penalty is imposed by a court's arbitration rules, it can be exacted even if the other side did not request attorney fees in its pleadings. ∎

Chapter 8

Settling a Lawsuit

How You Can Help Your Lawyer

The vast majority of all civil lawsuits are settled before trial; at some point in the litigation the parties, through their lawyers, almost certainly will engage in serious settlement negotiations. Some opposing parties discuss settling their lawsuit several times during the litigation process. Other parties might never talk about settlement until a judge requires it on the eve of trial. This Chapter explains how and when settlements are negotiated, how a judge can help settle a case, how settlement payments are determined and structured and what settlement documents are necessary to formally end a lawsuit.

Section I: Setting Settlement Goals and Starting Negotiations

1. Can my lawyer tell me what my case is worth?

One of the most common questions clients ask their lawyers in the early stages of a lawsuit is "What do you think would be a fair settlement of my case?" Most good lawyers will not offer a simple answer. There is no mathematical calculation or legal formula for deciding whether a settlement is "fair." Until the facts in the case have been fully developed, the lawyer will not even know the range of reasonable settlement possibilities.

Although a lawyer cannot tell a client whether a particular settlement would be fair or satisfying to the client, it is part of the lawyer's job to discuss realistic settlement possibilities as the litigation moves along. A lawyer can assess how much the Defendant might be willing and able to pay (including any limits on insurance coverage), what non-monetary settlement options might be available, what legal maneuvers might strike a serious or fatal blow to either side and what a jury might award the Plaintiff, based on the lawyer's local experience and jury verdicts in similar cases. The lawyer should adjust these assessments after each significant development in the case; if a damaging piece of evidence appears, a party or other key witness does particularly well or poorly in a deposition or a judge's ruling seriously helps or harms the client's case, these settlement possibilities will change.

Ultimately, it is the client who must decide whether to accept or reject a particular settlement. Although the lawyer can provide useful advice and information, only the client can decide whether a particular settlement meets the client's needs.

2. How can I decide how much to offer or accept to settle my lawsuit?

Lawyer and client must begin discussing settlement in the early stages of the case; negotiations with the other side might begin even before the first pleadings are completed. From the beginning, lawyer and client should sketch the general outlines of a settlement that might be both satisfactory to the client and realistically obtainable from the other side. However, this assessment will certainly change as the case goes along. The client's chances of winning may seem to go up or down (and probably both). Mounting litigation costs and attorney fees may sap the client's willingness to continue fighting the lawsuit. And both parties' ability to meet or accept certain settlement terms may change. As a result, a client and lawyer usually must periodically revise the settlement goals they set earlier in the case.

Some of the primary factors to consider in setting, and revising, settlement goals include:

- **Likely outcome.** In setting a settlement goal, client and lawyer must first consider the cost of failing to settle: Is the case likely to end before trial? What is likely to happen if the case goes to trial? Which party will win? How much will the loser have to pay? These assessments must be adjusted periodically, depending on developments during the litigation. (Question 6 discusses moments in a lawsuit when the odds might shift and therefore when settlement deadlocks are likely to be broken.)

- **Expense of litigating.** Client and lawyer must also consider the cost of litigating. If a party wins the case only after a long and expensive legal battle, the victory might be hollow. If a party loses at trial and also has to pay the other side's litigation costs, the pain of failing to settle the case will be that

much sharper. And if a party might have to pay the other side's attorney fees after losing at trial, the party must consider this huge potential expense in setting a reasonable settlement goal.

- **Satisfactory amount of money.** Both a Plaintiff seeking money and a Defendant being asked to pay it must arrive at a settlement amount with which they would be satisfied. This amount is not necessarily what the litigant would "like," or thinks would be "fair." A lawyer tries to negotiate an amount that would please the client; if the other side eventually agrees to that amount, that's great. But in setting settlement goals, lawyer and client must agree on a figure that the client would consider satisfactory given all the risks, costs and other stresses of litigation—not what the client would request from a genie in a bottle.

- **Realistic amount of money.** It's one thing for a Plaintiff to decide on a settlement amount that would be satisfactory. But if that amount is more than Defendant can pay, it is not a realistic settlement goal. Plaintiff must factor in the other side's assets and income (about which some information might be available through discovery —see Chapter 4). If the other side has insurance coverage for the dispute, Plaintiff must consider the *policy limits* —the maximum such insurance would pay. In most cases, these insurance policy limits are the most that can be hoped for in settlement. Only a party that has considerable personal or business assets will be able to pay beyond the insurance coverage.

- **Feasible non-monetary solutions.** If money is not the only goal of the litigation, the parties must figure out what arrangements between or among them will work for the future. For example, if the dispute is about control of a business or property, is there a practical way for the parties to divide or share ownership or control? If dividing control wouldn't work, could one side buy out the other? If the lawsuit concerns employment or tenancy, is a continuing relationship possible? If not, can the parties agree to part company permanently after one side compensates the other? Similarly, if the dispute is over services performed, could one party complete or redo the work, or would that merely invite more trouble?

- **Time, effort and anxiety of litigation.** A party might want to set a relatively low settlement goal—even if the party has a good chance of winning at trial—simply to get out of the lawsuit. Litigation can take years, eat up enormous energy and cause considerable stress and anxiety. Many people are unwilling to pay this price, even to get a higher monetary award. Instead, they choose to settle their lawsuits early for less than they might have won had they fully litigated the case.

Giving Your Lawyer "Settlement Authority"

Offers of settlement pop up at surprising times, in unexpected places. Whenever opposing lawyers find themselves in the same room—the courtroom (even in an altogether different case), the coffee room during a break in a deposition or the steam room at their local health club—they might talk about settlement. The same is true whenever they talk on the phone. At any of these impromptu sessions, the lawyer for the other side might make a crucial concession or float a settlement figure you would accept.

Human emotions rule much of what goes on in a lawsuit. At different times, the party on the other side might be more or less willing to fight; a settlement offer made one day might not remain on the table the next. Because of this fast-changing negotiating weather, you and your lawyer must talk regularly about your settlement goals —what you would accept or offer to settle the case. If you give your lawyer *settlement authority*—permission to settle the case without your approval once your settlement goals are met—the lawyer might be able to take advantage of a sudden and perhaps fleeting opportunity to settle the dispute. In cases with many complicated issues, this kind of settlement authority might not be practical. But if your main goal is just to win or to avoid paying money, giving your lawyer the authority to accept a certain settlement figure might allow you to grab an offer that would otherwise disappear.

3. What is typically included in a settlement?

In a settlement agreement, each of the parties gives up something. Whatever else it might include, a settlement requires the Plaintiff to end the lawsuit and not to file another concerning—lawyers say "arising out of"—the same dispute. In exchange, the Defendant agrees to dismiss any countersuit against Plaintiff. One side usually pays money to the other. If the dispute involves questions of ownership, control or possession of property or a business, those matters, too, are resolved; either party or both might agree to give up or transfer control or ownership of the asset. One or both parties might agree to perform certain acts, or refrain from certain conduct, in the future. In lawsuits with more than two parties, settlement may be negotiated between one Plaintiff and one Defendant, or by all parties simultaneously. (See Section IV.)

The parties can negotiate and settle any dispute raised in the Complaint or Cross-Complaint. Ideally, a settlement should resolve every claim, counter-claim and request for damages in the lawsuit. A settlement usually decides some or all of the following issues:

- how much money Plaintiff will be paid by one or more Defendants (or to Cross-Complainants by one or more Cross-Defendants), as compensation for damages suffered by the Plaintiff (or Cross-Complainant)
- how, when and in what amounts settlement money will be paid

- the rights and obligations of the parties regarding any real or personal property or business interest that is a subject of the dispute
- the rights and duties of the parties under any contract or other ongoing relationship that is a subject of the dispute
- any actions either party will have to undertake or cease in the future
- who will pay each side's litigation costs and attorney fees, and
- whether the terms of the settlement will be confidential.

Because the goal of a settlement is to resolve every aspect of the lawsuit once and for all, the parties virtually always give up the right to sue each other for lawsuit-related claims. Plaintiffs (and Cross-Claimants) generally agree to accept the settlement amount as payment in full for their damages —even if they later discover that their damages were more extensive, or the Defendant's conduct was more harmful, than they realized. A settlement ends the lawsuit, regardless of what either party later learns about the underlying dispute.

4. What is early neutral evaluation?

At the beginning of a lawsuit, the opposing sides usually have very different ideas about what an appropriate settlement would be. Even a lawyer and client on the same side may have very different ideas about how much a case is "worth." Because of these differences, early settlement negotiations often go nowhere. To bridge this gap before too much time and litigation expense go by, both parties might find it useful to get an informal, outside opinion about the case. The lawyers and parties can get a more realistic picture, which might help them come up with more reasonable settlement goals.

Lawyers for the parties can arrange an outside, neutral evaluation of the case informally, using a lawyer who is known, or whose good reputation is known, to both. The best choice would be a lawyer with expertise in the subject of the dispute. This evaluator might read informal written briefs summarizing the case, hear short presentations from both lawyers, then deliver an unofficial opinion about which side is likely to win the case if it goes to trial and how much the verdict might be. Both sides can then use this unofficial opinion to adjust their views of the case, and perhaps to move closer to settlement.

The two sides usually split the cost of this outside evaluation. The neutral lawyer will probably charge an hourly fee, which might run to several hundred dollars for each party. However, if the evaluation brings an early settlement of the case, this is money well spent.

5. How do lawyers get informal settlement negotiations started?

There are no inappropriate times for lawyers to discuss settlement. Either side may initiate negotiations with the other side at any point in the litigation, regardless of what is going on in the lawsuit. For tactical reasons, however, lawyers often carefully choose the moment to open settlement discussions. Many lawyers believe that appearing too eager to settle makes the other side tougher in negotiations. So, lawyers engage in a certain amount of gamesmanship. A lawyer tries to signal willingness to negotiate without appearing to wave a flag of surrender. Lawyers may initiate settlement discussions in a variety of ways, from sending a formal written settlement offer to making a casual remark during a break in a deposition.

Formal Offer of Settlement

In most courts, one side can use a procedure known as an *Offer of Judgment* or *Offer of Compromise* to call the other side's negotiating bluff. If the Plaintiff seeks only money damages, the Defendant may send the Plaintiff a formal offer stating the settlement amount the Defendant is willing to pay. Plaintiff then has a short time—usually 10-14 days—to accept this offer. (In some states, Plaintiffs may also make these offers, agreeing to settle the case if the Defendant offers a certain amount.)

If the other side accepts the offer, the case is over. If the offer is rejected, the rejecting party increases his or her risk in going to trial. If the rejecting party loses at trial, or wins less than what the other side offered, the rejecting party must pay the other side's court costs. These costs may include the sizable fees charged by expert witnesses. In some courts, the rejecting party also has to pay the other side's attorney fees from:

- the date the formal offer was rejected
- the date the formal offer was made, or
- the beginning of the case.

If you have made a reasonable offer to settle but the other side is stalling, your lawyer may want to send an Offer of Compromise. The risk of having to pay court costs may jar the other side out of its delaying tactics. Even if the other side rejects the offer, you will have the right to collect court costs if the other side wins less at trial than you had formally offered.

6. When are settlement negotiations most likely to succeed?

Although settlement negotiations may take place during any phase of the litigation, settlement is more likely at certain moments, such as:

- **Immediately following the pleadings.** When the first roar of the lawyers has died down, the parties sometimes step back and reconsider their options. Once Complaints and Amended Complaints, Demurrers and Answers have been filed, with accompanying lawyer saber-rattling (and the first round of costs and attorney fees), warring parties often consider trying to settle their dispute. When faced with the stark realities of lengthy litigation, a party may view compromise with the other side as the lesser evil.

- **After a surprising piece of evidence turns up.** During discovery (see Chapter 4), a witness might testify much differently than expected, damaging documents might turn up unexpectedly or an analysis of figures or physical evidence might provide some surprises. If the witness or evidence is important to the case, both sides might rethink their odds of winning the lawsuit. The party who lost ground because of the surprise might be willing to offer more favorable settlement terms.

- **After a party's deposition.** The sheer misery of being bombarded with hostile questions during a deposition might lead a party to consider a settlement. Even if the deposition experience does not shake up a litigant, the litigant's performance may have shaken the lawyer's belief in the strength of their case. Conversely, a party might do superbly in a deposition, impressing the lawyers for both sides and thereby improving that party's settlement position. Because so much often rides on a party's own testimony, the days following either party's deposition are often a good time to reevaluate the case and initiate settlement talks, or jump-start negotiations that have been stalled.

- **Immediately before or after an important motion.** Certain legal maneuvers —such as a Motion for Summary Judgment or Motion for Summary Adjudication of Issues (see Chapter 5, Section VIII)—can drastically change the course of a lawsuit, or end it entirely. Before a judge rules on these crucial motions, the parties' fear of losing may lead them to offer more favorable settlement terms. Parties are also more likely to settle immediately after an important motion is decided. The court's ruling on the motion may have significantly shifted each side's position. Before embarking on more litigation, the side that lost the motion might be willing to change its settlement offer sufficiently to forge an agreement.

- **The eve of trial.** After almost all the litigating is done, the court will hold one or more formal conferences intended to help settle the case before trial. (See Section II.) Even if these formal sessions fail to produce a settlement, the looming reality of trial—plus whatever progress toward settlement was made during the formal conference—may lead the parties to make last-minute settlement offers. So much pressure builds in the days right before trial, so much is at risk, that many lawyers and litigants blink. One side makes a last ditch offer to settle, which is welcomed by the other lawyer and client who are just as pressured and anxious. Probably more cases settle in the two or three weeks before trial—many on the very morning of trial, while everyone waits for an available courtroom—than during any other period of the long litigation process.

How to Help Your Lawyer Set the Tone for Settlement Negotiations

Your lawyer's ability to negotiate a settlement is determined in part by his or her relationship with the lawyer on the other side. That relationship depends in part on prior dealings between the lawyers and on the quality of your lawyer's legal work during the litigation. But it also depends on the posture you want your lawyer to take on your behalf: how you want your lawyer to approach the lawsuit and the other side.

Initially, you might direct your lawyer to be as aggressive and unyielding as possible, because you are angry at, or want to intimidate, the other side. But the other party may ignore your lawyer's posturing, and you might later decide you want to settle the case despite your feelings toward the other party. By then, your lawyer might have a hard time getting the other side to negotiate reasonably—the other side might read this changed attitude as a sign that you have lost confidence in your chances of winning the case, or that you have lost the will (or the cash flow) to keep fighting.

In contrast, if you ask your lawyer to make it clear from the outset that you are open to negotiations, your lawyer will find it easier to discuss settlement without appearing to admit "weakness." However, this strategy only works if your lawyer simultaneously demonstrates that you are able and willing to litigate thoroughly if negotiations are not fruitful.

Section II: Getting Help From the Judge: Settlement Conferences

7. How do judges assist in the settlement process?

Although the parties may engage in informal settlement negotiations at any time, most courts also require them to participate in a more formal settlement procedure. This *Settlement Conference* (sometimes called a *Mandatory Settlement Conference*) is presided over by a judge (or court referee or commissioner), who listens to both sides' views of the dispute and of the likely outcome of the case. The judge then serves as a kind of mediator, attempting to close the gap between what one side offers and the other is willing to accept.

Some courts schedule more than one Settlement Conference per case and encourage their judges to spend a lot of time and energy trying to coax the parties into settlement. In other courts, the judges do little more than observe negotiations between the parties. Regardless of the formal procedures, the success of these Conferences often depends on the personality, style and judicial philosophy of the settlement judge.

The settlement judge is selected according to the court's local rules. In large master calendar court systems, the settlement judge probably has not presided over any pretrial proceedings in the case, and will not preside over the trial if there is one. In direct calendar court systems, one judge usually hears all matters pertaining to a specific case, including the Settlement Conference. But in some of these courts, a Settlement Conference is sent to a judge other than the one who is assigned to preside over the trial. The purpose of this policy is to ensure that the trial judge is not influenced by what one party did or refused to do in settlement negotiations.

8. When do Settlement Conferences take place?

The court usually schedules a Settlement Conference during the later stages of the lawsuit, after a date has been set for trial. The judge might attend briefly to other lawsuit business, but will focus primarily on trying to settle the case. (In many courts, settlement might also be discussed at earlier conferences held to address discovery and scheduling issues, such as a Case Management Conference, Pretrial Conference or Status Conference. See Chapter 9, Sections I and III.)

Some courts hold a Settlement Conference several months before the trial. However, most courts schedule a Conference—sometimes in addition to an earlier one—in the two or three weeks before trial, when the parties are usually most willing to settle.

In addition to any Mandatory Settlement Conference, a party can almost always ask the court to set up an additional conference, if the other side agrees. Most judges are happy to try to settle cases; if both parties request a *Voluntary Settlement Conference*, the court will usually oblige and schedule one at virtually any point in the litigation. This extra Settlement Conference may be particularly useful if the lawyers for both sides believe they are close to reaching a settlement but one party or the other is stubbornly unwilling to go the extra few yards necessary to reach agreement. Having a judge speak directly to the litigant at that extra Settlement Conference sometimes provokes just enough movement to settle the case.

Mediation Might Work If a Settlement Conference Falls Just Short

Often, a Settlement Conference judge is able to bring the parties close to settling, but not quite all the way to an agreement. At that point, mediation may be a good idea. (See Chapter 6.) A mediator can spend extra time with the parties to bridge the last gap between them—time a judge might not have. And a mediator may be more skilled than a judge at helping the parties overcome their last bit of resistance. Also, the parties can speak for themselves in mediation, something that most Settlement Conferences do not allow. If the parties are interested in going to a mediator, a judge will likely put the case on hold for a brief time—a couple of weeks, perhaps—while the parties try to mediate a resolution.

9. Where are Settlement Conferences held?

A Settlement Conference does not take place out in a courtroom with all the lawyers and clients together in front of a public audience (what lawyers call in "open court"). Instead, the conference takes place in *chambers*, the judge's private office next to the courtroom, so that the lawyers and judge will be encouraged to speak freely about the case and about the parties. To further this openness, no court reporter puts what is said "on the record" unless and until a settlement has been reached.

Much of the Conference May Go On Without You

Although almost everything said in a Settlement Conference is about you and the other party, neither of you will get to hear much of it. You might be asked into chambers for the judge to get a sense of your appearance and personality—that is, how you would appear to a jury. You might also be asked in to hear the judge's view of a crucial issue, instead of hearing it second-hand, through your lawyer. And if you and the other side reach a settlement, the judge might bring you into chambers to make sure you fully understand and agree to its terms. Otherwise, the judge and the lawyers will do most of the talking behind closed doors, without you. This permits the judge and the lawyers to talk freely—sometimes with brutal frankness and disparagement—about the case, about you and the other parties and witnesses.

Because you won't hear most of what goes on, you must rely on your lawyer's ability to negotiate. By the time you reach a Settlement Conference, your lawyer will have a detailed knowledge of the facts and law of the case, your settlement goals, each side's strengths and weaknesses and the best ways to maneuver the other side's lawyer. You must also rely on your lawyer's willingness to keep you precisely informed about the closed-door sessions—what terms are proposed by the other side, how your lawyer responds to those terms and what the judge has to say about the case, the parties and the settlement offers.

10. What happens during a Settlement Conference?

A Settlement Conference typically takes place in phases. The judge speaks with each lawyer and client together, then separately with Plaintiff's lawyer, then alone with Defendant's lawyer and so on. The judge may go back and forth between the lawyers several times, then bring them together at the end of the process to hammer out details. If the parties do manage to reach an agreement, the judge usually calls all the lawyers and parties into chambers, along with a court reporter. The judge or a lawyer states the terms of the settlement "on the record"—officially recorded by the court stenographer—and the parties are asked to state that they understand and agree to those terms.

In the Settlement Conference, the judge acts as the classic devil's advocate, shifting arguments back and forth depending on the audience. When speaking with the Plaintiff's lawyer, the judge pushes the Defendant's point of view; the judge tries to get Plaintiff's lawyer to admit Defendant's strengths and Plaintiff's weaknesses, and to adjust Plaintiff's settlement position accordingly. When speaking with Defendant's lawyer, the judge reverses roles and argues from the Plaintiff's side. A good settlement judge will concede each party's strong points, even while arguing the other side's position.

A judge does not necessarily remain "neutral" during the settlement process. If a judge is convinced that one side has a stronger case, the judge will probably say so—and put more pressure on the other side to settle.

In each round of the negotiations, the judge tries to get each side to move a little closer to the other's position until, perhaps, an agreement can be reached somewhere in the middle. But the amount of settlement work any particular judge is willing to do depends greatly on that judge's personality. Some judges give up and send everyone home after one initial meeting with each party. Other judges push and push, propose innovative solutions, stay after regular court hours have ended and bring the lawyers and parties back another day—all in an effort to resolve a case the judge believes can be settled.

What Techniques Does a Settlement Judge Use to Convince the Parties to Settle?

Sometimes, a judge believes that one side is making a very fair settlement offer but the other side is being unreasonable. Or the judge might believe that both sides are stubbornly refusing to take the final, small step needed to reach an agreement. In either of these circumstances, a skilled settlement judge can become very persuasive.

Settlement judges use a variety of methods to persuade the parties. They often make forceful—sometimes almost browbeating— arguments to the lawyer for a stubborn party, warning the lawyer that no better offer will be forthcoming and going to trial would be a mistake. A judge might order the lawyer to "discuss" the settlement offer again with the client, in light of the judge's warnings. Or the judge might say the same thing directly to the client. These arguments,

particularly coming from a judge's position of authority, can be very effective in convincing a wavering lawyer or client to accept a settlement offer or to raise their own offer slightly to meet the other side.

Occasionally, a judge may use one party's special eve-of-trial request as leverage for or against that party. For example, one side might request a postponement of the trial date, over the strong objection of the other side. A judge can usually grant or deny such a request for any reason. If the case is close to settlement, the judge might let the other side know—without making any direct connection between the two matters—that the judge is likely to grant the other side's request if that party doesn't take the last little step necessary to settle the case.

11. Does my lawyer have to file any papers for the Settlement Conference?

Before the Settlement Conference, the lawyer for each party usually prepares a *Settlement Conference Statement* to send to the judge and the other parties. This document is intended primarily to educate the Settlement Conference judge about the case. It includes a history of the parties and the dispute, a discussion of the evidence, an explanation of the legal arguments to be made at trial and a description of any settlement offers that have already been made.

In the Settlement Conference Statement, each lawyer not only spells out the basic facts about the dispute but also, in the way those facts and the legal arguments are presented, tries to influence the judge's attitude toward the case. The lawyer hopes that, after reading the statement, the judge will enter the Settlement Conference already leaning toward that side's position. (As a result, one side's Settlement Conference Statement usually sounds very different from the other's.)

How You Can Help Your Lawyer Prepare for a Settlement Conference

Before a Settlement Conference, you and your lawyer should meet to do an updated evaluation of the case, including:

- what range of settlement the other side is likely to offer at the Settlement Conference

- how the judge is likely to view the case
- what the odds are of winning at trial, if the case is not settled, and
- what it might cost to go to trial.

Based on these factors, you and your lawyer can arrive at a bottom line for settlement—the absolute minimum you would accept, or maximum you would pay, to settle the case. If money is not the only issue, you must determine your baseline position on other important matters as well (for instance, keeping ownership of a business, holding title to property or requiring the other side to agree to stop certain conduct).

You and your lawyer must figure out your bottom line before entering the Settlement Conference; a settlement offer made during the conference might have to be accepted on the spot. If you don't accept, the offer might not remain on the table once the conference is over. The opposing side will begin immediately to spend time, energy and money to prepare for trial; its later offers might be somewhat less generous to account for these expenses.

Of course, the settlement negotiations might produce a much better result than your minimum or maximum position. But once you have decided on your bottom line, you can at least head for settlement negotiations knowing that whatever the other side offers or the judge suggests, your lawyer will understand the limits beyond which negotiations should not go.

The Settlement Conference Might Be Hard on You

The Settlement Conference might be a difficult experience for you, no matter how well you and your lawyer prepare for it. You may be seeing the other party for the first time in a long while. You may have to sit in the courtroom or hallway within sight of the other party, perhaps for hours, while the lawyers wrangle inside with the judge.

Also, when your lawyer reports what is being said in the judge's chambers, you will hear the full force of the argument against your side of the dispute, as presented by the other side's lawyer. You might even hear some things about yourself and your side of the dispute that are extremely unflattering.

Finally, there is the unexpected. No matter how thoroughly you and your lawyer prepare, surprises happen at Settlement Conferences. You might get blindsided by a damaging piece of evidence or legal argument revealed for the first time. Or, the other side or the judge may come up with a type of settlement offer that you and your lawyer simply have not considered. If so, you and your lawyer might have to make a difficult decision on the spot; the offer might not remain on the table after the conference is over.

12. What can the parties do if they don't reach an agreement at the first Settlement Conference?

If the conference goes well but the parties don't quite reach a settlement, or if some details need to be clarified before final terms can be reached, the lawyers might want to schedule another conference with the same judge. If the lawyers on both sides believe a settlement could be reached but they did not get much help from the Settlement Conference judge, they might try to schedule another conference with a different judge. Or the lawyers might urge their clients to mediate, if only one stubborn party is preventing a settlement. And regardless of whether the parties agree to further formal settlement procedures, the lawyers can always keep trying to negotiate a settlement between themselves.

Section III: Payment Options

13. Are there different ways a settlement amount can be paid?

In a standard lawsuit settlement, Defendant agrees to pay money to Plaintiff in exchange for Plaintiff ending the lawsuit. The money is usually paid in one lump sum within a short time after the agreement is reached or in a few periodic payments spread over a few months or a year. After receiving the money, Plaintiff's lawyer formally dismisses the lawsuit. If there are other issues in the settlement, such as changing title to property or a business, the parties prepare and exchange the necessary papers at the same time.

However, if the cash settlement payment would be large (over $100,000), a Plaintiff might suggest—or a Defendant offer—what is called a *structured settlement* rather than a lump sum payment. In a structured settlement, Defendant makes regular payments to the Plaintiff for a fixed number of years, but the payments end if the Plaintiff dies before the time is up; Defendant does not have to continue payments to Plaintiff's heirs. The total amount Plaintiff might receive over the full length of a structured settlement is much larger than a lump sum settlement in the same case would be.

14. Why would a Defendant agree to pay a larger settlement amount over time?

If there is a structured settlement, Defendant does not personally pay the full settlement amount. Instead, Defendant purchases an annuity—a contract to pay Plaintiff a set amount every month or year—for less than the lump sum amount Plaintiff would accept, and far less than the potential total annuity payments to the Plaintiff. Defendants purchase annuities from finance companies, which sell them for less than the total pay-out might be, as part of a calculated economic bet. The annuity company gets to

hold and invest the bulk of the money over the payment years, keeping the earnings. Because the payments stop if Plaintiff dies, the annuity company factors into its price the odds (based on Plaintiff's age, health and other actuarial factors) that Plaintiff will die before the company has to pay the full amount.

15. What factors should the Plaintiff consider when deciding whether to accept a structured settlement?

A Plaintiff expecting a large settlement offer should be prepared, through discussions with counsel and perhaps a financial adviser, to consider a structured settlement. Factors to consider might include:

- If payments are stretched out over many years, Plaintiff's initial payment will be small. Will the first installment meet Plaintiff's current financial needs? If not, can Plaintiff's lawyer get the other side to offer an initial lump sum payment, followed by a slightly smaller annuity?
- An annuity ends if the Plaintiff dies before the payments finish. Is the Plaintiff likely to live long enough to collect the bulk of the money? Or would the Plaintiff be better off collecting a smaller lump sum immediately, investing it and passing those assets to others on the Plaintiff's death?
- Monthly payments will not give the Plaintiff a single large sum. Will this

unnecessarily limit the Plaintiff's ability to invest the money? Or is the Plaintiff or the Plaintiff's family likely to "blow" a large lump sum soon after receiving it?

- Plaintiff might have to pay income tax on the settlement received (except for settlement amounts paid for physical injuries, which are generally not subject to income tax). Would spreading the payments out over a number of years offer Plaintiff any tax advantages?

16. Does a structured settlement affect my lawyer's contingency fee?

If the Plaintiff's attorney is working on a contingency fee basis, that fee would be calculated as a percentage of the *present value* of the structured settlement payments —a hypothetical amount that approximates how much the annuity could be sold for if it were a commodity exchanged on an open market. The Plaintiff and Plaintiff's lawyer need to know this present value to determine whether the structured settlement increases or decreases the lawyer's contingency fee, and by how much. (Most lawyers hire a specialist to calculate this present value figure.) Plaintiff and lawyer should discuss this matter when the lawyer is advising the client about the pros and cons of accepting a structured settlement versus a lump sum. If the lawyer would receive a lower fee in a structured settlement, lawyer and client might try to adjust the

terms of the annuity, or the terms of the fee agreement, to make up for this shortfall.

Section IV: Partial Settlements

17. If there are more than two parties, can some of them settle their part of the lawsuit while others continue to litigate?

Yes. There is often more than one party on either or both sides of a lawsuit. For example, a driver and passenger injured in an accident might seek damages from both the driver of the other car and that car's owner, or the driver's employer if the driver was on company business, and perhaps a city or county that carelessly maintained a dangerous roadway. In this situation, one or both Plaintiffs might settle with the other driver but continue to litigate against the driver's employer or the government agency. Similarly, a Defendant might settle with one of the Plaintiffs whose damages are clear but continue to litigate with a Plaintiff who is claiming much more than the Defendants think the case is worth.

Settlements in these multiple-party cases can present problems. A Defendant might not have enough money to fully compensate all Plaintiffs. Conversely, each of several multiple Defendants might want to settle the case separately, for as little as possible, to shift the burden of compensating Plaintiff to the remaining Defendants.

Because of these complications, an individual party sometimes refuses to settle with any other party unless and until *all* have reached a mutual settlement agreement. In many other cases, however, a Plaintiff will settle all claims against one Defendant, dismiss that Defendant from the lawsuit and continue fighting the remaining Defendants. Similarly, one of several Plaintiffs might settle with the Defendant, leaving the other Plaintiffs to continue the litigation. A settlement between certain parties that leaves other parties in the lawsuit is known as a *partial settlement.*

18. When does it make sense for a Plaintiff to reach a partial settlement with one of several Defendants?

A Plaintiff might benefit from settling quickly with one Defendant while continuing to fight the others. The money Plaintiff receives can help fund the litigation or provide ready cash for other needs. Also, by eliminating one Defendant—and that Defendant's lawyers—from the proceedings, Plaintiff's lawyer might find it easier to manage the case. A partial settlement also gives Plaintiff some sense of security in the battle with the other Defendants. The Plaintiff can more comfortably risk going to trial with the remaining Defendants, and possibly losing, because some compensation is already in the bank.

A Defendant can also benefit from settling individually with the Plaintiff relatively early in the litigation. If the Plaintiff needs ready cash, Defendant might get away with paying a lower settlement than Defendant might face later in the case. Also, the cost of litigating a multi-party lawsuit can escalate quickly, even for a Defendant whose connection to the dispute is minimal; the more parties and lawyers involved, the higher the expenses are for everyone. By settling early, a Defendant can avoid the high costs and attorney fees of a long legal battle.

In some cases, though, a Defendant who settles a lawsuit while other Defendants continue litigating might later have to prove to a judge that the settlement amount bore a fair relation to Defendant's legal responsibility in the dispute. (See Questions 20-22.) This ensures that the settling Defendant's payment to the Plaintiff was not so small as to constitute a quick-money "conspiracy" to get Plaintiff some cash while letting Defendant avoid paying a fair share of Plaintiff's damages.

19. When does it make sense for one of several Plaintiffs to reach a partial settlement with a Defendant?

If several Plaintiffs sue a single Defendant who has only limited resources, an individual Plaintiff might choose to settle quickly, and for less money than might otherwise be reasonable, to insure some compensation. If Plaintiff waits, Defendant might spend most of its resources continuing to fight the lawsuit. Or Defendant might use up its

personal assets or insurance coverage paying settlements to the other Plaintiffs.

20. Can one party challenge a partial settlement made between other parties?

A Plaintiff might reach a settlement with
one Defendant while continuing to litigate
against the others. If so, the non-settling
Defendants might believe this partial settlement was not made in "good faith," meaning
that the amount paid was not a fair share of
the settling Defendant's actual legal responsibility for the damages. Instead, the partial
settlement might appear to be the settling
Defendant's unfair escape from responsibility
—buying out of the lawsuit by offering a
small but fast sum of money to a cash-
strapped Plaintiff. Plaintiffs are willing to do
this because, in most jurisdictions, any one
Defendant who was partly the cause of the
Plaintiff's damages may be held fully responsible for all of Plaintiff's injuries; so,
Plaintiff can continue to seek the full
amount of damages against any remaining
Defendant.

A remaining Defendant who believes that
such a partial settlement is unfair may challenge it in court. Or the Plaintiff and the
settling Defendant may go to court first, to
seek a judge's decision that the partial
settlement is fair. In either case, the moving
party files a *Motion to Determine Good
Faith of Settlement*. In this motion, each
party explains to a judge why it thinks the

partial settlement is fair or unfair. The court
will consider such issues as:

- the entire amount that Plaintiff is
likely to win
- each Defendant's relative share of
responsibility for Plaintiff's damages
- whether the partial settlement amount
is reasonably related to the settling
Defendant's portion of responsibility,
considering the total amount Plaintiff
is likely to win. "Reasonably related"
is a very loose legal standard; an
amount is "reasonable" unless it is
wildly disproportionate to the total
amount and to the settling Defendant's
potential legal responsibility
- if the partial settlement amount is not
reasonably related to the total, whether
the amount is fair anyway because
the settling Defendant cannot afford
to pay more, and
- whether there is any evidence that the
Plaintiff and settling Defendant have
cut some sort of backroom deal, such
as Plaintiff letting that Defendant off
for a small payment in exchange for
the Defendant helping Plaintiff prove
the liability of the remaining Defendants
by providing damaging testimony or
other evidence.

21. When should I seek a judge's prior approval of a partial settlement?

There are some potential advantages for a
settling Plaintiff and Defendant who reach a

22. When should I challenge a partial settlement between the Plaintiff and another Defendant?

A motion to challenge the good faith of a partial settlement is not that difficult or costly to make. So, at least in terms of time and money, if one Defendant senses that a partial settlement between the Plaintiff and another Defendant is an underhanded move, it is probably worth making the motion.

But sometimes there is good reason not to challenge the settlement. In some cases, one Defendant might be better off with the settling Defendant out of the case. The litigation might be less difficult or expensive once the settling Defendant is gone.

Also, because the settling Defendant will not be present at trial, the remaining Defendant might be better able to convince a jury that the absent Defendant was the real "bad guy" in the dispute, leading the jury to let the remaining Defendant off the hook. If the remaining Defendant and lawyer decide that it is good to see the settling Defendant go, they might choose not to challenge the partial settlement, even if it seems fishy. For example, in a construction dispute, a general contractor might not mind when a subcontractor settles with the Plaintiff. At trial, the general contractor might be able to produce witnesses who put all the blame on the subcontractor. If the subcontractor is not there to present a defense, the jury might more easily find that the general contractor did not cause Plaintiff's problems.

partial settlement to ask a judge to formally approve their agreement, rather than waiting to see if another Defendant challenges it in court. If the judge determines in advance that the agreement was made in good faith, Plaintiff can accept the settlement money and get on with the litigation against the other Defendants. The settling Defendant can get on with life without fear of being dragged back into the lawsuit. If a judge rejects the settlement, Plaintiff and the settling Defendant return to litigation or further settlement negotiations immediately, without the false security that the settlement is valid.

However, there is also a potential down side to seeking a judge's approval of a partial settlement. There is no way to know whether the motion would be necessary. In fact, it might kick a sleeping dog: the motion might provoke some opposition to the settlement from remaining Defendants who otherwise would not have interfered.

Section V: Finalizing the Settlement

23. What documents are prepared to formalize a settlement agreement?

In most cases, only a few documents are needed to finalize a settlement agreement. One lawyer usually prepares these documents, then the other lawyer reviews them. If the settlement involves anything other than a simple payment of money for dismissal of the lawsuit, the client and lawyer should review the settlement documents together to ensure that the client fully understands and agrees to the terms. Once a party signs and delivers settlement papers and the lawsuit is dismissed, the parties are stuck with the written agreement; they are not permitted to complain that the terms in the documents were different from what they believed the agreement to be.

Most settlements are reached in meetings or phone calls between the lawyers. One lawyer then puts the agreed terms in a letter and sends it to the other side. If the other side makes no changes or objections to what is stated in this letter agreement, those terms become final. If an agreement to end the lawsuit was reached at a formal Settlement Conference with a judge, the judge usually has the settlement terms officially recorded by the court stenographer with all the lawyers and parties present. If so, the lawyers might not bother with a letter agreement and instead will proceed directly to the *Release*.

Usually prepared by Defendant's attorney, the Release states that the Plaintiff agrees to "release" Defendant—to give up the right to pursue this case or to file any other lawsuit against Defendant—from liability for all claims Plaintiff has, or might have, arising out of this same dispute. For example, if a lawsuit involves building construction—one side complains about the quality of the work while the other complains about not being paid—the Release would end the current lawsuit and preclude all future lawsuits between those parties concerning that building project, even if the building owner later discovered different problems with the work.

If the parties have a continuing or complex relationship, Plaintiff's lawyer must make sure the Release does not require Plaintiff to give up the right to sue Defendant for claims unrelated to the present dispute. For example, if Plaintiff sued a neighbor for damage to Plaintiff's property caused by uncontrolled water run-off, the Release should not cover any other damage the neighbor might cause. The neighbor might also have a tree whose roots are busy destroying Plaintiff's pipes or a wall that is going to collapse onto Plaintiff's property. Because these problems are entirely unrelated to the water damage, they should not be included in the Release. Plaintiff's lawyer must make sure the language of the Release is not so broad as to cover these unrelated issues.

Keeping Settlement Terms Confidential

To protect their public image, many Defendants repeatedly deny—in court and out—any wrongdoing, even if they know they will eventually be forced to take legal responsibility for their actions. But a settlement is hard to deny. Paying a settlement indicates at least some small admission of responsibility, no matter how much Defendants claim it was merely to avoid the greater cost of further litigation. The settlement amount reveals how much the Defendant was able and willing to pay—and perhaps, the strength of Plaintiff's case.

Many Defendants want to avoid public revelation of a settlement, particularly if they are large businesses that may face other current and future lawsuits. So Defendants often demand two conditions as part of any settlement agreement. First, they want the settlement document to state that it is not an admission of any wrongdoing or legal responsibility. Second, they insist that the terms of the settlement, including any money paid, remain confidential: if Plaintiff or anyone associated with Plaintiff reveals the settlement terms, Plaintiff has to refund the settlement. Some Defendants even try to get the Plaintiff to agree not to discuss any of the events that led to the lawsuit. In some courts, a judge must approve any such confidentiality agreements.

If you're a Plaintiff, such demands may be very irritating. But if you do not agree to them, particularly with a large corporate Defendant, the entire settlement might be off. If Defendant insists on confidentiality, you will have to decide whether you are willing to continue litigating—perhaps all the way through trial—to preserve your right to talk freely about the dispute.

24. Once the parties have signed the settlement documents, how is the lawsuit officially ended?

A Plaintiff formally ends a lawsuit by filing a *Dismissal With Prejudice*, sometimes called a *Notice of Dismissal* or *Stipulation for Dismissal*. The term "with prejudice" means that the case cannot be filed again, even if one party has a change of heart. Once the Dismissal With Prejudice is filed, the party who filed the Complaint is forever barred—legally prevented—from filing a lawsuit against the same opposing party regarding that same dispute. Plaintiff's lawyer files this Dismissal after both sides have signed the Release and any other settlement documents, and the settlement money or other property has been exchanged. If Defendant filed a countersuit against Plaintiff (see Chapter 3, Section III), Defendant files a Dismissal of that action, too.

25. How can I be sure that the other side will honor our agreement?

Some settlements require more than a mere exchange of money or property. A settlement might require one or both parties to do, or not do, something in the future—for example, to refrain from operating a competing business. If the settlement includes promises regarding future conduct, the parties may file what is called a *Stipulation for Judgment* or *Judgment Pursuant to Stipulation* instead of filing a Dismissal. This document does not dismiss the lawsuit but instead declares an official outcome to the case—the "Judgment"—that spells out the terms by which each side must abide. If a disagreement later erupts about whether a party is conforming to the settlement, either side may file a simple motion to have a judge decide if the Judgment's terms are being violated. If the case had been dismissed instead, the settlement agreement would be legally considered just another contract, and enforcing it would require much more complicated court procedures, perhaps even an entirely new lawsuit.

The Lawyers Handle the Money

If you are a Plaintiff, you will probably receive some money, either from Defendant or Defendant's insurance company, to settle your lawsuit. But instead of going directly to you, the money first goes to your lawyer, who puts it in the bank in what is called a "trust" account—an account separate from the lawyer's own money. The payment is held in this account as a kind of escrow. Once you sign, exchange and file all the necessary settlement and dismissal documents, your lawyer will pay you your settlement amount out of this account. You can sign those final documents knowing that the money has already been given to your lawyer.

This escrow arrangement also ensures that the lawyer gets paid. Your lawyer may withdraw from the trust account any amounts the lawyer has advanced for litigation costs that you have not yet reimbursed. Your lawyer may also take out attorney fees, either unpaid portions of hourly bills already earned or the entire fee amount if the case was handled on a contingency basis.

26. Is the settlement process any different if a government agency is a Defendant?

If a Plaintiff sues a "public entity" (a federal, state or local government or government agency), reaching an agreement with the government's lawyer does not necessarily end the lawsuit. Instead, the Plaintiff has to wait—often for months—while the government lawyer gets approval for the settlement from the government agency itself.

Governments routinely approve settlements. On rare occasions, however, a government entity may question or disapprove a settlement. This seems to happen most often when the settlement includes payment from public funds for high private attorney fees. Local governments are particularly sensitive to public criticism for using local tax money to pay what are considered high fees to private lawyers who have sued them. If a settlement runs into this kind of roadblock, Plaintiff's lawyer might have to renegotiate. Often a minor change, perhaps involving slightly smaller attorney fees, does the trick. The government lawyer often knows why the settlement was rejected, and so might have ideas about how the terms can be changed to satisfy the government body and get the settlement approved.

27. Does a settlement negotiated on behalf of a minor or other legally dependent person require a judge's attention?

Yes. In the vast majority of cases, a settlement is made between the parties, without the need for court approval. But in a few circumstances, the parties must get permission before a settlement becomes final. This requirement applies to cases in which a minor or other legally dependent person is a party. In these cases, the lawsuit representative—guardian ad litem (see Chapter 3, Section IV)—of a minor or other dependent person must apply to the court for approval of the settlement terms. A judge examines both the settlement terms and the amount of attorney fees and litigation costs to be paid by the minor or other dependent person.

The court usually approves the attorney's rate—either contingency or hourly—at the beginning of the case. (See Chapter 3, Section IV.) At the end of the case, a judge reviews the billing to make sure there are no improper charges or inflated hours. The lawyer must file papers (called something like *Motion for Approval of Settlement on Behalf of Minor*) that describe the case and the settlement terms and outline the work the lawyer has done. Usually, no one needs to appear in court. If a judge finds something to question, however, the lawyers and parties might be notified to show up in court to explain. ■

Chapter 9

Trial

How You Can Help Your Lawyer

Although the vast majority of civil lawsuits are resolved before trial, a small number of cases are not. If and when a case does get close to trial, the pace of litigation steps up considerably. As a result, the client's general confusion about the lawsuit process tends to rise sharply, as do attorney fees and litigation costs. This Chapter slows things down a bit by explaining how a case is brought to trial, how lawyer and client prepare for trial and what the trial itself is really like.

Section I: Setting the Trial Date

This section explains what steps a lawyer must take to set a case for trial.

1. What must my lawyer do to get the case set for trial?

When pretrial litigation procedures—pleadings, discovery and motions—are nearly complete, either side may file a document informing the court that the case is *at issue* (ready to be set for trial). This document is typically called an *At-Issue Memorandum, Memorandum to Set Trial Date* or, in some courts, *Motion to Set Trial Date*. Once the proper document is filed, the court:

- picks a trial date and notifies the parties
- calls the parties into court for a Trial Setting Conference, or
- calls for a hearing on the Motion to Set Trial Date.

If there is a conference or hearing, the judge discusses the case with the lawyers and picks a date for trial.

In a few courts, there is no need to file any document notifying the court that the case is ready for trial. Instead, the lawyers simply wait for the court to schedule a Trial Setting Conference (sometimes called a Status Conference), at which the judge inquires about the progress of the litigation and chooses a trial date.

2. When can my lawyer file the document requesting a trial date?

In a court with a large volume of cases, a lawyer usually files a trial date request as soon as possible after most discovery and pretrial motions have been completed. The lag time between filing the request and the actual date the court assigns for trial might be as much as a year, so the earlier the request is filed, the sooner the trial. In less crowded courts, lawyers typically wait until all discovery and other pretrial procedures are completed before requesting a trial date.

3. What information does the trial setting document contain?

Each party's At-Issue Memorandum or Motion to Set Trial Date typically:

- describes the nature of the case
- states whether a jury is demanded or whether the party is instead willing to

have the case decided by a judge alone

- gives an estimate of the time required for trial, and
- describes the latest settlement offers.

In the memorandum or motion, the party may request a Pretrial Conference (in courts where such a conference is not mandatory—see Section III, below). The party may also argue that the trial should be set sooner than it ordinarily would, or be set within a specific window of time. (See Question 6 for a discussion of the reasons why a case might be specially scheduled.) The parties may also alert the court to any unusual features of the case that might require special handling at trial. For example, if one issue might end the case entirely—eliminating the need for the rest of the trial—both parties might want that issue heard first.

4. How does the other party's lawyer respond to a request for a trial date?

When one party files an At-Issue Memo or a Motion to Set Trial Date, the other side files a response. The party might file an At-Issue Memo of its own or another document agreeing that the case is ready to be set for trial, although perhaps disagreeing about certain case details or scheduling needs. Or the other side may file an opposition arguing that the case is not ready for a trial date and explaining why. A party might oppose setting the case for trial if:

- important discovery still needs to be scheduled
- discovery disputes are yet to be resolved, or
- significant pretrial motions have not yet been heard.

 Lawyer Fees Will Jump Once the Case Is Set for Trial. Your attorney fees and litigation expenses will begin to rise sharply when a trial date is set, or shortly thereafter. Your lawyer must begin preparations for trial fairly soon after the trial is scheduled. The earlier the trial date, the faster the lawyer has to crank up the trial preparation machinery. This can run up many lawyer hours fairly quickly, particularly if there will be a Pretrial Conference (see Section III). If you are paying your lawyer a contingency fee, your fee agreement most likely provides that the fee will rise automatically (for example, from 33% to 40%) when a trial date is set or within 60 to 90 days of trial. (See Chapter 1, Section III.) Litigation expenses also tend to rise soon after a case is set for trial; expert witnesses must be deposed and trial exhibits prepared, among other incidental costs.

Because of this abrupt rise in fees and costs, you should talk to your lawyer before he or she seeks to have the case set for trial, especially if you are likely to get an early trial date. If you believe that you are close to settling the case, you might want to have your lawyer try further negotiations before setting a trial date. On the other hand, sometimes the other side makes a reasonable settlement offer only after you force the issue by setting a trial date. In this situation, you might ask your lawyer to delay trial preparations for a short time after the trial date is set (but not so long as to jeopardize trial preparations), or hold off on raising your contingency fee, while a new round of settlement negotiations takes place.

5. How is the trial date set?

Once the court has been notified that the case is ready to be set for trial, it picks a trial date based on its own calendar. In *direct calendar courts* (in which a single judge handles every aspect of a case from the first motions all the way through trial), including federal courts, the judge assigned to the case is likely to call the lawyers in for a *Trial Setting Conference*. At this Conference, the judge asks the parties how long the trial might take, then finds a spot for it in that judge's individual court calendar. In *master calendar courts* (in which the trial judge is assigned only on the date of trial), there may be a Trial Setting Conference, or the court clerk's office might select a trial date based solely on the next available slot in the entire court's trial calendar.

6. Do my lawyer and I have any say in the setting of a trial date?

In some circumstances, a party may have a good reason for trial to be scheduled within a specific time frame. If so, the party may request a trial date within that period.

An older party may request an early trial date. Laws in most courts require that trials involving parties over the age of 65 or 70 automatically move to the top of the schedule (in order to ensure that person a day in court while he or she is still alive and relatively healthy). A lawyer who represents an older client may ask for this special scheduling in the At-Issue Memorandum or in a *Motion for Preference*. The party may also request an early trial date at the Trial Setting Conference.

A party may also request an early trial date if the legal cut-off point for trial is approaching. Many courts require that a case be brought to trial within a certain number of years from the filing or serving of the Complaint. If the case is not brought to trial within that time, it is dismissed and Plaintiff is not permitted to file it again. When a case is nearing such a final cut-off date, the lawyer for the Plaintiff may ask the court to specially assign a trial date within the permitted time period. A lawyer might make the same request if a party is seriously ill and needs the trial held as soon as possible. In either case, the lawyer may raise these concerns in the At-Issue Memorandum, or formally request an earlier trial by filing a *Motion to Advance Trial Date*.

Other circumstances might prompt a lawyer to ask the court for a trial date within a specific time frame. For example, if a party or key witness is only in the state during a certain part of the year, a lawyer might ask that trial be set during that time. If the lawyer or a crucial expert witness has other commitments later in the year, the lawyer might request a trial date before those other obligations begin. In these types of situations, a lawyer may file a *Motion to Specially Set Trial Date.*

7. Can the trial date be changed if a lawyer or party becomes unavailable, or is unable to prepare in time?

During the trial setting process, a lawyer informs the court of dates when the lawyer or client would not be available for trial because of prior commitments. But because trial dates are often set well in advance, a lawyer or client cannot always anticipate a conflict that later arises. A lawyer, client or key witness might develop a serious health problem that would prevent participation in a trial at the scheduled time. More often, though, a lawyer's work schedule creates the conflict.

If other commitments would prevent a lawyer from appearing at trial, or from properly preparing the case for trial, that lawyer usually must ask the judge for a *continuance* (postponement) by filing a *Motion to Continue Trial Date.* The other side may oppose it, just like any other motion. But even if the other side does not actively oppose a continuance, a judge might still deny it if the lawyer does not have a good reason for the request. Once a case is ready for trial, the court will not want to postpone it any longer than necessary.

A judge will consider several factors in deciding whether to postpone a trial, including:

- **Proximity to the trial date.** A judge is less likely to grant a request to continue trial made shortly before the trial date. By the time trial is near, the other side will already have spent much time, energy and expense preparing. However, judges do sometimes agree to continuances even on the morning of trial, if the delay is unavoidable. (See Question 8.)

- **Prior postponements.** A judge is less likely to grant a party's request to continue the trial date if the same party has previously obtained one or more postponements. Even if the other party requested a prior postponement, the judge might hesitate to grant another delay. Judges do not like to continue a trial too often regardless of who asks for it.

- **Likelihood of actually going to trial on the date.** In master calendar courts, many cases are scheduled for trial on the same date, but only a few will actually be sent to a courtroom for trial when the day arrives. (See Question 8.) The likelihood of any given case going to trial on the scheduled date depends mostly on how long ago the Complaint was filed or the trial date was set. If a case is fairly "new"—this is its first or second scheduled trial date—it might not go out to trial in a crowded master calendar court. A judge is more likely to grant a continuance for such a new case than for one with a realistic chance of beginning trial on the scheduled date.

- **Age of the case.** Judges do not like to postpone trials in cases that have been in litigation for a long time. Postponement might push the case close to the cut-off date when a lawsuit must be either tried or dismissed for good. Even if this cut-off is not imminent, judges do not like to delay cases that are already long in the tooth.

- **Length of delay.** A judge is more likely to grant a continuance for a week or two than for months. However, most court schedules are so full that asking for a short postponement results in a long one; the next available trial date might be months away.

- **Reason for continuance.** Some reasons for a continuance request are beyond the control of the asking party, such as an unexpected serious health problem for a lawyer, client or key witness. A judge has little choice in such a case but to postpone the trial. However, delays are most commonly requested because of scheduling conflicts, particularly with a lawyer's (or occasionally a client's) other courtroom appearances. The trial takes precedence over non-trial court appearances in other cases. The court might make an exception if an important court appearance is scheduled in another case while the case set for trial is not

likely to actually begin because of the court's crowded trial calendar. But sometimes, the conflict is between different trials in different courts. In these circumstances, judges follow these general rules in deciding which of the competing cases will take precedence:

- a criminal case takes precedence over a civil case
- a federal court trial takes precedence over one in state court
- a superior (or other higher branch) court trial takes precedence over municipal, justice or common pleas court, and
- a trial scheduled earlier takes precedence over a trial scheduled later in the same level court.

These are not inflexible rules, however. A judge may consider other factors—and even speak to the judge responsible for the other trial—in making a decision.

- **Prejudice to the other side.** The court will consider how a postponement might negatively affect the other side. The judge might deny a continuance simply because the other side does not want to wait any longer for trial. But if the other side offers specific reasons why a trial postponement would be harmful—for example, if a witness, attorney or party might not be available later—the judge will be even less likely to grant the continuance request.

8. Will my trial actually begin on the scheduled date?

What happens when a client and lawyer go to court on the morning of the first scheduled trial date depends on the court's calendaring system. In direct calendar courts, where the same judge hears the case from beginning to end, a high percentage of cases actually begin trial on the first date for which they have been scheduled. However, even in these courts trial does not always start on the first scheduled date. One party might ask for a last-minute postponement based on unforeseen and unavoidable circumstances. (See Question 7.) Or, the court may experience an unexpected judicial logjam—a criminal case, or a civil case with some emergency or priority, might suddenly take precedence over the scheduled trial.

Most master calendar courts are just the opposite—trials rarely begin there on the first date for which they are scheduled. All the lawyers and parties in cases set for trial on a particular date report to a central courtroom, usually the "department" of the *presiding judge*. This central court then sends as many cases to trial as there are judges and courtrooms available. For any given date, however, these master calendar courts schedule far more cases than the courts can accommodate. This ensures that no matter how many cases settle or need to be postponed right before trial, there are always enough trials to fill all the courtrooms. As a result of this massive overbooking, most cases set for trial on any given day are delayed.

9. What happens to my case if the trial does not begin on the scheduled date?

When no courtroom is available for trial, or when for any other reason a case does not begin trial on the scheduled date, the trial is postponed in one of several ways. The presiding judge in a master calendar court, or the trial judge in a direct calendar court, may simply pick another date some months off and immediately inform the parties. Or, the judge might bring the parties back to court later for another Trial Setting Conference, at which a new trial date is set. (See Question 5.)

Often, however, a judge asks the lawyers and parties to wait and see if a courtroom becomes available. In this situation, the judge keeps the case on *stand-by for trial*, sometimes called *trailing*. Although there is no courtroom presently available, the judge wants the lawyers and parties to remain prepared to go to trial in case a courtroom opens up in the next few days. Trailing is much more common in master calendar courts, where a trial might begin in any judge's courtroom that becomes available.

Courtrooms become available when another case sent to trial settles at the last moment or when another trial that has been going on for awhile finally finishes. As a result of this uncertainty, a case set for trial on one day might remain on stand-by for another day, several days or a week. Lawyers, parties and witnesses must remain ready to begin trial within a half-day's or a day's notice by the court. If no courtroom becomes available within a certain time determined by each court—often a week— the case is rescheduled to another date some months down the road.

It is very disheartening for parties and lawyers alike to remain keyed up for days then not go to trial. However, it is far worse for them to assume that the case will not be heard, call off the witnesses, unwind emotionally and start to make other plans— then get a phone call from the court announcing that trial will start in the morning.

Section II: Judge or Jury?

Although many people in the United States believe that they have an absolute right to a trial by jury, this is not necessarily correct, at least in civil cases. This section explains when a party in a civil lawsuit has a right to a jury trial and how a party might decide whether to request a jury, if one is available.

10. When do I have a right to a jury?

The Seventh Amendment of the United States Constitution guarantees a right to jury trial in federal court civil cases, but only for those types of cases that were historically

decided by a jury. This federal right does not apply to state courts, but each state has its own right to jury trial that closely resembles the federal standard.

The distinction between those lawsuits that historically entitled the parties to a jury —called cases *at law*—and those that required only a *court trial* (by a judge without a jury)—called cases *in equity*—is extremely fuzzy. Nonetheless, some categories of cases usually fall on one side of the line or the other. Generally, a jury is available for any case in which money compensation is sought. For example, a party is entitled to a jury in the trial of a personal injury, property damage or breach of contract case.

Cases which seek only to clarify a party's rights, to divide property or to order one of the parties to engage in or refrain from future conduct are usually considered lawsuits in equity. Historically, these cases were not tried by a jury and are still typically tried by a judge alone. Such cases include family law matters, lawsuits that seek injunctions, declaratory relief, accounting and dissolution of a partnership, quieting (settling disputed) title to real estate, mortgage foreclosure, rescission (voiding) of a contract based on fraud and specific performance (forced completion) of a contract.

However, there are exceptions even within these generally recognized categories. For example, some states allow a jury to decide cases seeking an accounting of business assets and liabilities but other states do not.

The same is true for eviction proceedings. And in a few states, even cases in equity are tried to a jury, if requested by any party. In contrast, some consumer protection or unfair business practice cases are tried by a judge only, even though they seek monetary compensation.

11. Am I entitled to a jury if the Complaint seeks both equitable relief and monetary damages?

Many cases include several causes of action (see Chapter 3, Section I), some in equity and others at law. For example, a Plaintiff's lawsuit might ask the court to rescind (void) a contract because of the Defendant's fraud (a claim in equity), and also ask the court to order Defendant to pay damages to Plaintiff for breach of that contract, a claim at law. In these mixed cases, either party is entitled to a jury. Both claims would be presented during the same trial, but only the claim at law would be submitted to a jury; the judge would decide the equity claim.

Sometimes, a Plaintiff's Complaint is solely in equity (a lawsuit seeking division of partnership property, for example) but the Defendant asserts a defense, or files a Cross-Complaint, alleging a cause of action at law (such as breach of contract). In that situation too, a jury would hear the Defendant's counterclaim (if a party requested it), while the judge alone would decide the Plaintiff's original claim.

12. If a jury is available in my case, should I request one?

A party might not want a jury trial, even if one is available. To make this decision, party and lawyer must consider the pros and cons of a jury trial versus a court (judge only) trial, including:

- **Speed in getting to trial.** In most courts, a case can get to trial much faster if there will be no jury. A court trial eliminates the need for jury selection, jury instructions and certain types of exhibits. If the litigation has already taken a long time and a party wants to avoid delay, the party might consider waiving (giving up) the right to a jury.
- **Expense.** If a litigant is paying hourly attorney fees, a jury trial will be more costly. Considerably more hours are required to prepare for a jury trial than for a court trial. A lawyer must prepare for jury selection and jury instructions. And the trial itself takes much longer; choosing the jury can take several days, and the entire trial moves more slowly because lawyers must tailor their presentations to the jury. The difference in expense to the client is not nearly so great if the lawyer is being paid a contingency fee, but even then the costs for jury trial are higher. The party requesting a jury must pay jury fees, which can quickly add up to more than a thousand dollars. (See Question 13.) Also,

the cost of expert witnesses, investigators and other outside trial assistants is likely to be higher because they will have to do more work—on jury selection, jury instructions and visual trial exhibits—if there will be a jury.

- **Emotional appeal.** In some cases, a jury is likely to sympathize with one party over another. For example, juries tend to side with individuals who have been economically damaged because of something done without conscience by a large corporation. Similarly, juries tend to look for a way to compensate people who have suffered serious physical injuries, even if the person causing the injuries did not act in a terribly careless fashion. Conversely, many lawyers believe that jurors are usually unsympathetic to an individual who sues a local government entity; those jurors are also local taxpayers whose tax funds will pay the verdict.

- **Technical detail.** Juries tend to be less sympathetic towards a party who is suing or defending based on a technical legal rule, particularly if the other side's behavior seems reasonable from a commonsense perspective. A jury might not look favorably on Defendant breaking a lease, refusing to live up to a contract or failing to pay a share of profits or royalties, for example, if Defendant took these actions solely because Plaintiff failed to sign a certain paper or file a particular document.

- **Risk of a hung jury.** One of the advantages of a court trial is that the parties know a judge will deliver a final verdict. With a jury, there is always the possibility of a deadlock—known as a hung jury—instead of a verdict. If the jury hangs, the parties have to try the case all over again (see Question 59). This would entail another long delay and significant added expense. In those courts that don't require a unanimous jury verdict, this risk is reduced.

13. How and when does a party formally request a jury?

A party who wants a jury trial may have to request it more than once. In federal court and some state systems, the party must include a jury request—sometimes called a *jury demand*—in the party's initial pleading (Complaint, Answer and/or countersuit). In those courts, a lawyer almost always includes a jury request in the pleadings, saving the real decision about a jury for later in the case. If the lawyer and client ultimately decide they do not want a jury, they may later drop the jury request without any penalty. In a few courts, a party might have to get the judge's permission to drop a jury request shortly before trial, or pay a monetary penalty to offset the other side's work in preparing to face a jury.

A jury demand must be included in the At-Issue Memorandum or Motion to Set

Trial Date. (See Section I.) In federal court, the jury demand must be repeated at a Trial Setting Conference. And in a few courts, a lawyer must file a separate Jury Demand document.

The party requesting a jury must also *post jury fees*. Each juror is paid a daily fee. The amount per juror (usually $10 to $50) varies from state to state. The party that requests a jury is required to offset part or all of these fees, and must deposit a certain set portion of the jury fees with the court several weeks before the scheduled trial date. A party that fails to make this deposit by a court-established deadline loses the right to a jury trial.

Section III: Pretrial Proceedings and Conferences

Once a trial date has been set, the lawyers turn their attention to how they want the trial itself to proceed. They might consider:

- whether certain subjects or types of evidence will be presented at trial
- the order in which evidence will be presented at trial
- whether the trial will be bifurcated (separated into two parts), to prevent evidence about one matter from prejudicing the jury's view of other matters, and
- how to shorten the trial.

Opposing lawyers might agree on some of these issues. If not, either lawyer may ask a judge to decide these matters before

the trial date. In some court systems, a judge addresses these issues whether or not the lawyers raise them. The judge requires both sides to attend a Pretrial Conference, during which a kind of script for the trial is created.

14. What is the normal order in which evidence is presented at trial?

Usually, the Plaintiff presents evidence about the Defendant's liability (legal responsibility) for damages Plaintiff has suffered, and evidence about the amount of those damages, during the first phase of trial (in any order Plaintiff chooses). Then the Defendant presents his or her evidence regarding both liability and damages. Finally, the Plaintiff may present some closing evidence, known as rebuttal, to respond to the Defendant's presentation.

15. Can a party request a change in the usual order of evidence at trial?

In some cases, the usual order of presenting evidence is changed to increase the chance of a fair trial. This happens most often when evidence about damages is so extreme that it might influence a jury's decision about liability. For example, if the Plaintiff in a personal injury case will never walk again, the jury might be so sympathetic that it would find a well-heeled Defendant fully liable even if the Defendant might not be fully responsible. The same problem might arise if someone's business or career was ruined or personal assets were wiped out.

In such a case, the Defendant's lawyer might ask a judge to *bifurcate* (separate) the trial into two distinct parts. In the first part, the jury would only hear evidence about liability. The jury would go on to hear evidence about damages only if it first found Defendant legally responsible for Plaintiff's injuries.

A party requests this type of division in a *Motion to Bifurcate Trial* or a *Motion for Separate Trials*. If the judge schedules a Pretrial Conference, the request may be made then, instead of in a motion.

You May Agree to a Non-Unanimous Verdict

In many court systems, a jury's vote must be unanimous in order to reach a verdict. But this requirement often results in a hung jury—a jury that can't reach agreement. If the jury hangs, the parties must go through the trial all over again. (See Section VIII.) To lessen this risk and the related delays and extra costs, some courts permit the parties to agree ahead of time to accept a less-than-unanimous verdict. Most judges approve these agreements; they usually like any reasonable proposition that decreases the likelihood of a hung jury (and possible need for a retrial).

---

16. Can the parties change the order in which legal issues are presented at trial to save time and expense?

In some lawsuits, a single legal issue might determine the outcome of the entire trial, or at least preclude the need to hear evidence on some other issues. For example, in a business dispute, the terms of a written contract might dictate all of the parties' rights. However, if the written contract was invalid for some reason, one of several other legal theories might apply. If a judge or jury first decides that the written contract was in force during the dispute, the parties would not have to introduce evidence and make arguments about any of the other non-contract legal theories. And that would save the parties considerable time and expense.

In such a case, a party may ask a judge to rule that the key issue be heard and determined first at trial, before and hopefully instead of other issues and evidence. This request is made in a *Motion to Determine Order of Trial*. The motion may be made any time after the trial date has been set. The request may also be made at a Pretrial Conference, if one is scheduled.

17. Prior to trial, can a party request that the judge exclude certain evidence?

Yes. During the course of discovery, one party might learn a particularly damaging or

party who wants to introduce the evidence that the other side will then be allowed to introduce related evidence that the jury would not otherwise be allowed to hear, or

- to wait and see how the trial develops before deciding what to do about the evidence.

inflammatory piece of information about the other side. For example, one party might have evidence that the other party had a previous similar dispute with someone else. Or a party might know embarrassing (and irrelevant) facts about the other party's personal life. In these situations, the party against whom the evidence might be used will want to know as soon as possible—in order to plan a response, if necessary—whether the jury will be allowed to hear that information at trial. Either party may ask the judge to decide, before trial, whether this evidence may be presented to the jury by filing a *Motion in Limine* (which means at the "threshold" of trial).

When a party makes such a motion, the judge may decide:

- not to permit any of the contested evidence to be introduced at the trial
- to permit all the contested evidence to be introduced, without restrictions
- to place limits on the evidence, either by permitting some parts to be admitted but not others, or by warning the

You May Want to Dismiss Part of Your Case Before Trial

At the beginning of a lawsuit, Plaintiff's lawyer may load up the Complaint with all kinds of Causes of Action (legal theories), unsure which ones the evidence will turn out to support. (See Chapter 3, Section I.) A Defendant might counter with multiple defenses in an Answer, or numerous legal theories in a countersuit. By the time trial rolls around, however, there might be insufficient evidence to support one or more of these theories. Presenting these unsupported legal theories at trial may look bad to the jury—and will certainly waste time and energy.

In these situations, Plaintiff's (or Defendant's) lawyer might drop these theories from the lawsuit before trial begins. A Cause of Action would have to be dismissed with prejudice at such a late date; it could never be litigated again. However, if there is no chance of proving that claim to a jury, Plaintiff (or counterclaimant) has little to lose by dismissing it.

18. What is a Pretrial Conference?

In the weeks shortly before a scheduled jury trial date, the judge may call the lawyers in for a *Pretrial Conference.* (If there will be no jury, however, the judge usually skips the Pretrial Conference and handles matters informally on the first day of trial.) The purpose of the Pretrial Conference is for the judge to find out what the lawyers expect to present at trial and to hammer out problems and procedural details ahead of time, rather than bogging down the trial itself.

Pretrial Conferences are more common, and more extensive, in direct calendar courts (including federal courts), in which a single judge is assigned to handle every aspect of a case, including trial. In master calendar courts, in which different judges hear different aspects of the case and the trial judge is not determined until the day of trial, Pretrial Conferences are usually held only in complex cases. Either party might also request a Conference to sort out particular procedural or evidentiary problems in advance.

19. What does a judge decide during a Pretrial Conference?

At a Pretrial Conference, a judge tries to streamline the trial by getting the parties to agree on the evidence and legal theories that will be presented to the jury. If the parties can't agree, the judge decides these issues for them. Before the Conference, a judge usually requires the lawyers to submit a *Trial Brief* or *Pretrial Conference Brief.* In this brief, each party must:

- spell out those facts that are uncontested
- outline the contested facts each side intends to prove at trial
- indicate what documents or exhibits each side wants to introduce into evidence, and
- list the witnesses each side intends to have testify.

At the Conference, the judge determines which facts both sides admit, so that evidence about those facts need not be presented at trial. The judge also determines what documentary or physical evidence may be introduced at the trial through "stipulation" (agreement between the parties) rather than requiring witness testimony. (See Question 39.) The judge might also make a formal ruling on the admissibility of certain evidence, eliminating the need for a separate Motion in Limine. (See Question 17.) The judge might determine the order in which evidence will be presented at trial. And the judge might decide what legal theories may—and may not—be argued to the jury.

20. What is a Pretrial Order?

The decisions made at the Pretrial Conference are formalized in a document called a *Pretrial Order,* a kind of blueprint that both sides must follow once the trial is under-way. The judge usually asks one side to prepare a draft of the Pretrial Order, which the other side can review, change or comment on before it goes back to the judge to be finalized.

 Pretrial Conference Preparation Is Expensive. If you pay your lawyer by the hour and an extensive Pretrial Conference is held in your case, you might be shocked to see the size of your bill for attorney fees *even before* you get to trial. For the Conference, your lawyer has to organize almost all the evidence and legal arguments in the case and present them in a brief to the judge. Because the judge's rulings at a Pretrial Conference often affect the outcome of the case, the lawyer must do a very thorough, and therefore expensive, job. Your consolation is that the lawyer would have had to do most of this work anyway to prepare for trial; the fees just get to you sooner.

Section IV: Preparing for Trial

A lawyer's performance in front of a jury is only as good as the lawyer's preparation. No amount of fast-talking in the middle of a legal tussle can substitute for having evidence, legal papers and arguments organized and readily available. A client must understand how much work a lawyer needs to put in during the weeks immediately before a trial, why the lawyer may not always be available to answer all the client's

questions and, if paying by the hour, why the lawyer's bill for that period is so large. Because a party's own testimony is often crucial to the outcome, the client, too, should thoroughly prepare.

21. What legal papers does my lawyer prepare for trial?

On movies and television, fictional trials take place entirely in the open courtroom—lawyers question witnesses, argue with the other lawyers and the judge and make opening and closing pleas to the jury. But in real life, much of the business of trial takes place on paper. Among the formal papers a lawyer must prepare for trial are:

- **Trial brief.** If there has not been a Pre-trial Conference before the trial judge, the lawyers must prepare a trial brief. This document describes each party's view of the facts and legal issues in the case. The trial judge uses these briefs to make informed decisions about jury questioning, evidence disputes and the propriety of the lawyers' opening statements to the jury. If there will be no jury, the brief prepares the judge to handle the trial efficiently.

- **Questions for prospective jurors.** During jury selection, the judge questions potential jurors and the lawyers pose additional questions in a process known as jury *voir dire* (having potential jurors "say the truth"). Many judges require the lawyers to submit ahead of time a list of voir dire questions they want the judge to ask. And some judges also want the lawyers to submit in advance the questions the lawyers want to ask potential jurors. Preparing these questions requires a great deal of time and care—they are intended not only to bring out information about the potential jurors but also to educate or prepare the jurors about issues or facts that will come up during trial. (See Section VI.)

- **Motion in Limine.** Unless a lawyer has already done so, the lawyer might need to prepare a Motion in Limine asking the judge to rule at the beginning of trial that certain evidence will or will not be presented to the jury. (See Question 17.)

- **Jury instructions.** Jury instructions are the rules of law a judge reads to the jury after all the evidence has been presented, explaining how the jury should apply those laws to the facts the jury decides are true. (See Question 55.) Although it may seem extremely premature for the lawyers to submit proposed jury instructions before any evidence has been heard, some courts require it. In these courts, the judge usually permits some changes or additions to these proposed instructions once all the evidence has been presented at trial.

Getting Ready ... But Not Too Fast

One of the most difficult things for a lawyer and client to manage in the weeks leading up to trial is the timing of preparations. Because of overcrowded court calendars, trials may be postponed to weeks or months after their scheduled date. Knowing this, a lawyer does not want to fully prepare if much of that work would only have to be repeated months later. On the other hand, lawyers and clients can't always be certain until the trial day arrives whether the court will actually postpone the case. And they can't afford to be caught unprepared should the case happen to be sent to trial on schedule.

If the trial has not yet been postponed by a week or so before the scheduled date, both lawyer and client must assume that the trial will go ahead on that date, and prepare accordingly. Nonetheless, there is still a good chance that the case will be postponed on the morning of trial. This kind of uncertainty is one of the many unpleasant, uncontrollable aspects of a lawsuit.

22. What preparations does my lawyer make immediately before trial?

The weeks just before trial are often frantic for a lawyer. The lawyer and lawyer's assistants must organize a tremendous number of people and documents. And the lawyer must do extensive studying, thinking and rehearsing. In addition to preparing the formal trial papers, a lawyer must attend to the following:

- **Witness testimony.** The lawyer reviews the client's deposition testimony (see Chapter 4, Section V) as well as any documents with which the client should be familiar. Then the lawyer meets with the client to prepare his or her testimony. The lawyer must carefully review the deposition testimony of other witnesses as well, plus the interrogatory responses and admissions of the opposing party, in order to have key portions at the lawyer's fingertips during trial. This prior testimony is used to *impeach* (contradict) a witness who says something different at trial than what that witness said during deposition. (See Question 48.) Most lawyers also prepare some of the actual questions they will ask the witnesses, even though many questions will be added or altered at trial, depending on the witness's answers to other questions.

- **Experts.** A lawyer must prepare any expert witness who will testify at trial. In particular, lawyer and expert must discuss how the expert can present information a jury will understand and believe. They must also discuss how to repair mistakes the expert might have made at his or her deposition.

 As Trial Nears, the Cost for Experts Shoots Up. At some earlier point in the litigation, your lawyer may have consulted an expert—for example, an engineer regarding a construction dispute, an accident reconstruction expert about a car crash, a doctor regarding the extent of a party's injuries or a real estate appraiser about a property value. The expert probably had a conversation with your lawyer, received some documents and provided your lawyer with a preliminary opinion about an aspect of the case. For that preliminary work, the expert probably charged for several hours work, an expense passed on to you for payment as a litigation cost.

As trial nears, however, an expert's workload rises tremendously. So do the expert's fees. If you are paying your lawyer by the hour, attorney fees for preparing the expert will also sharply rise.

To prepare for the expert's testimony, your lawyer will probably give the expert more documents to review. Then the lawyer and expert will meet in person to go over the expert's proposed testimony. In many cases, the expert's deposition will not be taken until close to the trial date. So in the weeks immediately before trial, the expert will have to prepare for and testify at the deposition, then prepare again to testify at trial. You will have to pay for all of these preparations.

- **Visual aid exhibits.** Most trial lawyers agree that jurors are greatly affected by visual displays. Lawyers find it easier to explain something to a jury (and for the jury to understand) if the lawyer can refer to a picture of some sort—a diagram, blow-up photograph, mock skeleton, list of key facts, over-size print of an opposing party's damaging statements or any other kind of visual aid. These exhibits are often prepared with technical assistance from a professional trial support service.

- **Opening and closing statements to the jury.** Plaintiff's side of the case is presented first at trial, so Plaintiff's lawyer must prepare to give an *opening statement* to the jury within a day or two after the trial date. (See Question 36.) Defendant's lawyer may also give an opening statement at the beginning of trial, though many defense lawyers prefer to give their statements right before they begin presenting their own witnesses in the second half of trial.

Some lawyers also prepare a closing argument ahead of time, as they already know what most of the evidence is going to show. Of course, they will have to change the argument somewhat as the trial progresses. But by planning their argument in advance, they can make sure to bring out witness testimony along the way that specifically supports the closing points they want to make for the jury.

How You Can Help Your Lawyer Prepare for Trial

Depending on the complexity of the case, your knowledge of technical matters about the dispute, and your lawyer's style in trying a case, you might provide valuable advice to your lawyer during the testimony of certain witnesses. If the lawyer wants you to take that role, you can prepare for trial by reviewing key documents, records and witness deposition testimony on these subjects.

More commonly, your only active trial participation will be giving your own testimony from the witness stand. To prepare for trial testimony, you should review the transcript of your deposition, as well as key points raised in other depositions about which any of the lawyers may question you. You should also review your answers to interrogatories, responses to requests for admissions and any documents that might come up during your testimony.

The final step in your preparation is to meet with your lawyer to practice—or at least discuss—your testimony at trial. You will already have a good sense of what testifying is like from the experience of being deposed by the other side's lawyer. You and your lawyer together can go over the strengths and weaknesses of your performance at that deposition —and discuss questions the opposing lawyer might ask at trial that were not asked at the deposition.

Unless there has been a non-binding arbitration (see Chapter 7), the trial will be your first opportunity to testify under the friendly questioning of your own lawyer. You and your lawyer might practice that testimony, too, to get a feel for how that works.

Of course, your lawyer will emphasize specific factual points for you to make. But another important goal of your testimony is to give the jury a positive overall impression of yourself and your conduct during the dispute. You and your lawyer should discuss the specific words you will use, the tone of your voice and even your facial expressions, in addition to the content of your testimony.

23. How much direction can I expect my lawyer to give me about my trial testimony?

A lawyer must perform a delicate balancing act when preparing a client for his or her trial testimony. On one hand, as a matter of legal ethics the lawyer is not supposed to tell the client what to say, even if it is the truth. Actual testimony is supposed to come from the litigant, not the lawyer. On the other hand, a lawyer knows that the same question might be truthfully answered in many different ways. The difference between one true answer and another can sometimes affect the outcome of a case.

Consider, for example, a case in which the client fell down stairs that had no handrail. "If there is a handrail, I always use it going down stairs," sounds much better than, "I didn't notice there was no handrail before I started down those stairs," even if both are accurate. A key issue in the case might be whether the client was likely to have used a handrail had there been one. Because such small differences can be important, a lawyer usually attempts to have the client understand what a very good answer would include, without telling the client exactly what to say.

Different lawyers approach this preparation differently. Some play it fast-and-loose, providing the client with a word-for-word answer but then adding, "but you answer however you think best." Other lawyers are more careful, explaining to the client what is important on a particular issue and what the lawyer is trying to achieve with a specific question, but never giving the client the exact words to say. When lawyer and client are preparing the client's trial testimony, the client should pay close attention to what the lawyer says about the key issues in the case and keep this in mind when preparing answers to specific questions. The client should also feel free to ask the lawyer about different ways the client might answer a question. As long as the different answers are both true and both come from the client's mouth, there is nothing wrong with the lawyer helping the client understand which answer would help the client's case the most.

Sections V-VIII: Trial

By the time a lawsuit finally gets to trial, the lawyers and parties might feel that they know everything possible about the dispute, the participants and the legal rules in the case. But they don't. Trials are always unpredictable, and the outcome is usually a shock to at least one party. However, the basic structure of a trial is well established. This section describes that structure and the roles played in it by lawyers, parties, witnesses, judge and jury.

In most respects, a trial proceeds in the same way whether or not there is a jury, though a *court trial* (judge only) is a bit less formal and usually much shorter. Where significant differences exist between the two types of trials, this section points them out.

Section V: Getting a Judge

24. When my case is called for trial, how is a trial judge selected?

In direct calendar courts, the same judge who has handled all aspects of the case from the beginning presides over the trial. In master calendar courts, however, the parties don't know who the trial judge will be until the case is actually assigned to a courtroom on the day of trial. The presiding judge in a master calendar court randomly assigns the case to a judge from a list of those available that day. However, if the presiding judge is aware of a potential conflict in a particular judge's calendar, that judge might be skipped.

25. Do I have any choice about the judge named to preside over the trial?

The parties have no say in the initial selection of a judge to preside over their trial. However, in some courts, any party may veto the judge by exercising what is called a *peremptory challenge* (a challenge requiring no explanation). Each side gets only one such peremptory challenge, which must be exercised immediately after the judge is named. In all courts, a party may object to a judge based on the judge's bias or conflict of interest. Such an objection is called a *challenge for cause.*

Peremptory challenges are used when a lawyer believes the judge will not be fair or reasonable towards the client, but cannot prove any specific bias. Perhaps the lawyer and judge have clashed previously. Or, the judge may have a difficult and cantankerous personality with which the lawyer does not want to wrangle during trial. Sometimes a lawyer exercises a peremptory challenge because of the judge's background or views. Some judges are known to favor corporate or insurance defendants over individuals. Others may have a reputation of being subtly unfriendly to lawyers and litigants of color, or to women lawyers. And other judges may be known in the legal community to have little sympathy for certain types of claims. ·

In any of these situations, a lawyer may exercise a peremptory challenge based on gut feelings rather than hard evidence.

Before doing so, however, the lawyer must determine what other judges are available to preside over the trial. A party has only one peremptory challenge; the lawyer does not want to use it to bounce little Napoleon only to find the case assigned to Attila the Hun.

In a challenge for cause, a party must demonstrate the "cause" for removing a judge—the judge's conflict of interest or actual bias in favor of or against one of the parties or lawyers. Such bias or conflict of interest is usually very difficult to prove, and so is not often alleged. An unsuccessful challenge leaves a party facing a judge whose impartiality, and perhaps integrity, the party's lawyer has just attacked.

A lawyer might successfully challenge a judge for cause if:

- the judge did legal work for the opposing party before being elected or appointed to the bench
- the judge worked in the same law office as opposing counsel in the case
- someone in the judge's family works for, or has a financial connection to, one of the parties, or
- the judge has a personal relationship with one of the parties.

However, a judge cannot be challenged for cause just because, as a lawyer, the judge frequently represented clients on only one side of similar cases—for example, always represented mortgage companies in foreclosure cases. Nor may a judge be disqualified because of a casual social relationship with one of the lawyers.

Unlike a peremptory challenge, a challenge for cause does not necessarily have to be made as soon as the case is assigned to the particular judge. Instead, the party must make the challenge as soon as that party learns that cause for disqualification exists.

If a party makes a challenge for cause, the case is put on hold for several days or weeks while another judge rules on the challenge. Unless the challenged judge immediately decides to withdraw from the case (*recuse* herself) instead of resisting the challenge, a challenge for cause almost certainly will require the trial to be rescheduled, which can delay the case for several weeks or months.

26. What happens when the parties and lawyers first arrive at the trial judge's courtroom?

Before any formal trial proceedings take place, the lawyers usually meet with the trial judge in chambers (the judge's office next to the courtroom). The scope of this initial meeting depends on whether trial is in a direct calendar court or a master calendar court.

Direct calendar courts. In a direct calendar court, the judge is already very familiar with the case and with the lawyers. Much of the trial's organizational business has already been taken care of in the Pretrial Conference and memorialized in a Pretrial Order. (See Section III.) Because the trial is already fairly well planned, this initial trial conference is likely to be brief. The judge and lawyers will go over the Pretrial Order and discuss matters of timing and details of jury selection not covered in the order. If the lawyers and judge did not discuss jury instructions at the Pretrial Conference, they will do so now. If there will be no jury, this informal conference will be much simpler. The judge might also handle much of the preliminary business in the courtroom rather than in chambers.

Master calendar courts. In a master calendar court, the initial informal conference on the morning of trial is the first time the judge sees or hears anything about the case. The judge uses that conference to become familiar with the case, listening to each side's lawyer describe the issues and the evidence each intends to introduce at trial. If the lawyers have prepared trial briefs, the judge might read them immediately before or after this initial conference. (See Question 21.) Similarly, if there has been a Pretrial Conference and order, the judge will discuss the order's terms with the lawyers. (See Section III.)

In this first meeting in a master calendar court, the judge goes over how trials are to be conducted in his or her courtroom, including how the lawyers will present questions for prospective jurors and when they must submit proposed jury instructions. The judge may even begin to discuss specific jury instructions. If so, this conference could take quite a bit of time. If there will be no jury, however, the initial conference is a much briefer affair.

Hurry Up and Wait

When the hour finally arrives for you and your lawyer to trudge down the courthouse hallway and into the courtroom where your trial is to take place, the lawyers almost immediately disappear behind closed doors to huddle with the judge. This informal conference might last for hours. Meanwhile, you will sit in the courtroom or hallway with nothing to do and no idea what is happening. Unfortunately, more of these private chamber conferences will probably occur throughout the trial.

When you first reach the trial courtroom, potential jurors are usually not yet present. Judges don't like to make jurors wait around in the courtroom until the trial is actually ready to begin. But the other parties most likely will be there. One of the things you must prepare for is facing the opposing parties during the many stretches of time when you must be in the same courtroom or court hallway, waiting for the lawyers, judge or jury. One thing you shouldn't do is start a conversation. It's not a good idea for opposing clients to talk to each other without their lawyers present.

Don't Rule Out a Last Minute Settlement Offer

By the time you walk into the courtroom to begin your trial, you might no longer be thinking about settling the case. But many lawsuits are settled inside the courtroom at the very cliff-edge of trial. At this point, lawyers and clients have reached high levels of anxiety. Either party might be eager to jump at even a slightly better settlement offer from the other side.

Right before trial, you and your lawyer should discuss the possibility of a last-minute settlement offer from the other side. What would it take for you to settle the case at this point? Similarly, you and your lawyer might want to consider proposing slightly improved settlement terms to see if the other side will bite at the last moment, allowing all of you to avoid the expense and risk of trial.

These last-minute settlements are sometimes brokered during the first informal meeting among the lawyers and the trial judge. Many judges will ask the lawyers if they would like the judge to make a last-ditch settlement try. If both sides agree, the judge might hold an abbreviated version of a settlement conference. (See Chapter 8, Section II.) With the beginning of trial only minutes away, a judge's coaxing might be all it takes to bridge the gap in settlement positions.

Section VI: Jury Selection

27. In a jury trial, how are the initial candidates for the jury selected?

Theoretically, every legal resident of the United States who is age 18 or over and mentally competent may serve as a juror. Most states and the federal system add some further restrictions, however. Jurors must be citizens, and be able to read and write English (regardless of how well they speak and understand it). In some places these latter requirements tend to create juries that do not accurately reflect the communities from which they are drawn, but such restrictions have been routinely upheld by state and federal high courts.

Each court compiles a list of potential jurors from voter registration lists for the county or other judicial district in which the court is located. This list under-represents minorities and the poor, who register to vote in lower percentages, but the higher courts have upheld the method. (To address this under-representation, some courts supplement voter lists with lists of driver's license holders.) From the list of potential jurors, a certain number are randomly chosen each week and notified to appear in court.

The potential jurors who appear in court on any given day are known as the *jury pool* or *jury array*. From this pool, a smaller group—called a *jury venire* (meaning "summoned")—is randomly chosen and sent to a courtroom in which a jury trial is scheduled to begin. The size of this smaller group varies depending on the size of a jury in that particular court and the estimated length of the trial. The longer the trial, the more potential jurors will be excused for personal or business "hardship" reasons, thus requiring a bigger initial group from which to choose.

Where Do I Look? How Do I Look?

Once trial begins, you will be face to face for long periods of time with the people who will determine the fate of your lawsuit —judge, jury, witnesses, opposing lawyer and opposing party. As the trial moves along, you will no doubt have strong reactions to what these various participants say. And if you are like most humans, what you are thinking will show up on your face.

As all the trial activity is swirling around you, try to keep in mind how you appear to the jury while you sit at the counsel table. Jurors won't expect you to be cool, calm and collected all the time. But neither will they like it if you yawn or look disgusted every time the opposing lawyer speaks, sneer whenever the judge makes a ruling against your lawyer or roll your eyes at everything a witness says. Be attentive and concerned, but don't act out every reaction in a constant exaggerated pantomime.

Should you look at the jurors themselves? Avoiding all eye contact with them throughout the trial is nearly impossible. You may certainly look their way on occasion, and smile or nod to the group of them as they file into the jury box at the beginning of court sessions. But try not to stare at any of them. Don't expect them to react visibly. And if any particular juror seems uncomfortable under your gaze, make a special effort not to look directly at him or her.

28. How are prospective jurors sent to the courtroom?

Once the trial judge and lawyers have concluded their informal conference, the trial judge calls the presiding judge (or jury commissioner's office) and asks that a group of prospective jurors be sent to the courtroom. Typically, 25 to 50 prospective jurors arrive in the courtroom. They are given an introductory speech by the judge generally describing the case and how long the trial is expected to last. Then the judge might ask if any of the prospective jurors needs to be excused from the case because serving on the jury would cause personal hardship. The judge talks to those prospective jurors who ask to be excused, usually permitting some to leave but refusing others' requests. (Some judges wait until prospective jurors are actually called into the jury box before discussing hardship requests.)

After the judge has finished these remarks, a panel of prospective jurors is chosen at random to enter the jury box for more detailed questioning about their background. The number of jurors initially called into the jury box is the same as the number of jurors who will wind up hearing the case. Different courts use different size juries— from 6 to 12 jurors—in civil cases.

Where in the Courtroom Do I Belong?

Courtrooms are full of barriers, benches, tables, chairs and rows of seats. When you first enter, you might see some people sitting in the audience and others scurrying around in front. Or, the room might be empty. Unfortunately, there are no signs indicating where the players in the courtroom drama are expected to sit and where some are not allowed to go. Although not all courtrooms are exactly alike, they are all similar enough that the picture on the facing page should give you a good place to start.

judge's bench. Where the judge sits. Only the lawyers (after first asking permission) and court clerks are permitted to approach the bench. Some informal conferences between judge and lawyers are held at the side of the bench, out of earshot of the jury.

door to chambers. Behind this door is the judge's chambers, or private office. During trial, the lawyers might be asked in for conferences. You and the other party, however, won't get behind this door except to agree to a settlement.

witness box. Immediately next to the judge's bench is the place where witnesses sit while testifying under oath. When you testify, you will also sit here.

court reporter. Immediately in front of the judge's bench, usually right next to the witness box, the official court reporter records on a stenography machine anything said by anyone in the courtroom. Almost all proceedings are *on the record* (the court reporter takes everything down),

though some preliminary business and side-bench conferences may be *off the record* (not reported) if the judge says so.

clerks and bailiffs. A court clerk (and sometimes a bailiff) usually sits at a table immediately in front of or to the side of the judge's bench. The clerks handle courtroom paperwork between the lawyers and the judge.

jury box. On the same side as the witness box, along one wall of the courtroom, is a separate section where the jury sits.

counsel tables. Between the judge's bench in the front of the courtroom and the audience area in the rear are two counsel (lawyers) tables. The parties also sit here, one side at each table. Traditionally, the Plaintiff's side sits nearest the jury box, but this is not true in every court. If there are multiple parties, there may be additional tables and chairs. Sometimes the parties sit behind their lawyers rather than next to them at the counsel table.

barrier. Behind the counsel tables is a barrier—the famous "bar" (lawyers take the bar exam in order to be "admitted to the bar")—that separates the legal community of lawyers, parties, clerks and judge from the general public. In some courts, paralegals, investigators and other non-lawyer assistants must remain behind the bar.

public audience. Trials are almost always open to the public. Behind the bar is an area for the audience, including friends and relatives. During jury selection, the prospective jurors sit in the audience.

Sample Courtroom

29. How does the jury selection process begin?

The judge starts jury selection by personally questioning the prospective jurors. This questioning begins what is known as jury *voir dire* (lawyers and judges mangle this term in a number of ways, but the most common pronunciation is "vwaar deer"). The judge usually begins by posing questions to the panel as a whole. These questions usually cover the jurors':

- personal knowledge about the case
- personal acquaintance with any of the parties, lawyers or witnesses (a list of which the judge reads aloud), and
- personal experience with similar disputes or lawsuits and with lawsuits of any kind.

Depending on a particular prospective juror's answer, the judge may follow up with more questions about that juror's experience. These questions are intended to determine whether the juror can be impartial in the present case. A judge often combines these questions with little speeches about how jurors must put aside any personal feelings and decide the case based only on the evidence that will be presented at trial.

Judges generally do not like to remove (in legal lingo, "excuse") jurors. If the first few questions do not clearly demonstrate a prospective juror's inability to be impartial, the judge usually drops the inquiry after giving one of the little speeches of encouragement. However, the lawyer for one side or the other is likely to pick up the line of inquiry if the lawyers are given a turn to question the prospective jurors. (See Question 30.) If, on the other hand, the prospective juror insists that his or her experience would make it impossible to fairly decide the case, the judge may excuse the person from serving. (If the judge does not do so at this stage, the lawyers will have the opportunity to remove this prospective juror later in the jury selection process—see Questions 32-33.) When a prospective juror is excused from the jury box, another is randomly called to fill that place and is asked the same introductory questions.

The judge might also ask more specific questions of individual prospective jurors, attempting to draw out information about their personal and work lives. And the judge might ask questions that pertain to the lawsuit itself, trying to find out whether a prospective juror has strong opinions about the particular type of dispute involved. (These are usually questions previously submitted to the judge by the lawyers.) Other judges leave most of this type of individual juror questioning to the lawyers. If any of this questioning demonstrates that a juror would have bias towards one side or the other, the judge may excuse that juror, whose place will be taken by another person randomly chosen from the panel.

30. Will my lawyer get to question prospective jurors directly?

At some point, the judge may turn juror questioning over to the lawyers. A few judges do all the questioning themselves, believing they do a more efficient job than the lawyers and/or that direct questioning by lawyers may make the jurors feel uncomfortable. Other judges do most of the questioning themselves but eventually allow the lawyers to ask a few questions of their own. Still other judges do only a minimal amount of questioning, then quickly turn the job over to the lawyers, permitting them wide latitude in what they may ask.

Individual prospective jurors are usually questioned one juror at a time. The judge and each lawyer ask questions of the same juror before moving on to the next. If the judge excuses a prospective juror from the jury box during this questioning, a new prospective juror is immediately called in to take that seat.

31. What do the lawyers hope to gain from the voir dire?

Lawyers want to accomplish several things during voir dire questioning of prospective jurors. First, they try to find out whether there is anything in a juror's background or attitudes that would make the juror likely to favor the other side in the lawsuit. For example, the Plaintiff's lawyer might want to know if a prospective juror has ever been a Defendant in a previous lawsuit—the experience of being sued may make the juror more likely to favor the party being

sued in the present case. Or the different lawyers representing an architect, a contractor and a subcontractor in a dispute over a building project all might want to know if a prospective juror has ever personally had any trouble with a construction project (and if so, who the juror thinks was to blame). Lawyers will also want to know if a prospective juror:

- thinks people tend to ask for "more money than they deserve" in lawsuits
- has strong feelings about corporations (if one is involved in the case), or
- has strong feelings about people who seek monetary compensation by filing a lawsuit (if the case involves such a claim) rather than finding some other way to settle the matter.

Lawyers also want to know whether there is anything in a prospective juror's background or attitudes that might affect how the juror would view a party or important witness in the case. For example, if a police officer will be a key witness in an accident case, does the juror have any personal relationship with a police officer or other police employee, or has the juror had a bad experience with one?

Lawyers also try to use the voir dire process to prepare the jurors for issues that might arise in the case. For example, in a contract dispute, a lawyer might ask whether a prospective juror believes someone has a right to end a business relationship that has gone bad. If a case includes testimony about foul language used by one party during the heat of the dispute, a lawyer might ask prospective jurors about their attitudes toward foul language—and even use the particular nasty words several times. This way, the lawyer can not only determine whether any of them might be bothered but also get all the jurors so used to hearing the words that they will not be shocked to hear them during testimony. Lawyers might also question jurors about a party's use of alcohol or drugs, divorce, non-marital cohabitation or any other subject that will come up in the trial and that might offend someone.

Finally, lawyers try, through voir dire, to get prospective jurors to like them. Lawyers want jurors to trust them, to believe what they say during trial and to want to decide in their favor—even if the jurors are not wild about the lawyers' clients. Sometimes, a client might think that a lawyer has failed to ask obvious follow-up questions of a prospective juror, has not probed deeply enough into a juror's feelings or background or has not responded strongly enough to a hostile remark from a prospective juror. But lawyers have to tread a fine line between seeking information and avoiding offending the jurors or making them look bad. If a lawyer already senses that a prospective juror would not be good for the client's case, the lawyer might not press any harder during questioning. Seeming to browbeat a prospective juror would not only make that juror uncomfortable, but the other jurors as well. Then the lawyer would have to face an entire jury that disliked the lawyer from the very start of the case.

What Role Do Jury Selection Experts Play?

Over the past few years, new players have emerged on the jury trial scene. Known as *jury consultants*, they assist lawyers in several ways. First, they help figure out questions a lawyer can ask prospective jurors during voir dire. They tell the lawyer what it might be useful to know about a prospective juror for a particular kind of case. And they help a lawyer phrase voir dire questions in a way that brings out the information without offending or embarrassing the prospective juror.

A jury consultant might also help a lawyer figure out how to approach the jury by using a "focus group." In this quite expensive process, the jury consultant puts together a group of half a dozen or so people intended to reflect the make-up of the actual jury. The lawyer makes a presentation to the group about the case, then the jury consultant interviews the group in detail about their reactions to the dispute, including which side they favored, how much they would award in damages and what they think of the lawyer's approach to the case. The lawyer can then use this information in shaping voir dire questions, evidentiary presentations and final arguments to the real jury.

Jury consultants might also sit in the courtroom during jury voir dire, observing the jurors' answers, suggesting further questions to the lawyer and helping the lawyer decide which prospective jurors to remove with peremptory challenges (see Question 33). Whether a lawyer uses a jury consultant in any particular case, and how extensively, depends on the type of case and whether lawyer and client believe the amount of the potential verdict justifies the expense.

32. If a prospective juror indicates a problem with being impartial, does that automatically disqualify that person from the jury?

No, it doesn't. Many times a prospective juror will reveal a bias toward or ill feeling against one side of the lawsuit. The juror may volunteer this information fairly easily and quickly (to get out of serving on a jury), or it might come out only after extensive questioning by the judge or lawyers. But this type of admission does not automatically disqualify someone from serving on the jury. Instead, the judge will question the juror further about whether the juror could "set aside" those feelings and decide the case based only on the evidence to be presented during the trial.

Depending on the juror's answers to this series of questions, one lawyer may believe that a prospective juror would probably not be fair to his or her side of the case. If so, that lawyer may make a *challenge for cause,* to have the juror removed. Because judges do not want to excuse prospective jurors unless it is very clear that the person could not be fair, judges do not easily accept challenges for cause. Instead, they may ask one or two more questions of the juror. Then, they might give a little civics lecture to the prospective juror about how important it is for all citizens to serve on juries and how all jurors must make an effort to put aside their personal feelings in order to decide a case fairly. After delivering this lecture to the juror, the judge usually asks the juror "Will you be able to put aside your personal feelings and judge the case solely on the evidence?" Most prospective jurors put in this spot say they will be able to decide the case impartially—whether they believe it or not. At this stage, they will be allowed to remain on the jury, although they might still be knocked off later by a peremptory challenge from one of the lawyers. (See Question 33.)

There is no limit to the number of jurors a lawyer may challenge for cause. However, lawyers do not make challenges for cause against all prospective jurors whose answers indicate that they might not be perfect jurors for that lawyer's side of the case. An unsuccessful challenge for cause leaves that prospective juror on the jury (at least temporarily) after having his or her impartiality questioned, which might make that person even less likely to be fair. If the judge is unlikely to remove the juror, challenging the juror for cause serves only to inflame whatever bias the challenged juror already has. And a lawyer who challenges many jurors for cause might make other prospective jurors clam up rather than answer questions fully, for fear that they, too, will have their impartiality called into question.

Some Jury Matters Might Take Place in Chambers

Voir dire questioning necessarily probes potential jurors' personal experiences and views. But answering these questions might sometimes force a potential juror to discuss quite private or otherwise embarrassing personal or family details. To minimize this embarrassment—and make it more likely that the juror will answer fully and honestly—some questioning might take place in the judge's chambers rather than out in the courtroom. Either lawyer may request this procedure, or the judge may order this closed-door questioning without a lawyer's request. Occasionally, such closed-door questioning is used for a juror who has strong feelings about the case or its subject matter, feelings the lawyers or judge might not want the other jurors to hear.

The judge and lawyers might also retire to chambers to discuss the lawyers' challenges for cause. The lawyers will want to speak freely about the jurors and the trial; the jurors should not hear this conversation. Moving into chambers is sometimes easier than carrying on these discussions in whispers at the side of the judge's bench, or trying to squeeze this work in when the jurors are out of the courtroom.

33. When can a lawyer remove a juror without having to prove "cause"?

Each side in a lawsuit is given the opportunity to exercise *peremptory challenges*, which allow a party to remove a prospective juror without the judge's permission and without even having to state a reason for the challenge.

In a civil case, each side typically can use three to six of these peremptory challenges, the number varying from court to court. In lawsuits with many parties, a judge may grant extra peremptory challenges—different parties on the same "side" may not be able to agree on how to exercise them. The peremptory challenges are exercised alternately: Plaintiff removes one juror, then Defendant, then back to Plaintiff, and so forth. After a prospective juror has been removed by a peremptory challenge, the replacement juror may be questioned and challenged for cause.

When Should You and Your Lawyer Exercise a Peremptory Challenge?

Most lawyers believe that picking a jury is crucial. Getting the "wrong" jury means that a favorable verdict is unlikely no matter what the evidence shows. The trouble is that nobody knows exactly how to select a jury that will favor the client's case. An individual juror's reaction to a particular case simply cannot be predicted by the broad categories into which the juror fits—age, gender, ethnicity, occupation, family situation or general attitudes toward lawsuits. Yet this is what the exercise of peremptory challenges often amounts to: speculating about how a prospective juror might decide the case by considering pieces of information about the juror's life and experience, then challenging those jurors the lawyer thinks would be least likely to support the lawyer's side of the case.

Some of these decisions are obvious. For instance, peremptory challenges are often used to remove jurors who were challenged for cause but whom the judge allowed to remain. For example, in a lawsuit by a female administrator for wrongful employ-ment termination, the employee's lawyer might have challenged for cause the human resources director for a large company, a corporate executive whose company had faced a similar lawsuit and an older man who said he had never considered hiring a woman for any management position in his business. If the judge rejected these chal-lenges for cause, the employee's lawyer would probably remove them with peremp-tory challenges. Because of their specific work experiences, they are likely to side with the employer/Defendant in the case (and they may be upset with the Plaintiff's lawyer for challenging them for cause).

Other uses of peremptory challenges amount to little more than a guessing game. And some trial lawyers reduce this process to an exercise of simplistic stereotypes—men make better jurors for a young and attractive woman client, for example, or young jurors cannot sympathize with an older litigant's complaints. But a lawyer can also use his or her experience in more sophisticated ways, reading between and behind the lines of prospective jurors' answers: Has a juror's facial expression, tone of voice or use of certain words, when combined with broad categories like occu-pation or age, indicated some lurking hostility? Very careful observation is the only tool available for this job.

A client watching the proceedings can be a lawyer's valuable assistant in this process. You should pay close attention to each prospective juror's answers, and give your lawyer the benefit of your observations by talking during breaks in the proceedings, or by passing notes while the judge or other attorney is talking—though *not* while your attorney is questioning a juror—about a juror who for any reason has made you uncomfortable.

A Lawyer May Bump Jurors Based on Race, Ethnicity or Gender

The basic premise of peremptory challenges is that each side may remove a certain number of prospective jurors without having to explain why, let alone prove that there is any good reason for the challenge. In certain cases, a lawyer might exercise these challenges along what are obviously racial, ethnic or gender lines. For example, in the case of a woman suing her employer for sexual harassment or discrimination, the employer's lawyer might use all of the Defendant's peremptory challenges to eliminate from the jury women who work outside the home. Or, in a case with an African-American Plaintiff or Defendant, the other side might use its peremptory challenges to excuse all the African-Americans in the jury box.

Unfortunately, this is legal. The law requires the court to draw the jury panel from a fair cross-section of the community, excluding no one on the basis of race, ethnicity or gender. And in criminal cases, the law forbids government prosecutors from systematically using race, ethnicity or gender to excuse individual prospective jurors from a case. A private lawyer in a civil lawsuit, however, is under no such legal restriction. Blatantly discriminatory peremptory challenges are therefore distressingly common.

34. When is the jury officially selected?

Once the peremptory challenge process is completed, and there are no outstanding challenges for cause, the jurors remaining in the box are officially impaneled (sworn in) as the trial jury.

35. What are alternate jurors and how are they selected?

If a trial is expected to last several weeks, the judge might order that two or more *alternate jurors* be selected. Prospective alternates are questioned, challenged and excused in the same way as the primary jurors. Alternate jurors sit through the entire trial and are available to step in if one of the serving jurors takes ill or is otherwise unable to continue. If no juror drops out, the alternate jurors are dismissed when the regular jury begins its deliberations toward the end of the trial. (A few courts do not use alternate jurors at all. Instead, they simply permit a jury to continue with a smaller number if one or more jurors drops out during the trial.)

Section VII: Witnesses, Evidence and Arguments

36. When do the jurors first hear a lawyer fully describe what the case is about?

The Plaintiff's lawyer formally begins presenting the case by making an opening statement to the jury. If there is more than one Plaintiff and they have separate lawyers, each lawyer presents an opening statement for his or her client. (In non-jury trials, a judge often dispenses with the opening statements—the judge already knows what the case is about through trial briefs and informal discussion with the lawyers.)

In an opening statement, lawyers give the jury an outline of the case by explaining what the evidence at trial is going to show. The lawyers do not say much, if anything, about the law. Instead, they describe what happened out in the real world, the events that landed the parties in court. The main purpose of the opening statement is to give the jurors an overall picture of what happened, so the testimony of individual witnesses will fit into a larger story and thereby make sense to the jury. Because a jury will expect to hear evidence to back up each party's opening statement, a lawyer must be careful not to promise "facts" to the jury that the lawyer will not be able to produce.

Of course, Plaintiff's lawyer tries to tell a story that makes Plaintiff look good and Defendant look bad, a story that might sound quite different from what Defendant's lawyer will say. But an opening statement is not an argument to the jury. A lawyer is not supposed to try to convince the jury who was legally right and wrong. If the lawyer strays from describing the facts into arguing why those facts show that Plaintiff was "good" and Defendant "bad," Defendant's lawyer may object. The judge may stop a lawyer from making such argument during opening statement, perhaps reprimanding the lawyer in front of the jury for the improper conduct.

37. When does the Defendant's lawyer give an opening statement?

When Plaintiff's lawyer has finished an opening statement, it is Defendant's lawyer's turn. However, Defendant's lawyer does not have to give an opening statement at this stage of the case. Defendant's lawyer may choose to wait until Plaintiff's witnesses have all testified and it is Defendant's turn to present evidence. Many defense lawyers prefer to wait until this later stage to give their opening statement so they can tailor it to respond to what Plaintiff's witnesses have said. Also, Defendant's version of the case will be fresh in the jurors' minds when Defendant's witnesses testify—hopefully, in a way that matches what Defendant's lawyer has said.

Don't Expect Fireworks in Opening Statements

Many clients hope to see their lawyers act like lawyers do in the closing scenes of television courtroom dramas—complete with fiery speeches to the jury, heart-wrenching pleas and fist-pounding oratory. Don't expect to see it in the opening statement. Until the actual evidence is presented, courts do not want lawyers' arguments to sway the jurors too far in either direction. Many lawyers push the boundaries of this rule, slipping in comments here and there about what the jury should think about the evidence. But a lawyer who strays too far in this direction risks irritating the judge at the beginning of trial, which can make the judge more difficult to deal with later. And if the judge harshly criticizes the lawyer, the jury might react negatively. Also, a lawyer who gets too creative in an opening statement might lead the jury to expect evidence that the actual witness testimony cannot provide.

38. How is evidence presented at trial?

For the most part, lawyers present information—formally speaking, they *introduce evidence*—by questioning witnesses in front of the jury (or judge alone, if there is no jury). In answering the questions posed by the lawyers, witnesses say what they have done and what they have seen. They explain why they have done something in a certain way, or not done something at all. They describe the regular practices of a business or organization. They also identify documents, photographs, business records and physical items, which permits the lawyer to formally introduce that material into evidence and show it to the jury. Witnesses may also explain what such documents or physical evidence contain, or how they were used.

A "Virtual" Witness May Appear

Usually, the judge or jury may consider a witness's statement only if that witness testifies in person at the trial. Even if the witness has already given statements or testified at a deposition about the dispute, that evidence cannot be introduced at trial unless the witness is also present to testify in person. No degree of personal inconvenience to the witness can excuse this requirement. This rule assures that the judge or jury has a chance to assess the witness's demeanor in deciding whether the witness is telling the truth. It also permits lawyers for each side to ask questions that might not have been covered in the witness's prior statements or testimony.

Courts make an exception to this rule, however, if the witness is physically unavailable. If a witness has died, is seriously ill or incapacitated or has intentionally avoided a court subpoena (by leaving the country, for example), a lawyer will usually be allowed to present some of the witness's previous testimony at trial. Crucial portions of the witness's deposition transcript may be read out loud to the judge or jury. If the deposition was videotaped, that tape might be shown. But a lawyer may present only formal deposition testimony, given when both sides had a full opportunity to question the witness. A lawyer may not show or read to the judge or jury other statements by the witness unless the witness was questioned on those statements during the deposition.

39. What is a stipulation and how is it used to introduce evidence at trial?

A lawyer can introduce a document or other evidence without having it identified by a witness if both sides have agreed ahead of time—"stipulated"—that the document is authentic (though they may disagree about its meaning or importance to the case). Both sides might be willing to stipulate in advance to a certain amount of evidence because it saves them both the time and energy of introducing it through a witness. Stipulations are particularly common when there has been an extensive Pretrial Conference in the case. (See Section III.) One of the things a judge tries to accomplish at such a conference is to convince the parties to stipulate to as much evidence as possible.

40. Do the judge and jury ever leave the courtroom to see evidence first-hand?

On rare occasions, a judge hearing a trial without a jury might personally inspect a location important to a case—the site of an accident, for example, or property involved in a dispute. Even more rarely, a judge might agree to transport the entire jury to inspect a site in person. On-site inspections are time-consuming and expensive. They also run the risk of distracting the jury, so judges permit them only when some crucial aspect of the case cannot be explained adequately through witness testimony and photographs.

Each Side Must Meet Its "Burden of Proof"

At trial, each party tries to convince the jury that its version of the dispute is the true one. But often, neither side particularly convinces the jury. In this situation, the outcome of the trial is determined by each party's *burden of proof*. On any particular issue in the case, one party or the other has the burden of proving its version to the jury. If it cannot do so—that is, if its version is not *more* convincing to the jury than the opposing party's—it loses that part of the case.

For most issues in a case, the party with the burden of proof must prove its case by what is called a *preponderance of the evidence*. The party must prove that its version is slightly more probable or that the evidence weighs in that party's favor even by such a slim margin as 51% to 49%. For other issues, however, such as proving another party's "malice," the party might need to meet a higher standard, proof by *clear and convincing evidence*. The judge instructs the jury at the end of trial about how to apply these burdens.

The Plaintiff has the burden of proof regarding each Cause of Action in the Complaint. (See Chapter 3, Section I.) The Defendant has the burden of proof only as to affirmative defenses in the Answer (see Chapter 3, Section II) and counterclaims (see Chapter 3, Section III). Because Plaintiff bears the burden of proof on most issues in most lawsuits, Plaintiff begins the presentation of evidence.

41. In what order do witnesses appear at trial?

Immediately after opening statements, Plaintiff's lawyer begins presenting evidence by *calling witnesses*. In this beginning stage of trial, known as *Plaintiff's case in chief*, Plaintiff's lawyer is supposed to call all the witnesses and introduce all the documents and other evidence necessary to prove the claims made against Defendant, including the damages Plaintiff has suffered as a result. Plaintiff's lawyer may call the witnesses and introduce items into evidence in any order the lawyer wants (unless a judge, in a pretrial ruling, has decided that the evidence must be presented in a different order for the sake of fairness or efficiency; see Section III). When the last of Plaintiff's witnesses finishes testifying in Plaintiff's case in chief, Plaintiff's lawyer announces to the court that Plaintiff "rests." Then it is Defendant's turn to call witnesses.

In this second stage of the trial, known as *Defendant's case in chief*, Defendant's lawyer presents witness testimony and other evidence to counter key aspects of Plaintiff's case. Defendant also presents evidence to establish any affirmative defenses that would prevent the Plaintiff from recovering damages. (See Chapter 3, Section II.)

Defendant Should Be Prepared to Break the Ice

Unlike a criminal case, in a civil lawsuit the Plaintiff may force a Defendant to testify about the facts of the case. In many courts, Plaintiff is allowed to call Defendant as a witness during the Plaintiff's case in chief. In fact, sometimes a Plaintiff calls the Defendant as the very first witness in the trial. A Plaintiff might do this to force the Defendant to testify before hearing what anyone else says or to guarantee that the Defendant's response to hostile questions by Plaintiff's lawyer is the first impression the Defendant makes on the jury. Plaintiff can also shape his or her own testimony to respond to what Defendant says. If you are a Defendant, discuss with your lawyer the possibility of being called to testify first. You should prepare not only for the questions you might be asked but also for your demeanor in front of the jury.

Defendants called to testify first will have another chance to testify. When you present evidence in Defendant's case in chief, you will have an opportunity to tell the jury about things that Plaintiff's lawyer does not give you a chance to say. And you will be able to respond to the testimony of Plaintiff and other witnesses. But you will not get a second chance to make a first impression on the jury, so prepare well for the possibility of being the first witness in the box.

42. Does each party have a second chance to put on evidence?

When the Defendant has finished presenting his or her case in chief, the Plaintiff gets another round, called *rebuttal*. Following the Plaintiff's rebuttal, the Defendant is given the opportunity (sometimes called "surrebuttal") to present evidence responding to this second round of Plaintiff's evidence. During rebuttal, each side is permitted to introduce witnesses or other evidence to contradict what witnesses for the other side said during its case in chief. And witnesses who have testified previously may be "recalled" to the stand during rebuttal.

During the rebuttal stage, the parties may introduce witness testimony or other evidence only to contradict previous evidence. No "new facts" about the dispute may be elicited, only different versions of facts that have already been introduced by the other side. Judges often find this limit on rebuttal evidence hard to enforce, however. A question about one topic might result in an answer that spills over into other matters. Also, some judges are more lenient about enforcing the rule than others.

43. In what order do the lawyers question a witness?

At trial, a witness is first questioned by the lawyer who has "called" the witness to the stand. This is known as *direct examination*. Then other parties may question the witness, a process known as *cross-examination.* During Plaintiff's case in chief, Plaintiff calls witnesses and directly examines them, then Defendant cross-examines those witnesses. During Defendant's case in chief, the order is reversed.

Following cross-examination, the party that originally called the witness to testify is allowed another round of questioning, known as *redirect examination.* The lawyer conducting the redirect examination is supposed to confine the questions to matters that first arose during that witness's cross-examination. In other words, the lawyer is not supposed to raise new subjects not originally covered in the direct examination of the witness unless, while being cross-examined, the witness brought up something new. Finally, the lawyers for the other parties may ask a few more questions, known as *recross-examination.* These questions are supposed to be limited to subjects raised during redirect examination.

44. What rules does the judge use to decide whether information may be admitted into evidence and therefore be seen or heard by the jury?

The presentation of information in a trial is governed by what are called the *rules of evidence.* These rules operate to ensure that the judge or jury only considers information that is reliable. The rules also seek to keep out prejudicial, inflammatory and just plain

unnecessary material. At trial, a judge uses these rules to immediately stop questions to, and answers by, a witness that might improperly influence the jury, as well as to keep the jury from seeing improper documents. (If there is no jury, a judge is usually more flexible in the questions, answers and documents allowed.)

Among the most significant rules of evidence are:

- A lawyer may not ask questions on subjects that are not directly related (*relevant*) to issues that are to be decided by the lawsuit. Lawyers may not wander into subjects that might make a witness look bad (or good) in the eyes of the jury unless they are directly connected to the dispute.

- During direct examination, a lawyer may not ask questions in a way that suggests the desired answers, known as *leading questions* ("Mr. Jones, as you neared the intersection, did you slow down and look carefully in both directions?").

- A lawyer may not ask questions that intentionally intimidate a witness— known as *argumentative questions.* For example, a lawyer may ask "Was it your regular business practice to consider a person's age when evaluating someone for promotion?" but not "Isn't it true that you always found a way to deny promotions to older workers?"

- Except for experts qualified as such by the judge (see Questions 49-51), witnesses may not offer opinions or draw conclusions about events outside the courtroom. Instead, they may only testify about their first-hand knowledge of events.

- In many instances, a lawyer may not ask—and a witness may not testify about—what the witness heard another person say outside the courtroom (known as *hearsay evidence)*. Repeating others' words tends to be highly unreliable, like the children's game of "telephone." The hearsay rule also prohibits some documents and other writings from being read to or seen by the jury. The hearsay rule has many exceptions, however, and lawyers and judges often spend a fair amount of time during trial arguing about whether certain hearsay statements are "admissible" (may be introduced into evidence).

The Court Whisperers

Although it irritates parties and jurors alike, the lawyers and judge sometimes gather at the side of the judge's bench to argue in whispers, off the record—without the court reporter transcribing what is said—about some point of trial procedure. One of the lawyers may ask the judge if they may "approach the bench." Or the judge might call the lawyers aside. These "sidebars" are held so that they can freely discuss matters the jury should not hear, without taking the time to call a court recess. This often happens when there is a disagreement about whether certain matters are proper subjects for the questioning of a witness. As frustrating as they are, these one or two minute conferences are better than the alternative: a full recess of 15 or 20 minutes every time one of these minor disputes flares up.

45. How does a judge decide whether a question is proper or a writing is admissible into evidence?

When a lawyer believes that another's lawyer's question to a witness is legally improper, the lawyer may state an *objection* to the question. The lawyer does so by interrupting immediately after the question has been asked, before the witness answers. The interruption must include not only the word "Objection" but also a statement of the legal basis for objecting. A lawyer may object to either the form of the question (a "leading" question, for example, or an "argumentative" or "vague" one) or the question's substance (such as questions asking for "hearsay" or privileged information). Similarly, if the lawyer believes that a document or other writing shown to a witness could not properly be shown or read to the jury—technically, is not *admissible evidence*—the lawyer objects before the witness or the lawyer offering the document reads any of it out loud. (The opposing lawyer is entitled to see any document before a witness may discuss it.)

The judge then decides whether the objection is proper. This decision is not always cut-and-dried, so judges sometimes ask the lawyers to give short arguments about an objection. If the judge decides that the question is proper, the judge declares the *objection overruled* and the witness answers. If the question is improper, the judge declares the *objection sustained*. The witness may not answer until the lawyer rephrases the question or asks a different one.

If an attorney objects to a document, the judge either allows its *admission into evidence*, in which case it may be read and shown to the jury, or denies its admission. Occasionally, a judge will permit some portions of a writing to be admitted while excluding other parts. In that case, only the permissible parts may be read out in court. If the judge allows such a document to be shown to the jury, the inadmissible portions must first be deleted ("redacted").

The Jury Shuffle

No trial runs without a hitch. The lawyers and judge often disagree about proper procedures, rules of evidence or witness testimony. And in some cases, the jury should not hear these disagreements. The lawyers and judge need to say things, even describe potential evidence, which might unfairly influence the jury. So, from time to time, the lawyers and judge huddle at the side of the judge's bench to resolve these disagreements out of the jury's earshot.

However, some issues cannot be resolved without lengthy argument. A judge might try to postpone these arguments until a normal break in the court schedule when the jury is not present—lunch, the end of the court day or the beginning of court on the next day. But sometimes a decision cannot wait; in these situations, the judge will call an immediate court recess during which the jury leaves the courtroom until the matter is resolved.

46. What happens if the jury hears inadmissible evidence before the opposing lawyer has a chance to object?

Occasionally, a witness answers a question before a lawyer can manage to squeeze in an objection. Sometimes the question is proper but the witness's answer is not—this might happen if a witness refers to what someone else said ("hearsay") in the answer or volunteers an opinion about some facts. If an improper question is answered, or a proper question is answered improperly, the judge looks for a way to undo the damage. Lawyers often refer to the judge's efforts as trying to "unring" a bell, meaning that once the jurors hear an answer, they cannot erase it from their memories. Nonetheless, the judge usually immediately instructs the jury to disregard an improper answer or an answer to an improper question. The judge may also warn a lawyer or witness not to repeat the same type of improper question or answer. And at the end of the trial, during instructions to the jury, the judge will remind the jurors that it is their duty to ignore any information the judge has ruled improper.

The Noisiest Lawyer Is Not Necessarily the Best

Often a client watches the lawyer for the other side jump up and down, object to many questions and answers and make long, strong and sometimes loud arguments, even about seemingly minor matters. At the same time the client's own lawyer objects only occasionally, quietly and without fanfare. "What's the matter with my lawyer?" the client might wonder. "Why does the other lawyer always grab so much attention?"

A good lawyer does not always hog the spotlight. Judges get irritated with lawyers who quibble about every detail, and doubly so with lawyers who blab loudly and at length every time a thought crosses their mind. And judges tend to act on their irritation by making life difficult for the noisy lawyer throughout the trial. Jurors, too, might get peeved by a lawyer who always interrupts the proceedings.

On the other hand, a lawyer who lets some improper questions slide by if they relate to unimportant matters, and makes objections and legal arguments calmly though firmly, will likely earn the respect of judge and jury alike. Of course, there are times when a lawyer must step in and object. But a smart lawyer will do it without using a bullhorn or turning cartwheels, and will ask the judge to take care of any continuing problems rather than repeatedly trying to shout them away.

47. Is there anything a judge can do if a lawyer or witness says something to improperly influence the jury, or engages in serious misconduct during trial?

Sometimes a witness blurts out something that is both improper and highly prejudicial to one side or the other. Or, a lawyer might persist in asking improper questions or making offhand remarks in front of the jury even though the judge has already warned the lawyer about this behavior. If a lawyer repeatedly engages in improper conduct, the opposing side may ask that the judge impose *sanctions* on the offending lawyer. Sanctions are a kind of personal fine the lawyer must pay, in an amount the judge determines at the end of the case. The imposition of sanctions usually has a sobering effect on a lawyer who is getting out of hand. The judge may also immediately instruct the jury to ignore the lawyer's improper remarks, and will do so again at the end of the case.

However, if a lawyer asks questions or makes other remarks in front of the jury that clearly and seriously prejudice the opposing side, imposing a fine will not undo the damage. Similarly, a judge's warning to the jury to ignore a lawyer's or witness's highly prejudicial remark might be as effective as telling a cat to ignore a mouse. For example, a lawyer might improperly ask whether the opposing side had been sued previously for similar conduct. Or, while testifying, a party might disclose a settlement offer the other side had rejected.

In such cases of extreme misconduct, the party that is unfairly prejudiced by the misconduct may ask the judge to declare a *mistrial*. A mistrial means that the trial is immediately ended, the jury delivers no verdict in the case and the parties must start a new trial, with a new jury, from the beginning. (The new trial would not start immediately. Instead, the parties would have a new date scheduled, probably months later.)

Because of these extreme consequences —wasted effort and lengthy delay—a lawyer usually does not ask a judge to declare a mistrial unless the damage done in front of the jury seems serious and irreversible. However, tactical considerations sometimes make a mistrial more attractive. For instance, if a lawyer believes his or her side is losing the trial, the lawyer will be much quicker to ask for a mistrial. Also, the waste and delay might be partially offset if one party or that party's lawyer is clearly responsible for the mistrial. In that case, the other side may ask the court to order the misbehaving side to pay their court costs and attorney fees for the trial that was abruptly ended.

48. What happens if a witness at trial says something different from what that witness said previously?

By the time of trial, most witnesses—including each party—will have given sworn testimony and other statements concerning the dispute, most of which the lawyers will have gathered during the discovery process. (See Chapter 4.)

Sometimes, a party or other witness testifying at trial contradicts what that witness said in previous statements. If so, the lawyer cross-examining the witness may read the prior statement out loud to the witness—in front of the jury—and ask the witness to explain any discrepancies between the two. Confronting a witness with prior inconsistent statements is known as *impeaching a witness*. By raising these inconsistencies, a lawyer can challenge the reliability of a witness's recollection. If the discrepancies are large or frequent, particularly regarding crucial facts in the case, the jurors might doubt the truthfulness or accuracy of the witness's entire trial testimony.

After one lawyer impeaches a witness, the other side has a chance to repair the damage. The other side may "rehabilitate" the witness by asking questions that give the witness a chance to explain the disparities between the two statements. The other side may also read to the witness and jury any prior statements that are consistent with the trial testimony, in an effort to show that the one inconsistent statement was merely an innocent error.

49. What role do expert witnesses play at trial?

The testimony of expert witnesses is often crucial to the outcome of many kinds of

cases. For example, engineers testify about faulty construction, accident-reconstruction experts talk about how a collision happened and accountants testify about how much money a business lost or a partnership is worth. An expert may testify about any type of test, procedure or analysis that is generally recognized as valid in the expert's field. And, unlike other witnesses, experts are allowed to give their opinion about those aspects of the dispute that are within their expertise and beyond the common knowledge of jurors. For example, a soil engineer may testify about how a landslide occurred: landslide reconstruction is an established part of soil science but is not a field in which most jurors are generally knowledgeable. On the other hand, a lie detector expert is not allowed to testify in most courts: there is no general agreement in the world of physiology or psychology about the reliability of lie detectors.

50. What must a lawyer do to qualify a witness as an expert?

The lawyer who calls an expert to testify must establish two things. First, the lawyer must establish the witness's credentials as an expert in the field. Then the lawyer must establish that the expert will testify about a procedure generally accepted in the expert's field. The lawyer does this at the beginning of the expert's testimony by asking a series of questions about the witness's education and experience, and about the state of the science, profession or other field in which the witness is expert. This process of establishing the witness's credentials and subject matter is known as *laying a foundation* for the expert's testimony.

Following these "foundational" questions, the lawyer who has called the expert to the stand asks the judge to certify the witness as an expert for this case. If certified, the witness may testify not only about evidence he or she examined and tests or analyses that were performed on the evidence but also his or her own opinion about the evidence—that a wall collapsed because it was improperly built, that a business lost a certain amount in potential earnings following breach of a contract or that a piece of real estate is worth a certain sum.

The Jury Might Never Get to Hear the Expert's Opinion

In most cases, a lawyer only uses an expert witness who is obviously qualified in his or her field and whose opinion is based upon clearly established procedures in that field. However, sometimes an expert is asked to testify about a very specialized topic that has not been frequently considered. The witness might have no track record on that particular topic, although clearly an expert in the general subject. For example, an actuary who specializes in figuring out how much a deceased person would have earned over a "normal" lifetime might have no experience with the lifetime earning pattern of a ballet dancer or a website entrepreneur. Or, an expert's opinion might not be supported by an established history of testing or research. For example, an accident reconstruction expert might be of the opinion that talking on a cell phone while driving severely heightens the risk of accident, but the ex-pert might not be able to point to sufficient research to support that opinion.

In such situations, the opposing side may be able to prevent the jury from hearing anything from the expert. Instead of waiting to try to challenge the witness's opinion during cross-examination, the opposing lawyer may ask permission for what is called *witness voir dire*. During voir dire of an expert, the lawyer asks questions about the expert's background or field of expertise, in order to see if the expert should be allowed to testify. The jury leaves the courtroom while this voir dire takes place. If, after the voir dire, the judge decides the expert may not testify, the jury will never hear any of the expert's opinion. If the judge decides the expert may testify, the opposing side may still attempt to discredit the expert's opinion by asking similar questions during cross-examination.

51. What can the other party's lawyer do to oppose an expert's testimony?

As with any other witness, the other side has an opportunity to cross-examine an expert. The other side may challenge an expert's credentials, the analysis or testing procedures used and the expert's conclusions and opinions. The other side may also ask questions to impeach the expert, including questions showing that an expert always testifies for the same side in every lawsuit, consistently values property higher than any other expert or always tilts consistently in one direction. The other side may also call its own expert witnesses, to contradict the first expert.

52. Are closing arguments and jury instructions connected?

When the last witness has testified and the last document or other piece of evidence has been admitted into evidence, the trial moves into its final stage. The lawyers give *closing arguments* (sometimes called *final arguments*) to the jury, then the judge gives *jury instructions* on how to apply the law to the evidence in the case. If there is no jury in the case, the lawyers make closing arguments to the judge.

In closing arguments, the lawyers make legal points that favor their respective clients, and try to soften the impact of those arguments that seem to favor the other side. Because the judge's instructions to the jury will include all the legal rules the jury is to apply to the case, the lawyers need to know what instructions the judge will give before making their closing arguments. So the judge and lawyers will confer in the judge's chambers before closing arguments to discuss jury instructions proposed by both sides. The judge decides which of the proposed instructions will be given, which will not and which will be given in modified form. Once the judge has decided on the jury instructions, the lawyers are usually given a brief time to incorporate that information into their closing arguments.

53. In what order do the lawyers give their closing arguments?

Plaintiff's lawyer has the first chance to speak to the jury in closing argument. If there are several Plaintiffs with different lawyers, each Plaintiff's lawyer gives a closing argument before any Defendant does. Plaintiff's closing argument is followed by a closing argument from the lawyer for each Defendant. Then Plaintiff's side gets a final chance to speak to the jury in what is called *rebuttal argument*. This second round by Plaintiff's lawyer is the last closing argument—Defendant's side does not get a rebuttal argument.

The Judge May End the Trial Without Letting the Jury Decide

Sometimes, all of the witness testimony and other evidence presented in the Plaintiff's case in chief simply does not prove a valid legal case against the Defendant, even before the Defendant presents any contradictory evidence. A Defendant usually will have already convinced the court to dismiss a Plaintiff's legally insufficient case through one of several pretrial motions. (See Chapter 5.) Nonetheless, a case that once was sufficient may fall apart at trial. A crucial witness for Plaintiff might fail to appear at trial, or might appear only to contradict Plaintiff's testimony. Perhaps one of Plaintiff's witnesses testifies to a crucial fact that provides a legal escape hatch for Defendant. Or, Plaintiff might be unable to find an expert to provide necessary technical support. If, for any reason, Defendant believes that Plaintiff has not proven a case, Defendant may ask the judge to dismiss the case before Defendant's own case in chief and without sending the case to the jury. This request to end the trial is called a *Motion for Directed Verdict, Motion for Nonsuit* or *Motion for Judgment As a Matter of Law*. If granted, it ends the lawsuit in Defendant's favor and forever bars Plaintiff from filing it again.

Defendant may make, or renew, the same request after both sides have presented their evidence but before the case is sent to the jury. At this point in the trial, the Plaintiff may make a similar motion, asking the judge to declare Plaintiff the victor without the jury deciding the case. Plaintiff might do this if Defendant has produced very little evidence, the sum of which fails to contradict Plaintiff's claims.

Although these motions are frequently made, they are rarely won. They are frequently made because they take little time or effort. They are rarely won because regardless of how little evidence one side has produced, the right to a jury trial is extremely important. Judges do not want to deprive any litigant of that right except in the most extraordinary circumstances.

54. Are there any limits on what a lawyer can say in closing argument?

Closing argument is a lawyer's grand telling of the entire lawsuit story. The lawyer tells the jury who the parties are, what happened in the dispute, what the consequences were and how legal rules should be applied to the case, all from the point of view of the lawyer's client. A lawyer need not follow any mandatory or even standard structure in closing argument; lawyers argue in a wide variety of styles. Some lawyers keep it short and sweet, focusing only on the crucial facts. Others go on at great length, looking at every nook and cranny of the case in great detail. Some provide a simple, connect-the-dots road map for the jury, with a calm, matter-of-fact delivery. Others engage in theatrics, making dramatic speeches.

Sometimes, the judge limits the length of closing arguments. The trial judge may set a limit on the time each lawyer is permitted for closing argument, with a much shorter time for Plaintiff's rebuttal argument. Some judges give lawyers plenty of time—all day, if need be. Other judges worry that jurors can only concentrate for so long, and so give the lawyers less time. If there is no jury, a judge is likely to restrict severely the time allowed for closing argument. Judges are experienced in assessing evidence and legal rules; they do not need nearly as much

guidance or persuasion from the lawyers as jurors do.

Within this wide latitude, there are some rules that restrict the kinds of things a lawyer may say. First and foremost, a lawyer must stick to the evidence. A lawyer may not refer to "facts" about the dispute that the jury did not see or hear in court (referred to as "facts not in evidence"). And the lawyer must refer to evidence—witness testimony and the contents of documents— exactly as it was presented. If a lawyer misstates the evidence presented or refers to information the jury did not see or hear, the opposing side may object. The judge decides whether the objection is valid and either permits the lawyer to continue the argument as stated or forces the lawyer to rephrase the argument. Similarly, the lawyer must refer to legal rules exactly as they will be presented in the jury instructions.

Also, a lawyer is not supposed to appeal to jurors' emotions or prejudices during closing argument. This is a hard rule to define, and so a hard one to enforce. In general, it means that a lawyer is not supposed to ask jurors to ignore the evidence or legal rules, or to focus on who the parties are rather than on what they have done. Lawyers often abuse this rule in criminal trials—both the real and Hollywood versions—but judges force them to follow it more strictly in most civil cases.

Biting Your Tongue During Closing Argument

At the end of a stressful trial—which comes at the end of the long and exhausting litigation process—you might find it hard to sit quietly while the other side's lawyer offers the jury an uninterrupted story tilted in every way possible against you. Even though you know that your lawyer can tell your side of the story in the same way, hearing the evidence piled up in only one direction can be very frustrating. Your lawyer may be able to relieve some of this frustration by interrupting the other lawyer with an objection if the other lawyer mis- states some evidence, mischaracterizes a law or otherwise violates the rules regard- ing closing arguments. But your lawyer probably will not do this as often as you would like. Lawyers and judges follow an unwritten rule that a closing argument should not be interrupted unless there is a serious misstatement of fact or other attempt to unfairly influence the jury. Judges do not like one lawyer to interrupt the other over trivial matters and will scold a lawyer who objects too easily. Jurors, too, tend not to like petty interruptions while they are trying to concentrate on each side's final story. So, unless the other lawyer is seriously distorting matters, you and your lawyer will just have to stay quietly in your chairs, at least until it is your lawyer's turn to tell the tale.

55. What are jury instructions meant to accomplish?

Jury instructions serve several purposes. They:

- explain the mechanics of the jury process, including how the jurors are to deliberate

- explain to the jury which party has the *burden of proof* regarding any disputed issue

- explain to the jurors how to apply the evidence to the appropriate legal rules. For example, in a contract dispute, there may be a set of instructions about how to decide whether there was a valid written contract, and another series of instructions on how to deter- mine legal responsibility if the jury finds that no written contract was in effect, and

- explain how the jury is to arrive at a verdict, including whether a verdict in that court must be unanimous or something less than unanimous. (See Question 56.)

Section VIII: The Verdict or Decision

56. How does a jury deliberate?

Once the jury has been instructed, it moves behind closed doors to begin *jury delibera-*

tions. If the jury is able to reach agreement, it brings in a verdict that decides who wins and loses the lawsuit. In some cases, however, the jury only answers a set of questions about the facts, which the judge then turns into a final decision. (See Question 58.)

The jury is permitted to take into the jury room any document, exhibit or other item formally admitted into evidence during the trial. Jurors may also use their own notes from the trial, if the judge permitted them to take notes. No one else is in the room with the jurors while they deliberate and no one monitors what they say among themselves. The jurors have sworn to follow the judge's instructions—to discuss only the evidence presented and the legal issues as explained to them—but there is no one to check whether, or how well, they do so. This freedom from official control is one of the great strengths of the jury system, leaving the ultimate decision about the lawsuit in the hands of common folk rather than professionals or representatives of government.

At some point during deliberations, the jurors will take a vote in an attempt to reach a verdict. In some states, a verdict requires a unanimous vote, unless the parties have agreed otherwise ahead of time. (See Section III.) In other states, however, a verdict may be reached with less than a unanimous vote. The jurors may vote, then discuss, then vote again, as many times as they wish in their efforts to reach a verdict.

57. May the jury communicate with the lawyers or the judge during deliberations?

Once deliberations begin, the jurors hear nothing more from the lawyers, litigants or witnesses. If the jurors have a question about their deliberations—what a certain instruction means or what a certain witness said—they send the question to the judge, in writing.

In some courts, the lawyers must be present when a judge reads any note from the jury, and must be given an opportunity to comment on how the judge should respond. In other courts, the judge reads the request first, then decides how to proceed. If the jury's request is a simple one—asking to see some evidence that is not in the jury room, for example—the judge might notify the lawyers by phone then send the jury what it needs, or provide the jury with a written response explaining why they may not have what they requested.

If the question is more difficult to answer, the judge calls the lawyers into court and lets them argue—without the jury present—about how the judge should respond. For example, if the jury asks to hear the court reporter read a certain portion of a witness's testimony, one lawyer might argue that the jury should hear more of that testimony than the jury has specifically requested, to keep the part it did request in the proper context. The judge then either sends a written response to the jury or brings them back into court to hear a rereading of an instruction, to receive additional instruction or to hear the reading (by the court reporter) of portions of a witness's testimony. The lawyers and parties are permitted to be present while the jury is back in court, but they may not address the jury.

58. What types of verdicts may juries reach?

In most cases, a jury is instructed to return what is called a *general verdict*: a simple decision stating which party wins the case and how much, if anything, the losing party must pay the winner. A general verdict may also include other relief—such as title or

right of possession to property—for the Plaintiff or countersuing Defendant. In a general verdict, the jury does not explain how it arrived at its decision nor what it concluded about any specific issue included in the instructions.

In some cases, a jury may instead be instructed to return a *special verdict*. In this type of verdict, the jury answers a series of questions posed by the judge but does not make a final decision about who wins the lawsuit. These answers address the crucial factual issues in the case. The judge then takes the jury's answers regarding the facts and applies them to the appropriate laws, drawing legal conclusions to arrive at a final verdict.

Where to Go, What to Do?

While the jury is deliberating, there is nothing for you and your lawyer to do. You simply wait. But where? And for how long? Jury deliberations might take a couple of hours or a couple of days. At any point during those deliberations, the jury might ask a question, or make a request of the judge, that will require the presence of your lawyer. Because of this uncertainty, most lawyers return to their offices while awaiting a verdict. They know that even in a simple case, a jury usually takes several hours just to choose a foreperson and go over the evidence and instructions. However, a lawyer must stay within 15 or 20 minutes of the courthouse, in order to get back to court in a hurry if the jury needs further instructions or wants testimony repeated. So, if your lawyer's office is not close by the court, your lawyer might wait (with a phone handy) somewhere else nearby—the court cafeteria, another lawyer's office or your place of business. If you don't wait with your lawyer, you must be somewhere within telephone reach and, if you want to be in court when something happens, within 15 or 20 minutes of the courthouse.

59. What happens if the jury can't reach a verdict?

If a jury has been unable to reach a verdict for some time and the positions of the individual jurors are not shifting, the jury will report the deadlock to the judge. But a jury's first report of deadlock does not necessarily end the deliberations. Instead, a judge is likely to reread to the jury the standard instructions about how they are to discuss the evidence and law among themselves, and how they are to attempt to reach agreement. Then the judge sends them back into the jury room to try again.

If a jury reports more than once that it is deadlocked, a judge may resort to another tactic. In most courts, a judge may explain to the jurors that there will have to be another trial if they do not reach a verdict. The judge may then remind the jurors that another trial would be very expensive for the litigants and for the court system, and that there is no reason to believe that a new jury would be able to do any better than they can. The judge may then ask the jurors to try again for a verdict, and send them back into the jury room. This speech to the jurors—combining guilt and coercion—is known among lawyers as a "dynamite charge" because it is intended to explode a hole in the deadlock.

Sometimes, despite long hours of deliberations and repeated efforts by the judge, the jury is still unable to reach a verdict. The judge must then decide whether the jury is hopelessly deadlocked. The longer the trial has taken, the longer the jury will be kept deliberating. If a prior trial in the case also failed to reach a verdict, a judge might require even more effort by the present jury. The judge might ask for information on how many votes have been taken and the jury's latest vote count (without asking which party the vote favors). If there have been few votes and only one juror stands in the way of a verdict, a judge is likely to force the jurors back into more deliberations. If there have been numerous votes and there are still several jurors on each side of a verdict, the judge is more likely to decide that the stalemate cannot be overcome.

If a deadlock cannot be broken—in lawyer parlance, if there is a *hung jury*—the judge dismisses the jury from the case and declares a *mistrial*. A mistrial means that the present trial is over but the lawsuit continues with nothing resolved. The parties have to try the case all over again, in what is called a *retrial*. A retrial does not begin immediately but is scheduled for a later date.

60. If the jury reaches a verdict, how is it communicated to the parties and lawyers?

If the jury reaches a verdict, it sends a note to the judge. The judge's clerk then gets in touch with the lawyers, who in turn let their clients know. When everyone has gathered again in the courtroom, the jury foreperson hands the written verdict form(s) to the judge. The judge reviews the verdict form to make certain that it has been completed and signed, then has the court clerk read it aloud. After the reading, the judge may ask the jury foreperson if this is the true and correct verdict they reached.

61. May a lawyer request that individual jurors be questioned about the verdict?

The lawyer for either party may ask for a *jury polling*. To poll the jury, the judge asks each juror individually if the verdict read by the clerk was in fact the verdict they intended. The purpose of this jury polling is to make sure that no juror was confused about the verdict. On rare occasions, polling also reveals that a juror felt coerced into agreeing to a verdict that he or she did not in fact want to join. Jury polling is a particularly good idea if there is a special verdict (see Question 58), about which jurors are more likely to be confused.

62. If there was no jury for the trial, how does the judge deliver a verdict?

In a court trial—a trial before a judge but no jury—the judge may deliver a decision immediately after closing arguments. The judge informs the parties of the key points —who wins and how much compensation the loser must pay—and follows it up later with a detailed decision in writing called *Findings of Fact and Conclusions of Law.* Often the judge asks the winning party's lawyer to prepare a draft of these findings and conclusions, conforming to the decision the judge announces in the courtroom. The other side then has an opportunity to comment on the winning side's draft, making sure the winning lawyer accurately describes what the judge decided.

Often, the judge does not decide the case right away but instead takes the case *under submission*: a period of private consideration similar to a jury's deliberations. After a week or two (most courts have time limits of seven to 30 days within which a judge must make a decision) the judge sends each lawyer the written verdict with findings and conclusions.

63. What is the purpose of a judge's Findings of Fact and Conclusions of Law?

The judge's written Findings of Fact and Conclusions of Law are the equivalent of a jury's verdict. But unlike a jury verdict, they spell out in detail what facts the judge found to be true and how the judge applied those facts to the laws that pertain to the issues in the case. The findings and conclusions declare who wins and loses the lawsuit, what damages the loser must pay and what other relief is granted to the winning party (for example, an injunction, title to property or a business or termination of a contract). The findings and conclusions may also include an award of court costs and attorney fees, if appropriate. However, the amount of those costs and fees usually has to be determined at a later date through an additional court proceeding. (See Chapter 10.)

But It's Not Over

It might take a few days for the smoke to settle following a verdict at trial. If you've won, you may be surprised and elated. If you've lost, you may be shocked and angry. Perhaps you won less or lost more than you expected, so you might feel disappointed but not devastated. Whatever your reaction to the verdict, you will undoubtedly experience a letdown that the long litigation process is finally over.

Except it's not over yet. Almost immediately after the verdict, there is more work to be done. The lawyers will struggle over the amount of costs, and perhaps attorney fees, the winner can recover from the loser. The losing party and lawyer must consult about whether to try to overturn or appeal the verdict. The winning party, too, might consider an appeal. At the same time, the winner must formalize the Judgment and begin figuring out how to collect from the other side. (See Chapter 10 for a discussion of these post-trial procedures.)

Chapter 10

Appeals and Other Post-Trial Proceedings

In the days and weeks following the verdict, both the winning and losing parties—and their lawyers—must consider a number of further legal procedures. The winner has to formalize the Judgment, establish the amount of litigation costs, and perhaps lawyer fees, the losing side will pay and begin considering how to collect the Judgment from the other side. The losing side must immediately consider whether to try to overturn the verdict in the trial court or appeal the verdict to a higher court. The winner may also consider an appeal, if the verdict provided less relief than expected. And each side must respond to procedures initiated by the other side.

Section I: The Winning Party's Final Moves

The winner's work is not over once the judge or jury reaches a verdict. To secure the full benefits of victory, the winning party must transform the verdict into a Judgment. The winner must also obtain a court order setting forth the amount of costs and, if appropriate, attorney fees to which the winning party is entitled. Then, the winning party has to collect the Judgment.

1. How does a verdict become a Judgment?

A verdict decides the outcome of a case, but a lawsuit is not formally concluded until

the verdict is translated into a *Judgment*. A Judgment is the court's formal order declaring the end result of the lawsuit—who won, who lost and what relief was granted. A Judgment entitles the winning side to use the power of the court to:

- force the loser to pay whatever compensation the judge or jury awarded, and
- enforce whatever other relief was granted in the verdict, such as transfer of title to property, division of assets, assumption of control over a business or ending obligations under a lease or contract.

For a verdict to become a Judgment, the trial judge's clerk must report the verdict to the court clerk's office. The court clerk's office then registers the verdict as a Judgment in the court's records, often in a separate Judgment book or file. The clerk then sends a form—commonly called *Notice of Entry of Judgment*—to all parties in the case announcing the entry of the Judgment in the court's official records. In some courts, the lawyer for the winning party prepares the Notice of Entry of Judgment and files it with the court clerk.

2. How can I get the losing side to pay my litigation costs?

In most courts, the losing side in a trial is ordered to pay the winning side's litigation costs. These costs may include court filing fees, the expense of serving the Complaint and subpoenas, deposition costs, jury fees, regular and expert witness fees and the costs of preparing trial exhibits. (See Chapter 1, Section III.) They do not include an attorney's regular office expenses or a party's personal costs or income lost while preparing for the case or attending court hearings or trial. And they do not include attorney fees; different rules determine whether the losing side has to pay the winner's lawyer. (See Question 3, below.) There is no pre-set limit or maximum amount of litigation costs that may be reimbursed by the losing side. The amount varies greatly from case to case.

To obtain a court order awarding costs, the winning side must submit a list of its reimbursable expenses to the trial judge. This list—typically called a *Memorandum of Costs* or a *Costs Bill*—details each expenditure. The winning party's lawyer must also file an affidavit or declaration stating that the listed amounts were actually spent and are billable to the client (as opposed to expenses that are paid by the lawyer as part of office overhead). The winning party typically must file this list within ten to 30 days after the Judgment is entered and serve a copy on the losing party.

The losing party may oppose the Memorandum of Costs or Costs Bill by filing a *Motion to Tax Costs* or *Challenge to Costs*. This opposition may attack any particular expense as outside what the court permits as a reimbursable cost, or as an excessive amount for an otherwise proper category of cost. The judge then decides what amounts

are proper and makes an *Award of Costs*. The losing party must pay this amount to the winning party on top of whatever other compensation amount was specified in the verdict.

3. How can I get the losing party to pay my attorney fees?

Normally, each side in a lawsuit pays its own attorney fees, regardless of who prevails in the case. However, in some kinds of lawsuits, the losing side may be ordered to pay the winning side's attorney fees for the entire litigation. (See Chapter 3, Question 12.) These cases include:

- contract dispute lawsuits in which the contract itself provides that the losing party will pay the winner's fees
- lawsuits relying on state or federal statutes that include an attorney fees provision, and
- certain suits by and against the government.

If the winning side believes it is entitled to attorney fees, the lawyer for that party must submit a request for fees to the trial judge. The request—often called a *Motion for Award of Attorney Fees*—must explain the legal basis for the claim of attorney fees, detail all the lawyer's hours spent on the case and indicate the lawyer's hourly rate. The lawyer must also submit a declaration or affidavit describing the hours worked on the case and supporting the lawyer's hourly fee. In some cases, the lawyer also submits declarations or affidavits from other lawyers in the same field and geographical area, stating that the lawyer's hourly fee is appropriate.

The losing side in the lawsuit may file an opposition to the Motion for Attorney Fees contending that:

- there is no valid legal basis for an attorney-fee claim
- the hours claimed by the winning party's lawyer are unreasonable, or
- the hourly rate charged by the winning lawyer is excessive.

Because a lawyer's fee award for an entire lawsuit, including trial, typically runs into many thousands of dollars, oppositions to these requests tend to be extensive and vigorous.

4. How does a judge decide a Motion for Attorney Fees?

A judge ruling upon a Motion for Attorney Fees must decide whether:

- the winning side is legally entitled to any attorney fees at all
- there are any limits on the amount of fees (some laws that grant the right to collect attorney fees also put a cap on how much may be awarded)
- the hourly fee charged by the lawyer is reasonable (generally, it may not be higher than the top level of fees charged by other lawyers of similar experience for comparable work in the same geographic area), and

- the hours claimed by the lawyer are fair, given the amount and quality of work performed.

This can be a time-consuming process (taking weeks or even months), and not all judges do it carefully. Some judges actually compare the number of hours billed with each piece of legal work produced to see if the time matches the effort. Other judges glance over the bills more casually, only examining closely those items that the opposing side disputes.

Once the trial judge makes a decision concerning the award of attorney fees, that decision becomes part of the Judgment in the case. In some courts, the Judgment does not become final until the judge rules on the attorney fees request. In other courts, the Judgment may become final while the attorney fees request is still pending. Once the judge rules on the matter, the Judgment is then modified to include the attorney fees award.

5. May I appeal the verdict even though I won at trial?

It is commonly understood that a party who loses at trial may appeal the verdict. But it is not always easy to determine who has "won" and who has "lost." The verdict may favor one side over another but not nearly to the degree the "winner" had sought or believes the evidence supported. For example, a person suing for personal injuries sustained in an accident may have been awarded only a fraction of his or her damages. Or someone suing over lost employment might have been awarded some general damages but not nearly enough to cover his or her lost income.

If the "winning" party can point to any errors by the judge or misconduct by the opposing lawyer that might have led to the poor result, that party may be able to successfully appeal the verdict. The procedure for initiating the appeal process is the same for the winner as it is for the losing party. (See Questions 15-16, below.)

6. Can post-trial legal maneuvers by the losing party delay my right to enforce the Judgment?

A party that loses at trial has several procedures available to attempt to undo the verdict. In the trial court, the losing party may:

- ask the trial judge to enter a different Judgment from the one dictated by the jury's verdict (see Question 8, below), or
- file a Motion for a New Trial, asking the judge to erase the verdict and to order that the trial be done again from scratch, with a new jury. (See Question 9, below.)

While either of these procedures is pending, enforcement of the Judgment usually is delayed (*stayed,* in legal parlance). These procedures usually take just a few weeks to resolve, however, and so cause only brief

delay. If the losing party files an appeal, a much longer delay is possible.

The procedure for initiating an appeal is quite simple. Often, the losing party starts the process within a few days or weeks of the verdict even if that party does not know yet whether it will seriously pursue the appeal. (See Question 15, below.) In a few courts, simply initiating an appeal stays execution (enforcement) of a Judgment. But in most courts the filing of the first appeal papers does not automatically stay the Judgment. Instead, the appealing party must make a special request for a stay, either to the trial court or the appeals court. And in many courts, execution of the Judgment is stayed only if the appealing party posts a surety bond, which guarantees payment of the Judgment if the appeal is lost. (See Question 17, below.) If the Judgment is stayed pending an appeal, the delay could last two or three years or more, depending on the backlog of work in the particular appeals court system.

Getting the Losing Side to Pay

Collecting money you have won in a Judgment is sometimes as difficult as winning it in the first place. You can use court-supported collection procedures to enforce your Judgment if the other side has the money and just won't pay. (See Question 7, below.) But these collection efforts won't do much good if the losing party does not have enough money to pay the full amount of the Judgment. Collection efforts might even be counterproductive if they drive the other side into bankruptcy, which could result in you receiving nothing or at best only a small fraction of your Judgment amount. Moreover, you might not be permitted to begin collection efforts if the other side has obtained a stay while appealing the Judgment, a process that could take years. (See Question 17, below.)

If you anticipate trouble collecting your Judgment, you might have to consider settling the case *after* the Judgment, even though you could not settle the case before trial. In such a *post-Judgment settlement* arrangement you might agree to a lower total payment on condition that you receive the entire reduced amount immediately. Or, you might agree to receive the full amount but only over time, in regular payments.

7. How do I enforce the Judgment?

Winning a Judgment is one thing, but forcing the other side to abide by it is another. Some Judgments are self-executing, meaning they go into effect immediately, without any actions by the parties. For example, a Judgment that awards one party title to property goes into effect immediately (though to secure the title, the winning party may need to record the Judgment with the County Recorder or other office that keeps track of title to real property). A Judgment that releases the winning party from further obligations under a contract or lease might also require no further action by the parties or the court.

Judgments that award monetary damages to the winning party are another matter, however. Money does not automatically transfer itself, and the losing side may not be all that anxious to fork over the Judgment amount. If the losing party is covered by an insurance policy, the insurance company usually pays the Judgment within several weeks, if there are no post-trial motions or stays on appeal. (See Section II, below.) But if there is no insurance coverage, the losing party might not hand over the money without a struggle. The same is true if the Judgment requires the losing side to give up control of physical property or to take some other action (closing a competing business, rehiring the winning party or completing unfinished work, for example.)

If the losing side has the ability to comply with the Judgment but does not do so within a matter of weeks, the winning party has a number of options to enforce the Judgment. To collect money damages, the winning party might:

- attach (*garnish*) the losing party's wages

- execute a *lien* against property owned in whole or in part by the losing party, or
- apply to the Sheriff's Department for seizure of (*levy on*) the losing party's assets.

The winning party can also obtain a court order finding the losing party in contempt of court, forcing the losing party to comply with the Judgment or face sanctions.

You Might Have to Pay Extra to Collect Your Judgment

Collecting a Judgment when the losing party will not pay up can be a long and frustrating process. It can also be expensive. Losing parties have many ways to stall. (See Section II, below.) If you are paying your lawyer by the hour, many more bills could be headed your way after the trial is over. You may even have to hire a different lawyer—the lawyer who represented you during the main litigation might not handle difficult collection matters.

If your trial lawyer will be paid for the case on a contingency fee basis, the lawyer has a great personal interest in helping you collect the Judgment—until the other side pays, the lawyer doesn't collect a fee. Nonetheless, most contingency fee agreements do not cover legal work necessary to collect the Judgment. You will either have to negotiate a separate, hourly agreement to have your trial lawyer do the collection work or hire a different lawyer to do it.

If you hire your contingency-fee trial lawyer to do the collection work, the hourly rate the lawyer charges should be 40–50% less than the lawyer's regular hourly fee. After all, the lawyer is working to collect his or her own fee as part of your Judgment. If you hire another lawyer to do the collection work, you and your trial lawyer should split the new lawyer's fee in the same contingency fee proportion as your Judgment amount: if your trial lawyer will get $^1/_3$ of your award, for example, he or she should pay $^1/_3$ of the cost of collecting it.

Section II: The Losing Party's Final Moves

The party who lost at trial does not necessarily have to pay the full amount of the Judgment right away, or immediately give up control of a business or property as required by the Judgment. There are several ways the losing party can seek to have the Judgment overturned, including:

- asking the trial judge to alter the Judgment
- requesting that the judge erase the verdict and order a new trial, and
- appealing the Judgment to a higher court.

The losing party can also delay the winning party's enforcement of the Judgment, perhaps thereby coaxing the winning side to accept a settlement of less than was won at trial in exchange for ending the delay.

8. May I ask the trial judge to change a jury's verdict?

The purpose of the jury system is to take the ultimate decision in a lawsuit out of a judge's hands and give it to non-lawyer citizens. That purpose would be defeated if a judge could easily overturn the jury's verdict. Nonetheless, in a few unusual circumstances, a judge may directly modify a jury's verdict without holding a new trial. The losing party may ask for such a change in the Judgment by filing a *Motion for Judgment Notwithstanding the Verdict* (often

referred to by a shorthand of its Latin version, *Motion for Judgment NOV*) or a *Motion to Vacate Judgment*.

Such a motion must be made rather quickly after the verdict, within ten to 30 days. In some courts, the motion may not be made at all unless the party made a Motion for Directed Verdict before the case was sent to the jury. (See Chapter 9, Section VII.) As with any other motion, the other side may—and in this circumstance certainly will—file an opposition to the request.

The odds of winning a motion to reverse the jury's verdict are extremely small. A judge must deny such a motion if there is "any evidence" to support the verdict. A judge will reverse a verdict—that is, declare

that the party whom the jury found against is actually the winner—only if the verdict was obviously based on emotional considerations rather than facts and laws. For example, a judge might reverse the verdict if a jury awarded compensation to a severely injured person even though there was no evidence that a well-heeled corporate Defendant was legally responsible, or the jury held a big company legally responsible for its employee's wrongdoing off the job.

A party's chances of winning a Motion for Judgment NOV are somewhat better if the party seeks to modify the jury's verdict rather than overturn it completely. This might happen when a jury has made a mathematical miscalculation. For example, a party in a contract dispute might have sued for damages of $50,000, but the jury somehow botched up the numbers and awarded $60,000. If both sides had agreed at trial that only $50,000 was at issue, a judge might simply reduce the Judgment to $50,000 without ordering a whole new trial.

A judge might also modify a jury verdict that awards the Plaintiff large punitive damages. (See Chapter 3, Section I.) Judges are not always as keen on punitive damage awards as juries tend to be. Judges frequently reduce a punitive damage award if the amount seems out of proportion to the general damages awarded. In these situations, a judge might also order a "conditional new trial"—that is, the judge will order a new trial unless the Plaintiff agrees to accept a reduced amount of compensation. (See Question 12, below.)

You Might Want to Talk to the Jurors

If you lose in a jury trial, you might want to ask the jurors why they returned a verdict against you. Your lawyer might also want to talk to jurors to learn, for future reference, whether something in the lawyer's trial strategy went awry or something the other lawyer did was particularly effective. But talking to jurors might also serve a different, more concrete and immediate purpose. In these conversations, a juror might reveal some improper jury conduct that could lead to the granting of a new trial. (See Question 9, below.)

A few courts prohibit any lawyer or party from contacting jurors after the trial is over. This rule protects jurors from harassment and assures that they can decide the case without having to worry about explaining themselves afterward. In most courts, however, there is no rule against contacting jurors after the verdict. Nonetheless, jurors might be reluctant to talk. Many jurors are uncomfortable talking to the lawyers, and particularly to the litigants. This is doubly true for the losing party, whom the jurors may feel too embarrassed to face. And jurors are under no obligation to speak about their experience, even if they are permitted to do so.

However, if your lawyer is puzzled by the verdict—particularly if it was not a unanimous verdict—the lawyer may want to contact the jurors to find out what happened. This initial contact is best left to your lawyer, from whom jurors would probably be less nervous hearing.

9. If a serious error or misconduct occurred during trial, may I ask for a new trial?

A trial judge sometimes decides, after a verdict, that an error or misconduct during trial was so serious that the jury's verdict should not stand. In these situations, if the judge decides not to grant a motion for Judgment NOV (see Question 8, above), the judge might order an entirely new trial with a different jury. If the trial judge believes that the error at trial was so serious that an appeals court would reverse the jury's verdict anyway, granting a new trial saves the time, effort and expense that the parties and courts would otherwise spend grinding through the appeal process.

Any party may file a *Motion for New Trial*. In some courts the motion must be made within ten days of the verdict. In others, a party may have ten to thirty days after Entry of Judgment. Many courts require a party to file what is called a *Notice of Intent to File Motion for New Trial* within a short time limit, but permit extra time to prepare the supporting legal documents.

The judge who presided over the trial decides the Motion for a New Trial. Because that judge spent the trial attempting to avoid, prevent or remedy such serious errors, he or she will seldom be convinced that a new trial is required. Nonetheless, it does sometimes happen. The types of errors that are most likely to result in an order for a new trial are:

- jury misconduct (Question 10, below)
- new evidence (Question 11, below)
- lack of evidentiary support for damages (Question 12, below)
- misconduct by witness or attorney (Question 13, below), and
- judicial error (Question 14, below).

10. May I ask for a new trial because of juror misconduct?

Jurors generally take their job seriously and follow the judge's instructions carefully. But sometimes an individual juror, or the entire group, violates those instructions in such a significant way that the integrity of the jury is compromised. If so, a party may *impeach the verdict*—challenge the jury's conduct—and request a new trial. Juror misconduct might happen before or during jury deliberations, inside the courthouse or out. Some examples:

- an individual juror might not have answered fully or truthfully during voir dire (see Chapter 9, Section VI) about some matter that could have affected the juror's vote
- a juror might have spoken with a party or lawyer, contacted a witness, visited the scene of the dispute, consulted an expert or done Internet research on the subject of the litigation
- a juror may have read newspaper accounts of the trial although ordered not to do so by the judge
- inside the jury room during deliberations, an individual juror might have

been bullied into joining the others in a verdict

- the jurors as a group might have considered matters beyond what the instructions allowed, or
- jurors may have arrived at a damages amount by taking a mathematical average of individual juror figures rather than coming to an actual agreement.

Judges order new trials for jury misconduct outside the jury room far more often than for misconduct during deliberations. The courts are extremely protective of the privacy of the jury room. Only in extraordinary circumstances does a judge permit a juror to be questioned about what went on inside the jury room during deliberations. On the other hand, jury misconduct outside the jury room can be demonstrated through a sworn statement by some third party who witnessed an individual juror's misconduct or knows that a juror withheld information during voir dire.

11. May I ask for a new trial based on new evidence?

Occasionally, new evidence emerges after trial which, had the jury heard or seen it, would likely have altered the verdict. Such evidence justifies a new trial only if:

- the evidence is admissible in court
- the evidence is so significant that it clearly would have changed the jury's view of the case

- during trial, the evidence was unknown to the party who now seeks a new trial, and
- the party was not able to discover the evidence before trial, even with diligent efforts.

For example, a party's failure to discover a crucial witness who could thoroughly contradict the other party's testimony might not justify a new trial unless that witness had actively avoided detection or the other side had hidden the witness's identity.

12. May I ask for a new trial if the damages award was not supported by the evidence?

Sometimes a judge believes that the jury has awarded compensation far beyond what the evidence warranted, although the verdict is proper in all other respects. Perhaps the jury felt great sympathy toward the winning party and so went overboard in awarding compensation. Or the jury might have felt great animosity toward the losing party and punished it with a heavy damages amount even though the evidence did not justify the award.

If the compensation amount seems completely unsupported by the evidence, the judge has several alternatives. (Simply modifying the verdict to fit the evidence is not an option in this situation. See Question 8, above.) The judge can order an entirely new trial. Or, the judge can order what is called a *partial new trial* on the issue of damages (compensation) only. That is, the judge could maintain the first jury's verdict regarding who won and who lost but order a new trial with a new jury solely on the question of how much the damages should be.

A third alternative is to order what is called a *conditional new trial*—a kind of take-it-or-leave-it settlement offered by the judge to the winning party. The judge comes up with a "fair" compensation figure, or an amount the judge believes is the highest "reasonable amount" supported by the evidence. The judge then gives the winning party the option of accepting this amount as a reduced verdict—what is known in legalese as a *remittitur*—or having the judge order an entire new trial. Because of the cost, delay and uncertainty of a new trial, the winning party often is willing to accept this amount even if it is far less than what the jury awarded. (In a few courts, a judge may also increase a jury's award—called an *additur*—but this is much less common than reducing a verdict amount.)

13. May I ask for a new trial because of misconduct by a witness or attorney?

When misconduct by a lawyer, a party or a key witness occurs during a trial, the lawyer for the party adversely affected may object and ask that the judge declare a mistrial. (See Chapter 9, Section VII.) If the trial judge does not believe that the misconduct requires a mistrial, he or she will instruct the jury to ignore what it heard and saw, and will warn the witness or lawyer not to repeat the misconduct. Usually, if the judge did not declare a mistrial at the time, the judge is unlikely to order a new trial once the trial is over based on the same misconduct.

However, the same type of misconduct may have continued throughout the trial despite the judge's warnings, or may have combined with other acts of misconduct. By the end of the trial, the cumulative effect may have made a fair jury verdict unlikely. In that case, the judge may accept the losing party's contention that the only remedy is a new trial. A party can only make a Motion for New Trial if that party objected, during trial, to the misconduct on which the motion is based. The party is more likely to succeed if a mistrial was also requested when the misconduct occurred, but this is not a formal prerequisite to a Motion for New Trial.

14. May I ask for a new trial based on judicial error?

It is unusual for a judge to admit having made an error during a just-completed trial. It is far more unusual for a judge not only to admit a mistake but also to agree it was so serious that it warrants a whole new trial. Nonetheless, a judge might grant a new trial based on his or her own mistake. This most often happens when the judge's ruling either permitted or excluded a key witness or an entire line of evidence. Most of a judge's decisions during trial are about whether one question is proper or one piece of evidence should be admitted. But sometimes a judge is asked to decide whether an important witness may testify at all (a particular expert, for example), or whether an entire line of questioning is proper (for example, whether a party's history of similar conduct should be heard by the jury). Such a decision may have a profound effect on the jury's perception of the case.

At the time of the ruling, the judge might not have seen how important it was to one party's chance of success in the trial. By the end of the trial, however, the judge might realize the serious effect of the ruling. A judge might be convinced by affidavits from jurors, if they are willing to cooperate with the losing party's lawyer, demonstrating how important the judge's decision was to their verdict. If the judge concedes that an error was made, and the course of the trial after the ruling makes it clear that the mistake was important, the judge might be willing to grant a new trial.

15. How long do I have to file an appeal of the verdict?

The process of appealing a verdict to a higher court must be initiated very soon after the Judgment. The party who wants to appeal must file a *Notice of Appeal* or a *Notice of Intent to Appeal* within ten to sixty days (depending on each court's rules) following the Entry of Judgment. In some

court systems, the notice is filed with the trial court. In others, the notice is filed with the appeals court.

Filing a Notice of Appeal or Notice of Intent to Appeal does not obligate a party to complete the long and expensive appeals process. However, the party must file the notice within the short time limit following the Judgment to ensure the opportunity to follow through with an appeal.

16. Should my trial lawyer handle my appeal?

A lawyer's obligation to represent a client during litigation, as spelled out in the representation or fee agreement (see Chapter 1), usually ends with the Entry of Judgment and any post-Judgment motions in the trial court. It does *not* include an appeal. A separate agreement must be reached with a lawyer to handle the appeal. However, the rules of professional responsibility in many courts require a trial lawyer to file a Notice of Appeal for a losing client, or at least to inform the client when and where the Notice of Appeal must be filed.

A client should consider several factors in deciding whether the trial lawyer should handle the appeal. Some trial lawyers simply do not work on appeals. If the trial lawyer does handle appeals, the client must decide whether the lawyer who "lost" the trial should continue working on the case. On one hand, the trial lawyer already knows the case intimately, and might therefore have the best chance of succeeding on appeal. And because the trial lawyer knows the case, he or she might not have to spend long hours—for which the client would be billed—becoming familiar with the facts and legal issues.

On the other hand, the client may have lost confidence in the trial lawyer, or simply feel that another lawyer could bring a fresh approach to the case. And the trial lawyer might be sick of dealing with the case or the client and feel that another lawyer could do a better job.

Is My Trial Lawyer's Poor Work Grounds for an Appeal?

You may have heard some of the horror stories about lawyers in criminal cases who sometimes barely represent their clients at all—a lawyer who sleeps through part of the trial, is drunk most of the time or is sleeping with the prosecutor. In criminal cases, a Defendant is entitled by the Constitution not only to a lawyer but to the *effective assistance of counsel*. So, this kind of dereliction of duty by a lawyer can be grounds for a successful appeal.

The same right to effective counsel does not apply to civil cases. If your lawyer has done a lousy job litigating your case, you have two options. You may hire another lawyer to handle an appeal. This other lawyer might find a serious enough error by the opposing trial lawyer or the judge to justify overturning your loss in the trial court, despite your own trial lawyer's miserable performance.

The other option is to consider filing a lawsuit against your trial lawyer for legal malpractice. This is a big, and probably expensive, step. You may need to hire a lawyer who specializes in legal malpractice cases. And legal malpractice lawsuits are very difficult to win. On the other hand, almost all lawyers have legal malpractice insurance coverage. So if there is at least a reasonable argument that your lawyer's sloppy job amounted to malpractice, the insurance company might be willing to pay you something to settle the claim, even if it would not pay you everything you lost in the original lawsuit.

17. If I file a Notice of Appeal, does that stop the Judgment from going into effect?

Once a Judgment has been entered in the trial court's records, the winning party may enforce that Judgment—collect monetary compensation, transfer title to property, etc.—through several court-supported procedures. (See Section I, above.) However, the losing party can sometimes delay enforcement of the Judgment—in legalese, obtain a *Stay of Judgment* or *Stay of Execution of Judgment*—as part of the appeal process.

In some courts, merely filing a Notice of Appeal automatically stays the Judgment. The stay then remains in place while the appeal is "pending," which means as long as the party pursuing the appeal pays the appropriate appeals court filing fees, puts up the required *costs bond* (an amount calculated to pay the other side's court costs on appeal, should the appealing party lose) and files the required documents and appeal briefs. In other courts, filing a Notice of Appeal does not automatically stay the Judgment. Instead, the party filing the appeal may obtain a stay only by posting with the court what is called an *appeal bond*. This surety bond guarantees that the amount of the Judgment will be paid to the winning party if the appeal ultimately fails to overturn the Judgment. Because the fee for such surety bonds is usually quite high, only litigants who are serious about following through on the appeal—or those who have a lot of money—are likely to stay enforcement of the Judgment.

Finally, the losing party can obtain a stay of the Judgment while the appeal is pending by making a *Request for Stay Pending Appeal* to the trial court or appeals court. If the party appealing can show a strong legal basis for the appeal and significant harm—personal financial ruin or serious damage to a business—if the Judgment were to be executed but later reversed on appeal, then the trial court or appeals court might grant a stay with a minimal surety bond or without any surety bond at all. If the trial court grants a stay, the appeals court will probably review it and decide on its own whether and on what terms to continue the stay.

A Stay on Appeal Might Lead to a Deal

If you lost at trial after several long, hard years of litigation, the prospect of spending two or three more expensive years appealing the case might not seem very attractive. And depending on what happened during the litigation, you may have little chance of winning an appeal. There are also considerable expenses that must be paid almost immediately—filing fees, a costs bond and perhaps a surety bond—in order to secure a Stay of Judgment.

On the other hand, obtaining a Stay of the Judgment by filing an appeal might put pressure back on your lawsuit opponent. The other side might not be in position to wait two or three more years before getting the compensation or other relief it won at trial. And the cost of a lawyer to handle the appeal might put a drain on the other side's cash flow that it cannot easily absorb.

As a result of this pressure, the winning party might consider an offer to settle the case for less than it won at trial. Cases are frequently settled after a Judgment, either on easier terms than a lump sum payment, or for a lower total figure, or both. If other kinds of relief—transfer of control of a business or property, for example, or an order to refrain from certain conduct—were part of the Judgment, a stay on appeal might pressure the other side to grant you more time to comply. And the possibility that a stay would prevent that other relief from being enforced for two or three more years might also push your opponent to agree to more favorable settlement terms.

■

Index

A

Acknowledgement and Receipt, 3/18

Action. *See* Lawsuit

Additur (increased jury award), 10/12

Admissible evidence, 5/9, 9/45

Advance of costs, 1/26

Affiant, defined, 5/9

Affidavit of Good Cause, 4/17

Affirmative defenses, 3/24

Alternate jurors, 9/37

Alternative Dispute Resolution (ADR), 6/2
  See also Arbitration; Mediation

Amended Complaint, 3/27
  Defendant's request for, 3/19
  how to file, 3/20-21
  judge's reasons for allowing, 3/21
  Plaintiff's initiation of, 3/20

American Arbitration Association, 7/4

Answer, 3/19
  cautions advised for, 3/23
  definition/types of, 3/22
  failure to file by deadline, 3/24-25
  of general denial, 3/22
  helping your lawyer prepare, 3/23
  with multiple Defendants, 3/24
  of specific admissions and denials, 3/22

Appeal bond, 10/15

Appeals
  of jury verdict, 10/4-5, 10/13-14
  and lawsuit delays, 5/21
  of pretrial ruling, 5/20
  with Stay of Judgment, 10/15, 10/16

Appearance, special versus general, 3/26

Appellate Court, 5/20

Application. *See* Motion

Application for Order, 5/8

Application for Order Shortening Time, 5/7

Application for Preliminary Injunction, 5/26,
  5/28-29

Application for Temporary Restraining Order,
  5/24

Arbitration
  advantages of, 7/10
  binding versus non-binding, 7/3
  disadvantages of, 7/12-13
  documents required for, 7/15-16
  format/mechanics of, 7/4, 7/18-19
  mandatory, 7/5, 7/8-9
  Plaintiff's election of, 7/5, 7/7
  preparation for, 7/16-17
  selection of arbitrators for, 7/9-10
  stipulation to, by both sides, 7/5-6, 7/10
  testimony, in-person, 7/15
  testimony, order of, 7/19
  testimony, sworn statement, 4/34, 7/11, 7/15

How You Can Help Your Lawyer

with the Answer, 3/23
with the Complaint, 3/11
with a countersuit, 3/29-30
with depositions, 4/29-30
with interrogatories, 4/12
with judicial arbitration, 7/16-17
with Motion for Change of Venue, 5/36
with Motion for Summary Judgment, 5/52-53
by preparing for your own deposition, 4/37-38
with Request for Admissions, 4/25-26
with Request for Production of Documents, 4/16-17
with response to Request for Production, 4/19
to set the tone of settlement negotiations, 8/9-10
with Settlement Conference, 8/14
with a Temporary Restraining Order, 5/25
with trial preparation, 9/20-21

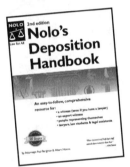

Remember:

Little publishers have big ears.
We really listen to you.

Take 2 Minutes & Give Us Your 2 cents

Your comments make a big difference in the development and revision of Nolo books and software. Please take a few minutes and register your Nolo product—and your comments—with us. Not only will your input make a difference, you'll receive special offers available only to registered owners of Nolo products on our newest books and software. Register now by:

PHONE
1-800-728-3555

FAX
1-800-645-0895

EMAIL
cs@nolo.com

or **MAIL** us
this registration card

------- fold here -------

Registration Card

NAME _____ DATE _____

ADDRESS _____

_____

CITY _____ STATE _____ ZIP _____

PHONE _____ EMAIL _____

WHERE DID YOU HEAR ABOUT THIS PRODUCT? _____

WHERE DID YOU PURCHASE THIS PRODUCT? _____

DID YOU CONSULT A LAWYER? (PLEASE CIRCLE ONE)   YES   NO   NOT APPLICABLE

DID YOU FIND THIS BOOK HELPFUL?   (VERY)   5   4   3   2   1   (NOT AT ALL)

COMMENTS _____

_____

_____

WAS IT EASY TO USE?   (VERY EASY)   5   4   3   2   1   (VERY DIFFICULT)

We occasionally make our mailing list available to carefully selected companies whose products may be of interest to you.

❏ If you do not wish to receive mailings from these companies, please check this box.

❏ You can quote me in future Nolo promotional materials.
   Daytime phone number _____.

UNCL 1.2

Nolo in the NEWS

"Nolo helps lay people perform legal tasks without the aid—or fees—of lawyers."

—USA TODAY

Nolo books are ..."written in plain language, free of legal mumbo jumbo, and spiced with witty personal observations."

—ASSOCIATED PRESS

"...Nolo publications...guide people simply through the how, when, where and why of law."

—WASHINGTON POST

"Increasingly, people who are not lawyers are performing tasks usually regarded as legal work... And consumers, using books like Nolo's, do routine legal work themselves."

—NEW YORK TIMES

"...All of [Nolo's] books are easy-to-understand, are updated regularly, provide pull-out forms...and are often quite moving in their sense of compassion for the struggles of the lay reader."

—SAN FRANCISCO CHRONICLE

fold here

- -

Place
stamp here

Nolo
950 Parker Street
Berkeley, CA 94710-9867

Attn: UNCL 1.2